EDUCATIONAL
Administration
A Decade of Reform

Joseph Murphy
Patrick B. Forsyth
Editors

CORWIN PRESS, INC.
A Sage Publications Company
Thousand Oaks, California

in collaboration with
The University Council for Educational Administration

For information address:

Corwin Press, Inc.
A Sage Publications Company
2455 Teller Road
Thousand Oaks, California 91320
E-mail: order@corwinpress.com

SAGE Publications Ltd.
6 Bonhill Street
London EC2A 4PU
United Kingdom

SAGE Publications India Pvt. Ltd.
M-32 Market
Greater Kailash I
New Delhi 110 048 India

Printed in the United States of America

Library of Congress Cataloging-in-Publication Data

Educational administration: A decade of reform / Joseph Murphy, Patrick B.
   Forsyth, editors.
      p. cm.
   Includes bibliographical references and index.
   ISBN 0-8039-6608-3 (cloth: acid-free paper)
   ISBN 0-8039-6609-1 (pbk.: acid-free paper)
   1. School management and organization—United States. 2. Educational change—
   United States. 3. Educational leadership—United States. I. Murphy, Joseph, 1949-
   II. Forsyth, Patrick B.
      LB2805 .E285 1999
      371.2'00973—dc21
                                                                        98-40186

This book is printed on acid-free paper.

99 00 01 02 03 04 05 10 9 8 7 6 5 4 3 2 1

Production Editor: S. Marlene Head
Editorial Assistant: Kristen L. Gibson
Typesetter: Judy Richards
Cover Designer: Tracy E. Miller

Contents

About the Editors

Joseph Murphy is Professor in the Department of Educational Leadership at Peabody College of Vanderbilt University. He is also Director of Research and Senior Research Scientist at the Peabody Center for Educational Policy.

Prior to moving to the university, he served as a school administrator at the school, district, and state levels. His most recent experience was as Executive Assistant to the Chief Deputy Superintendent of Public Instruction in California.

He currently chairs the Interstate School Leaders Licensure Consortium and is a former vice president of the American Educational Research Association (Division A, Administration). He is coeditor (with Karen Seashore Louis) of the AERA *Handbook of Research on Educational Administration*.

His primary interest is in school improvement, with emphases in the areas of policy and leadership. Recent volumes in these areas include *The Privatization of Schooling: Problems and Possibilities*; *School-Based Management as School Reform: Taking Stock,* with Lynn G. Beck; and *Restructuring Schooling: Learning From Ongoing Efforts* (all with Corwin Press); and *The Educational Reform Movement of the 1980s: Perspectives and Cases* (edited).

He also works in the area of leadership preparation and training. Recent books in this area include *The Landscape of Leadership Preparation: Reframing the Education of School Leaders* (Corwin Press); *Ethics in Educational Leadership Programs: An Expanding Role,* with Lynn G. Beck (Corwin Press); *Preparing Tomorrow's School Leaders: Alternative Designs* (edited); and *Approaches to Administrative Training* (edited with Philip Hallinger).

Patrick B. Forsyth is Executive Director of the University Council for Educational Administration and Corporate Secretary of the National Policy Board for Educational Administration. After teaching in New York City and New Jersey, he completed his doctoral study at Rutgers University in 1977. Forsyth's research interests are in the sociology of organizations and urban school administration. In 1983, he became the first recipient of the Jack A. Culbertson Award for outstanding contributions by a junior professor to the field of school administration for his research on the professionalization process. Among his other writings are *Effective Supervision: Theory Into Practice,* with Wayne K. Hoy; *Leaders for America's Schools: The Report and Papers of the National Commission on Excellence in Educational Administration,* with Daniel E. Griffiths and Robert T. Stout, editors; and *City Schools: Leading the Way,* with Marilyn Tallerico (Corwin Press). In 1989-1990, Forsyth chaired the study group for the National Policy Board for Educational Administration that produced *Improving the Preparation of School Administrators: An Agenda for Reform.*

About the Contributors

Nelda Cambron-Mccabe is Professor, Department of Educational Leadership, Miami University, Oxford, Ohio. Her current work focuses on systems thinking in school organizations and reconstruction of leadership preparation programs. She also coordinates several aspects of the Danforth Foundation's Forum for the American School Superintendent. Her most recent publication (coauthored with McCarthy and Thomas) is *Public School Law: Teachers' and Students' Rights* (1998).

The late **David L. Clark** was Kenan Professor of Education at the University of North Carolina—Chapel Hill, where he taught courses in organizational theory, policy studies, and educational research. Clark contributed to education for nearly half a century, serving on faculty and as dean at several universities. His research and publications, particularly in the field of federal education policy, were extensive. Clark also served in positions in the U.S. Office of Education and the U.S. Department of Education as well as in public school administration. He was honored by Phi Delta Kappa as one of its 33 Distinguished Educators and by the Association of Teacher Educators as one of 70 Leaders in Education. In 1994, Clark received the Roald F. Campbell Lifetime Achievement Award from the University Council for Educational Administration.

Daniel E. Griffiths is Dean Emeritus and Professor Emeritus of the School of Education at New York University. He is a prolific author, having written or edited 11 books and some 300 articles, reviews, evaluations, and research reports. Griffiths' most recent interest is nontraditional research and theory. His latest article is "The Case for Theoretical Pluralism" in the October 1997 issue of *Educational Management & Administration*. Since retiring in 1986, he has chaired the National Commission on Excellence in Educational Administration, traveled widely, played lots of golf, and taken up gourmet cooking, in addition to writing an occasional article.

Ann Weaver Hart is Dean of the Graduate School and Professor of Educational Leadership and Policy at the University of Utah. Her research interests include leadership succession and development, work redesign and organizational behavior in educational organizations, and academic freedom and scholarship in graduate education, and she has published broadly in these areas. Hart has served as the editor of *Educational Administration Quarterly* and is the founding editor of the *International Journal of Graduate Education*. Her most recent books include *The Principalship: A Theory of Professional Learning and Practice* (1996) with Paul V. Bredeson and *Designing and Conducting Research: Inquiry in Education and Social Science* (1996) with Clifford J. Drew and Michael L. Hardman.

Martha M. McCarthy, Chancellor Professor and Chair of the Educational Leadership Program at Indiana University, specializes in education law and policy. Previously Codirector of the Indiana Education Policy Center and Associate Dean of the Faculties at Indiana University, she has also been a public school teacher and central office administrator. She has written extensively and made numerous presentations regarding various aspects of students' and teachers' rights, church-state relations, curriculum censorship, equity issues, education reform efforts, and characteristics of educational leadership faculty, students, and preparation programs. Recently, she coauthored *Continuity and Change: The Educational Leadership Professoriate* (1997) and *Public School Law: Teachers' and Students' Rights* (4th ed., 1998).

Diana G. Pounder is Professor and Associate Chair in the Educational Administration Department at the University of Utah. Her teaching and research emphasis is human resource administration. Her current research addresses teacher teams and collaboration in schools, work group effectiveness, and the impact of group work design on teacher/school outcomes. Previous empirical research addresses leadership as an organization-wide phenomenon, educator selection, gender equity in compensation, and administrator preparation reform. Her publications appear in *Educational Administration Quarterly*, *Journal of School Leadership*, the *High School Journal*, *Education Law Quarterly*, *Journal of Personnel Evaluation*, *Journal of Educational Equity & Leadership*, and others.

Charol Shakeshaft is Professor of Administration and Policy Studies at Hofstra University. From 1987 to 1998, she served as chairperson of that department. Her research has focused on equity issues in schools and on the impact of technology on learning.

Scott D. Thomson has served as a teacher and high school principal in Palo Alto, California, as superintendent of Evanston Township High School District in Illinois, as Executive Director of the National Association of Secondary School Principals, and as Executive Secretary of the National Policy Board for Educational Administration. He also has been an instructor at Stanford and Northwestern Universities and an adjunct professor at George Mason University in the field of educational leadership. He has authored 58 articles in nationally distributed journals and magazines and three chapters in published books, and he has edited two books and several major documents, including NCATE's *Curriculum Guidelines for Programs in Educational Leadership.*

Eddy J. Van Meter is a Professor of Education and Chairperson of the Department of Administration and Supervision within the College of Education at the University of Kentucky. He also has served as a College of Education faculty member at Kansas State University. His teaching and administrative experience was obtained in New Mexico and Texas. He is the author of more than 50 publications on topics relating to school leadership and administration, and his current scholarly interests focus primarily on issues of school, institutional, and educational reform.

Introduction

DANIEL E. GRIFFITHS

The second half of the 20th century has seen two major attempts to improve the administration of American schools. The first was a rather grand effort initiated by the American Association of School Administrators (AASA) and royally supported by the Kellogg Foundation, whereas the second was a much more modest enterprise initiated by the University Council for Educational Administration (UCEA) and supported by a wide array of foundations, educational administration organizations, universities, and some 1,300 people who participated in meetings, wrote papers, critiqued drafts of reports, and gave advice.

The first effort, known as the Cooperative Program in Educational Administration (CPEA), was largely located in eight university centers, whereas the second, identified as the National Commission on Excellence in Educational Administration (NCEEA), had a small central staff housed in the UCEA headquarters, then located at Arizona State University, that interacted with virtually all elements of the educational administration community. The two efforts to improve educational administration differed in more than scope and financing. The CPEA consisted of eight regional centers, each going its own way. The centers varied in their foci, methods, and the extent to which they involved others in their activities. The NCEEA, on the other hand, was a highly centralized operation that produced a report that was delivered to the membership of the UCEA. The purpose of this book is to examine the extent to which the recommendations contained in the report have been acted on and how well they have been implemented.

In a sense, the second effort at improving administration grew out of the first in that the UCEA was formed by the heads of the eight CPEA centers under the leadership of John Norton and Daniel Davies of the Middle Atlantic Center, located at Teachers College, Columbia University, and was substantially funded for the first 10 years of its existence by the Kellogg Foundation. Other funding came from the university members, grants, and publications.

Cooperative Program in Educational Administration

To say that the CPEA was a grand effort is no exaggeration. The story of the first 5 years of the CPEA is well told by Hollis Moore (1957) in a volume titled, *Studies in School Administration.* It all began immediately after the end of World War II. In January 1946, an advisory committee on educational projects to the Kellogg Foundation met in San Francisco. The three members, who were all prominent educators—Paul Hanna, Ralph Tyler, and Maurice Seay—recommended to the Foundation that it enter the field of school administration. The Foundation had, since its beginning in 1930, supported projects in community development, so a move into educational administration was a natural development. A year later, the Planning Committee of the American Association of School Administrators (AASA) issued a report stating,

> The initiation of studies and programs looking toward further professionalization of the superintendency through improved training programs, refined standards of selection by boards of education, and fuller and wider participation in the activities of the profession [should be made a part of the AASA program at once]. (Moore, 1957, p. 2)

The report was accepted by the membership of the AASA at its annual convention meeting in Atlantic City, New Jersey in February 1947.

In the same year, a new organization was formed. Largely due to the leadership of Walter Cocking, editor of the *School Executive,* a group of professors of educational administration met at the Endicott, New York estate of Thomas Watson, president of IBM. The end result of the week-long conference was the establishment of the National Conference of Professors of Educational Administration (NCPEA), which has been meeting annually ever since. Prior to the formation of the UCEA, the NCPEA played a very significant role in disseminating the results of the CPEA to the professors of educational administration at large. Following the formation of the UCEA, however, it did not change to adapt to the new environment and lost much of its appeal to the professorship. By 1992, the NCPEA leadership decided that the organization needed to change its goals and move in a different direction. It hired a part-time executive secretary, Donald McCarty, Emeritus Professor, University of Wisconsin—Madison, and expanded its activities to a year-round basis. The goal of the new organization was to improve the quality of preparation programs, stimulate research, speed the dissemination of new ideas, and, in general, encourage the professionalization of the professorship. The NCPEA also changed its name to reflect the change in functions; it became the National Council of Professors of Educational Administration (NCPEA).

Moore summarized the confluence of these events as follows:

These were the three most important ingredients in the movement which was to follow: a foundation interested in community uplift and aware of the key role of the school administrator in the process; a profession of practicing administrators speaking though their national Association in vague, yet sincere, terms about their hopes for "further professionalization"; and a rapidly developing unity and purpose among professors and researchers in the field of school administration. The three forces came together in point of time, and the result was rapid acceleration in building a profession of lofty stature. (Moore,1957, p. 3)

Although the three ingredients came together quickly, they did not mix as fast. In fact, it was 4 years before actual work got under way. The first big question was, of course, "What shall we do?" There was considerable discussion of the Flexner Report, which changed the way medical education was conducted: It moved medical education from commercial medical schools into the universities. A special subcommittee of the AASA proposed the appointment of a national commission to conduct "a comprehensive project for upgrading the professional competence of the superintendency of education" (Moore, 1957, p. 9). This proposal was submitted to the Kellogg Foundation, and, in early 1948, the Foundation rejected the idea of a commission to do a study. They did, however, accept the recommendation contained in the proposal that a series of regional conferences be held to review the basic idea of a national study and make recommendations as to what should be done. The Foundation would then decide what and how it would be done.

On August 7, 1950, the Foundation announced its decision: They would finance a "program to improve the quality and training of school administrators" (Moore, 1957, p. 18). Within days the NCPEA met at Cornell University for its annual weeklong conference. At the time, I was an instructor at nearby Colgate University and a part-time graduate student at Yale University. My major professor, S. M. (Sam) Brownell, urged me to go to the conference, and I did. I was completely unaware of the developments sketched above and was quite surprised at the excitement that permeated the meeting. The first five university centers had been announced, and the word was that there would be more, but who would they be? It should be kept in mind that in 1950, educational administration was low on the academic totem pole. Furthermore, it was a financially impoverished field, and the prospect of millions of dollars was mind-boggling. However, not everyone was excited; some were angry, and others thought it a matter of little importance. Many knew that they would be left out, and some thought the conference was focusing on the wrong things. After all, the Korean War was being waged, and that was what should be most important. The spokesman for this position was Ernest O. Melby, Dean of the School of Education at New York University. He was a powerful speaker, and he made an impassioned plea at a general session for the conference to turn its attention to the war. Sam Brownell, among others, responded. Brownell made the telling point—namely, that the Korean War was merely the first in a series of global brushfires that the United States, in its new role as the world's most powerful country, would be called upon to extinguish. When it was quite clear that the conference wanted no part of the war, Melby walked out in protest, but he walked out alone.

Clyde Campbell captured the excitement of the meeting when he wrote of the CPEA, "The mere announcement alone seemed to channel thinking in certain directions. In the minds of those present, past practices were being pushed aside for new trails to be blazed as soon as the 1950 Conference was ended" (Flesher & Knoblauch, 1958).

As the Foundation described the project, the country was to be divided into six regions, and "all sections will share information and have common objectives" (Moore, 1957, p. 18). The project's cost was estimated at $3,347,567. Within the year, grants were made to eight centers: Harvard University; University of Chicago; Teachers College, Columbia University; University of Texas; George Peabody College for Teachers; University of Oregon; Stanford University; and The Ohio State University. These centers operated with a high degree of autonomy and little central direction. Activities and goals varied widely among the centers: interdisciplinary seminars at Oregon, research at Chicago, interaction with universities in the region at Teachers College (which led to the formation of the UCEA), the study of the principalship at Texas, the development of the competency approach to administration at Peabody, and educational leadership at Ohio State. Although each had a focus, they all engaged in a variety of other activities as well.

Moore, writing as he did shortly after the end of the first 5 years of the CPEA, was very thorough in his review of the project. He discussed several major outcomes in the first chapter and devoted the rest of the book to a large number of other outcomes. He considered those he called "process" to be the most important. By that he meant that in the first 5 years of the CPEA, so many status studies, pilot centers, research projects, and experimental designs had been initiated that the way the field of educational administration conducted itself had changed. Activities of this sort were not the norm prior to CPEA. Whereas publications in educational administration were largely restricted to textbooks plus occasional articles in general purpose educational journals, Moore was able to list 303 publications produced by the centers (Moore, 1957, p. 23). He was right in his analysis because educational administration did become more of an academic field of study. In fact, although the term "reform" (so popular today) was not used at the time of the CPEA, educational administration as a field of study was truly *reformed.*

By the time the CPEA had run its full course (the first 5 years plus a 4-year extension), the full impact of Moore's evaluation was evident. Under the leadership of the Middle Atlantic Center at Teachers College, Columbia University, departments of educational administration in 35 major research universities came together to form the University Council for Educational Administration. The stated purpose was that the UCEA "should promote, through inter-university cooperation, the improvement of the professional preparation of administrative personnel in the field of education" (Culbertson, 1995, p. 50). Even a cursory look at the UCEA over the years since its formation would lead objective observers to agree that by 1985, substantial progress had been made toward fulfilling the purpose. The reformation of academic educational administration was firmly established. But without being overly dramatic, it can be said that the storm clouds were gathering.

The National Commission on
Excellence in Educational Administration

By the middle of the 1980s, criticism of American public schools had assumed the dimensions of a frenzy. Led by *A Nation Prepared* (Carnegie Forum on Education and the Economy, 1986), every aspect of the public schools came under attack. A review of the research revealed the following troubling aspects in the field of educational administration:

- Lack of a definition of good educational leadership
- Lack of leader recruitment programs in the schools
- Lack of collaboration between school districts and universities
- The discouraging lack of minorities and women in the field
- Lack of systematic professional development for school administrators
- Lack of quality candidates for preparation programs
- Lack of preparation programs relevant to the job demands of school administrators
- Lack of sequence, modern content, and clinical experiences in preparation programs
- Lack of licensure systems that promote excellence
- Lack of a national sense of cooperation in preparing school leaders (National Commission on Excellence in Educational Administration, 1987, pp. xvi, xvii)

Quite in contrast to the period following World War II, when leadership was taken by the American Association of School Administrators and the Kellogg Foundation, in 1985 leadership was assumed by the UCEA. In addition, whereas the Kellogg Foundation forced the rejection of a commission approach (and history has proved them to have been right), the UCEA adopted the approach. The decision to go the commission route was not difficult to make because there was no way to fund an operation comparable to the CPEA. Furthermore, a commission made more sense at this point in time. The reform of the profession of educational administration had been accomplished earlier, a national organization (UCEA) was in place, and the issues facing the professoriate were matters of policy. The UCEA Plenary Session approved the formation of a blue-ribbon commission on April 30, 1986. The story of the commission is detailed by Patrick Forsyth in Chapter 3.

The commission published two reports: one, a brief overview containing the recommendations, which was titled *Leaders for America's Schools* (1987); and a second with the same title containing the recommendations and background papers (Griffiths, Stout, & Forsyth, 1988). The report opened with a listing of the most significant recommendations, followed by a vision of school leadership and 35 recommendations directed at the public schools, professional organizations, universities, state and federal policymakers, and the public. The most significant recommendations follow:

- Educational leadership should be redefined.

- A National Policy Board on Educational Administration should be formed.
- Administrator preparation programs should be modeled after those in other professional schools.
- At least 300 universities and colleges should cease preparing educational administrators.
- Programs for recruitment and placement of ethnic minorities and women should be initiated by universities, school boards, state and federal governments, and the private sector.
- The public schools should become full partners in the preparation of school administrators.
- Professional development activities should be an integral component of the careers of professors of educational administration and practicing administrators.
- Licensure programs should be substantially reformed. (National Commission on Excellence in Educational Administration, 1987, p. xiii)

Perhaps the most crucial of these was the recommendation to create a National Policy Board, whose major responsibility it would be to monitor the implementation of the commission's recommendations. The Board was established very shortly after the publication of the 1988 version of *Leaders for America's Schools.* It was hosted by the University of Virginia, and the late David L. Clark was the first executive secretary. All was then in place for the improvement of the preparation of educational administrators: a set of recommendations from a blue-ribbon panel; the UCEA, which was organized to implement the recommendations; and the Policy Board to oversee their implementation.

What to Expect

There have been many efforts to "reform" education, although, as pointed out above, remarkably few in educational administration. Reforms have focused largely on teacher education, curriculum, and school organization. The question must be raised as to why, when so much time, money, and effort have been expended, the schools are not in better shape than they are at the present time. Putting the question differently, what should be a reasonable set of expectations following a national reform effort?

My basic premise when thinking about what to expect from a national reform effort is that education is not amenable to radical change. This is an important premise, because Americans have been conditioned by media hype to anticipate big, exciting results from everything. If the results are not new, extreme, or radical, then the reform has not been worth the effort—so it would seem. This kind of thinking eliminates the possibility of change by improving quality, because changes in quality usually occur in small increments. Furthermore, changes in quality of education occur largely in what goes on between teacher and student, and this is very difficult for a national reform movement to influence. As a matter of fact, most teachers (and I include professors) do not even know when a reform effort is under way. Increased financing and what it buys—technology, smaller class size, health services, and so on—all contribute to quality, but they can only enhance the relationship between teacher and student.

Because the NCEEA was established to improve the quality of educational administration in the United States, school administrators must be developed who will head schools that will produce graduates who have the skills, character, and attitudes to grow a greater America. To accomplish this goal, improvements must made in four major elements:

- University faculty
- Graduate students
- Resources
- Environment

What changes should be expected to occur as a result of the activities of the NCEEA and the follow-up work of the UCEA and the National Policy Board? We should expect that professors would engage in activities to expand and focus the knowledge base of educational administration and to develop new and better ways of disseminating it. We should look forward to selecting students for entrance into graduate programs in educational administration based on evidence that they have administrative talent, not just appropriate college grades and good graduate record scores. There should be some increase in the resources available to schools and universities for selecting and educating administrators. And finally, the environment in which school leadership takes place should gradually grow to include all of the relevant actors: teachers, parents, community leaders, and universities.

What can reasonably be expected, then, is a change in the direction of the major elements cited above and a gradual, incremental change in the quality of educational administration. A close reading of this book should let us know if, indeed, this is taking place.

References

Carnegie Forum on Education and the Economy. (1986). *A nation prepared: Teachers for the 21st century.* New York: Author.

Culbertson, J. (1995). *Building bridges: UCEA's first two decades.* University Park, PA: The University Council for Educational Administration.

Flesher, W. R., & Knoblauch, A. L. (Eds.). (1958). *A decade of development in educational leadership.* The National Council of Professors of Educational Administration.

Griffiths, D. E., Stout, R. T., & Forsyth, P. B. (Eds.). (1988). *Leaders for America's schools: The report and papers of the National Commission on Excellence in Educational Administration.* Berkeley, CA: McCutchan.

National Commission on Excellence in Educational Administration. (1987). *Leaders for America's schools: The report of the National Commission on Excellence in Educational Administration.* Tempe, AZ: The University Council for Educational Administration.

Moore, H. (1957). *Studies in school administration: A report on the CPEA.* Washington, DC: American Association of School Administrators.

To friends and colleagues in the profession

PART I

Setting the Stage

1

A Decade of Change:
An Overview

JOSEPH MURPHY AND PATRICK B. FORSYTH

For at least the past dozen years, educational administration has been in the throes of considerable turmoil—disquiet that appears to be accompanying the shift from a scientific to a postscientific era in school administration. As was true in preceding periods of major transition in the profession, the present ferment is being fueled by devastating attacks on the current state of preparation programs, critical analyses of practicing school administrators, and references to alternative visions of what programs should become. If anything, the rhetoric today seems both more strident and more comprehensive than that found in earlier eras of reform. As the following statements indicate, the seriousness of the rhetoric has also increased:

> School administrators risk becoming an anachronism if their preparation programs in schools, colleges, and departments of education do not respond to calls for change in preparing them for professional leadership functions. (American Association of Colleges for Teacher Education, 1988, p. 1)

> I am thoroughly and completely convinced that, unless a radical reform movement gets under way—and is successful—most of us in this room will live to see the end of educational administration as a profession. (Griffiths, 1988b, p. 1)

> Educational Administration as a field is at a delicately critical phase. In fact, there is a rumbling in the clouds above us—they are no longer merely on the horizon—which could in fact blow the whole field of Educational

Administration apart, for both practitioners and the scholars in the field. (Beare, 1989, p. 3)

It is our position that although the current era of turmoil was foreshadowed by analysts almost at the same time that the theory movement broke over the profession (Culbertson, 1963; Harlow, 1962), and although it began to pick up momentum in the 1970s with the publication of Greenfield's (1975) insightful critique, it was not until the mid-1980s that the balance was tipped toward widespread critique and large-scale reform. This volume is designed to chronicle the efforts that have unfolded since that critical mass of energy was achieved. To anchor the work, we use the release of the National Commission on Excellence in Educational Administration's (NCEEA; 1987) report, *Leaders for America's Schools*, as our starting point. We then unpack reform initiatives that have begun to take root since 1987. Although the various authors are sensitive to the critical reviews that generated the momentum for change, because most of that work has been presented elsewhere (Griffiths, Stout, & Forsyth, 1988a; Murphy, 1990, 1992), the primary focus here is on narrating the struggle for change during the past decade.

A Snapshot of the Book

The book is organized to deal with the broad sweep of change in the introductory and concluding sections while highlighting specific areas of reform (e.g., the professoriate) in the middle chapters. In this introductory chapter, we tackle two assignments. We provide a brief analysis of the forces that threw the extant dynamics of educational administration into question and that have served as blueprints for the construction of new perspectives of the profession. It is here that reviews of critical analyses are concentrated. We also chronicle the major events that define what is likely to be remembered as the most prolific and intense period of reform activity in the short history of our profession.

Drawing on questionnaire data from 105 professors of school administration, Joseph Murphy paints a self-portrait of the profession in Chapter 2. Significant changes, critical events, and missed opportunities provide the material from which the picture is formed.

Chapters 3 and 4 are dedicated to examining a basket of important reform initiatives that were coordinated by the two leading organizational players of the past decade. Thus, in Chapter 3, Patrick B. Forsyth chronicles the story of the University Council for Educational Administration's (UCEA) efforts over the past decade in the service of a strengthened profession, whereas Scott D. Thomson reviews reform activities directed by the National Policy Board for Educational Administration (NPBEA) in Chapter 4.

The four chapters (5-8) that comprise the middle section of the book throw the floodlights on changes in specific domains of the profession. The three chapters by Ann W. Hart and Diana G. Pounder, Eddy J. Van Meter, and Joseph Murphy analyze issues associated with preparation programs for school leaders. Martha M. McCarthy, in turn, reviews changes in the professoriate and alterations in departments of educational leadership.

Based on unique positions afforded them as chroniclers of the profession, we asked four colleagues to provide "essays on the nature of the change process and the effects of that process, including critique about issues left unaddressed." Daniel E. Griffiths takes on that assignment as part of the introduction. The essays of Nelda H. Cambron-McCabe, David L. Clark, and Charol Shakeshaft are found in chapters 9-11. In the concluding chapter, we review the decade of reform with one eye to discovering important themes on the change landscape and the other eye to uncovering important gains and losses that have accrued in the profession from 1987 through 1996.

Pressures for Change[1]

A central theme of our work over the past decade has been that school administration is in the intersection between its past and its future—that it is struggling to loosen the bonds and routines that defined the profession from the mid-1950s to the mid-1980s during the theory movement. Although it is not clear to what extent those ties will be broken, and if they are, how the profession might be reconfigured, what is certain is that since the formation of the NCEEA, considerable effort applied in a relatively concerted manner has been directed to the reform of school administration. Indeed, in this volume, we argue that the decade defining the transition from the behavioral science era has been the most intense period of reform activity we have seen in school administration. Later in this chapter, and elsewhere in this volume, we document the full sweep of initiatives undertaken in the service of reform. Here, we briefly overview the reasons that the comfort of the status quo was thrown into question. Arguments are grouped into two clusters—those focusing on reform pressures from the environment and those emanating from critical analyses of the profession itself.

The Changing Environment of School Administration

In the next section, we examine forces internal to the academic arm of educational administration that are encouraging the profession to redefine itself. Although that is where the bulk of reform attention has been focused to date, it is important to emphasize that school administration is also finding it necessary to reshape itself in response to changing conditions in the environment—forces that, regardless of the internal health of the profession, demand a rethinking of the business known as school leadership. We review two sets of dynamics in this section—environmental forces associated with the evolution to a postindustrial world for the educational industry, and forces changing the nature of schooling of which school administration is a part.

The Evolution to a Postindustrial World

The changing economic fabric. It is almost a fundamental law that the economy is undergoing a significant metamorphosis as we head into the 21st century. There is widespread agreement that we have been and continue to be moving from an industrial to a postindustrial economy. Key aspects of the new economy include the globalization of economic activity, the demise of the mass-production economy, a privileging of information technology, an increase in the skills required to be successful, and an emphasis on the service dimensions of the marketplace (Marshall & Tucker, 1992). It is also becoming clear to many analysts that with the arrival of the postindustrial society, "we are seeing the dissolution of the social structure associated with traditional industrialism" (Hood, 1994, p. 12). The ascent of the global economy has brought an emphasis on new markets, "a loosening of the constraints of the labor market" (Dahrendorf, 1995, p. 21), and a "break[ing] of the state monopoly on the delivery of human services so that private enterprise can expand" (Lewis, 1993, p. 84). Along with these have come increasing deinstitutionalization, deregulation, and privatization.

There is a growing belief that "free market economics provide the path to prosperous equilibrium" (Thayer, 1987, p. 168)—a belief in "the assumption that left to itself economic interaction between rationally self-interested individuals in the market will spontaneously yield broad prosperity, social harmony, and all other manner of public and private good" (Himmelstein, 1983, p. 16). Supported by market theory and theories of the firm, and by the public choice literature, there is a "new spirit of enterprise in the air" (Hardin, 1989, p. 16)—a renewed interest in "private market values" (Bailey, 1987, p. 141) and the "virtues of private property" (Hirsch, 1991, p. 2), and a "promarket trend" (President's Commission on Privatization, 1988, p. 237) in the larger society. A view of individuals as "economic free agents" (Murnane & Levy, 1996, p. 229) is finding widespread acceptance. Although analysts are quick to point out the fallacy of this emerging belief in the infallibility of markets, there is little doubt that current alterations in the economic foundations of society are anchored firmly in a "belief in the superiority of free market forms of social organization over the forms of social organization of the Keynesian welfare state society" (Ian Taylor, cited in Martin, 1993, p. 48). As Starr (1991) notes, this expanding reliance on the market moves individuals in the direction of "exercis[ing] choice as consumers rather than as citizens" (p. 27). It leads organizations such as schools to emulate current private-sector business practices.

Shifting social and political dynamics. In the previous section, we addressed the changing economic substructures of a postindustrial state. In this section, we examine the shifting social and political foundations of the democratic welfare state that, in turn, act to help redefine the education industry and our understanding of school leadership.

The political and social environment appears to be undergoing important changes. There has been a loosening of the bonds of democracy (Barber, 1984). Thus, according to a number of scholars, "our American democracy is faltering" (Elshtain, 1995, p. 1), with a concomitant "loss . . . to our ways of living and working together and to our view of the worth of the individual" (Tomlinson, 1986, p. 211). The infrastructure of civil society also has been impaired. Analysts discern fairly significant tears in the fabric known as "modern civil society" (Dahrendorf, 1995, p. 23).

As a consequence of these basic shifts—the weakening of democracy and the deterioration of civil society, especially in conjunction with the ideological space that they share with economic fundamentalism—important sociopolitical trends have begun to emerge: (a) "a growing sense of personal insecurity" (Dahrendorf, 1995, p. 26), "unrest in the populace at large" (Liebman & Wuthnow, 1983, p. 3), and a less predictable "worldlife" (Hawley, 1995, pp. 741-742); (b) "the destruction of important features of community life" (Dahrendorf, 1995, p. 26); (c) shifts in the boundaries— both real and symbolic—between the state and alternative sociopolitical structures (Liebman, 1983a); and (d) an expanding belief that the enhancement of social justice through collective action, especially public action, is unlikely (Whitty, 1984).

The composite picture of self-destruction has been labeled "The Disunity of America" by Dahrendorf (1995, p. 23) and characterized as "the weakening . . . of the world known as democratic civil society" by Elshtain

(1995, p. 2). One strand of this evolving sociopolitical mosaic is plummeting support for government. In many ways, Americans "have disengaged psychologically from politics and governance" (Putnam, 1995, p. 68): "The growth of cynicism about democratic government shifts America toward, not away from, a more generalized norm of disaffection" (Elshtain, 1995, p. 25). As Hawley (1995) chronicles, "citizens are becoming increasingly alienated from government and politics. They do not trust public officials" (p. 741), and they are skeptical of the bureaucratic quagmire of professional control.

A second pattern in the mosaic is defined by issues of poverty. Many analysts, for example, have detailed the "concept and the phenomenon of the underclass" (Dahrendorf, 1995, p. 24) or the "trend toward private wealth and public squalor" (Bauman, 1996, p. 627). According to Dahrendorf (1995), this economically grounded trend represents a new type of social exclusion— the "systematic divergence of the life chances for large social groups" (p. 24). He and others are quick to point out that this condition seriously undermines the health of society: "Poverty and unemployment threaten the very fabric of civil society. Once these [work and a decent standard of living] are lost by a growing number of people, civil society goes with them" (pp. 25-26).

Consistent with this description of diverging life chances is a body of findings on the declining social welfare of children and their families. These data reveal a society populated increasingly by groups of citizens that historically have not fared well in this nation, especially ethnic minorities and citizens for whom English is a second language. Concomitantly, the percentage of youngsters affected by the ills of the world in which they live— for example, poverty, unemployment, illiteracy, crime, drug addiction, malnutrition, and poor physical health—is increasing.

According to Himmelstein (1983), society is best pictured as "a web of shared values and integrating institutions that bind individuals together and restrain their otherwise selfish, destructive drives" (p. 16). Some reviewers have observed a noticeable attenuation of these social bonds, or what Elshtain (1995) describes as a "loss of civil society—a kind of evacuation of civic spaces" (p. 5). The splintering of shared values and the accompanying dimi-nution in social cohesiveness have been discussed by Dahrendorf (1995) and Mayberry (1991), among others. Few, however, have devoted as much atten-tion to the topic of changing patterns of civic engagement and political par-ticipation as Robert Putnam (1995). According to Putnam, the "democratic disarray" (p. 77) that characterizes society and the polity can be "linked to a broad and continuing erosion of civic engagement that began a quarter-cen-tury ago" (p. 77). After examining citizen involvement across a wide array of areas (e.g., participation in politics, union membership, volunteerism in civic and fraternal organizations, participation in organized religion) he drew the following conclusion:

> By almost every measure, Americans' direct engagement in politics and government has fallen steadily and sharply over the last generation, despite the fact that average levels of education—the best individual-level predictor of political participation—have risen sharply throughout this period. Every year over the last decade or two, millions more have withdrawn from the affairs of their communities. (p. 68)

Another piece of the story, related to the themes of declining social cohesion and political abstinence but even more difficult to ignore, is the issue of "social breakdown and moral decay" (Himmelstein, 1983 p. 15) or rents in the "sociomoral" (Liebman, 1983b, p. 229) tapestry of society. Of particular concern is the perception that state actions have contributed to the evolution of social mores that are undermining the adhesiveness that has traditionally held society together—that "the welfare bureaucracy is irreversibly opposed to the established social morality" (Gottfried, 1993, p. 86).

The ideological footings of the emerging sociopolitical infrastructure are only dimly visible at this time. The one piece of the foundation that shines most brightly is what Tomlinson (1986) describes as the "ascendancy of the theory of the social market" (p. 211)—a theory that is anchored on the "supreme value [of] individual liberty" (p. 211). This emerging "high regard for personal autonomy, or liberty" (Gottfried, 1993, pp. xiv-xv) is both an honoring of individualization and a discrediting of collective action (Donahue, 1989; Katz, 1971). Social market theory suggests a "reduced role for government, greater consumer control, and a belief in efficiency and individuality over equity and community" (Bauman, 1996, p. 627). According to Whitty (1984), it includes the privileging of private over public delivery and "the restoration of decisions that have been made by professional experts over the last few decades to the individuals whose lives are involved" (p. 53). Whereas critics of social market theory and glorified individualism foresee "a weakening of democratic participation [and] social cohesion" (Tomlinson, 1986, p. 211), advocates contend that "the individual pursuit of self-interest is not a threat to the social bond, but its very basis" (Himmelstein, 1983, p. 16).

The Changing Nature of Schooling

As is the case with other organizations, schools are currently fighting to transform the way they think and act. From the collective effort of those who describe this change, a new vision of education quite unlike the "center of production" (Barth, 1986, p. 295) image that has shaped schooling throughout the industrial age is being portrayed. Embedded in this emerging view of tomorrow's schools are three central alterations: (a) at the institutional level, a change from professional to lay/professional control; (b) at the managerial level, a change from a bureaucratic operational system to more communal views of schooling; and (c) at the technical level, a change from behavioral to constructivist views of learning and teaching. Each of these fundamental shifts leads to different ways of thinking about school administration and school leadership.

Reinventing governance. Most analysts of the institutional level of schooling—the interface of the school with its larger (generally immediate) environment—argue that the industrial approach to education led to "the belief in almost complete separation of schools from the community and, in turn, discouragement of local community involvement in decision making related to the administration of schools" (Burke, 1992, p. 33). Indeed, a considerable body of literature suggests that one of the major functions of bureaucracy is the buffering of the school from the environment, especially from parents and community members.

Most chroniclers of the changing governance structures in restructuring schools envision the demise of schooling as a sheltered government monopoly heavily controlled by professionals. In its stead, they forecast the emergence of a system of schooling and, more important for our purposes here, improvement designs driven by economic and political forces that substantially increase the saliency of market and democratic dynamics. Embedded in this conception are a number of interesting dynamics, all of which gain force from a realignment of power and influence between professional educators and lay members of the community. To begin with, the traditionally dominant relationship—with professional educators on the playing field and parents on the sidelines acting as cheerleaders or agitators or, more likely, passive spectators—is replaced by a more equal distribution of influence. Partnerships begin to emerge. At the same time, the number of stakeholders in the schooling game increases, their legitimate influence expands, and the roles they play broaden. All of this, of course, reinforces the importance of democratic and market principles in schools and the vehicles by which these principles find expression—self-management, participatory governance, and choice.

Reinventing systems of organization. "In recent years, critics have argued that the reforms of the Progressive Era produced bureaucratic arteriosclerosis, insulation from parents and patrons, and the low productivity of a declining industry protected as a quasi monopoly" (Tyack, 1993, p. 3). There is growing sentiment that the existing structure of administration is "obsolete and unsustainable" (Rungeling & Glover, 1991, p. 415)—that the "bureaucratic structure is failing in a manner so critical that adaptations will not forestall its collapse" (Clark & Meloy, 1989, p. 293). Behind this basic critique is the belief that "bureaucracies are set up to serve the adults that run them and in the end, the kids get lost in the process" (Daly, cited in Olson, 1992, p. 10). It is increasingly being concluded that the existing bureaucratic system of administration is "incapable of addressing the technical and structural shortcomings of the public educational system" (Lawton, 1991, p. 4).

More finely grained criticism of the bureaucratic infrastructure of schooling comes from a variety of quarters. Some reformers maintain "that school bureaucracies, as currently constituted could [never] manage to provide high-quality education" (Elmore, 1993, p. 37); that, even worse, "bureaucratic management practices have been causing unacceptable distortions in educational process" (Wise, 1989, p. 301); and that those practices are "paralyzing American education . . . [and] getting in the way of children's learning" (Sizer, 1984, p. 206). Some analysts believe that bureaucracy is counterproductive to the needs and interests of educators within the school—that it is "impractical, and it does not fit the psychological and personal needs of the workforce" (Clark & Meloy, 1989, p. 293), that it "undermine[s] the authority of teachers" (Sackney & Dibski, 1992, p. 2), and that it is "incompatible with the professional organization" (Sackney & Dibski, 1992, p. 4). Still other critics suggest that bureaucratic management is inconsistent with the sacred values and purposes of education—they question "fundamental ideological issues pertaining to bureaucracy's meaning in a democratic society" (Campbell, Fleming, Newell, & Bennion, 1987, p. 73). Finally, some analysts contend that the rigidities of bureaucracy, by making schools "almost impenetrable by citizens and unwieldy to professionals" (Candoli, 1991, p. 31), impede the ability of parents and citizens to govern and reform schooling.

As might be expected, given this tremendous attack on the basic organizational infrastructure of schooling, stakeholders at all levels are arguing that "ambitious, if not radical, reforms are required to rectify this situation" (Elmore, 1993, p. 34), and that "the excessively centralized, bureaucratic control of . . . schools must end" (Carnegie Forum, cited in Hanson, 1991, pp. 2-3).

In its place, reformers are arguing for "a philosophy of devolved decision-making and school self-determination" (Dellar, 1992, p. 5) and for "policies . . . that unleash productive local initiatives" (Guthrie, 1986, p. 306). The emerging alternative vision of administration for tomorrow's schools includes methods of organizing and managing schools that are generally consistent with the "quiet revolution [in] organizational and administrative theory in Western societies" (Foster, 1988, p. 71). In the still-forming image of schools for the 21st century, hierarchical, bureaucratic organizational structures give way to systems that are more organic, more decentralized, and more professionally controlled—systems that "suggest a new paradigm for school organization and management" (Mulkeen, 1990, p. 105). The need to redefine school leadership is palpable.

Reinventing learning and teaching. From the onset of the industrial revolution, education in the United States has been defined largely by a behavioral psychological model of learning—a model that fits nicely with the bureaucratic system of school organization. In turn, this viewpoint nurtured the development of the factory and medical models of instruction that have dominated schooling throughout the 20th century. Under these two models, the belief that the role of schooling is to sort students into the able and less able—those who would work with their heads and those who would work with their hands—is deeply embedded into the fabric of schooling.

A shift in the operant model of learning is a fundamental dynamic of the struggle to redefine schools. Of real significance, if rarely noted, is the fact that this new model reinforces the democratic tenets embedded in the postindustrial views of governance and administration discussed previously. The behavioral psychological model that highlights the innate capacity of the learner is replaced by "cognitive or constructivist psychology" (Cohen, 1988, p. 19) and newer sociological perspectives on learning. Under this approach to learning, schools that historically have been in the business of promoting student adaptation to the existing social order are being transformed to ensure equality of opportunity for all learners.

The emerging redefinition of teaching means that teachers, historically organized to carry out instructional designs and implement curricular materials developed from afar, have begun to exercise considerably more control over their profession and the routines of the workplace. Analysts see this reorganization playing out in a variety of ways at the school level. At the most fundamental level, teachers have a much more active voice in developing the goals and purposes of schooling—goals that act to delimit or expand the conception of teaching itself. They also have a good deal more to say about the curricular structures and pedagogical approaches employed in their schools— "influences over the basic elements of instructional practice (time, material, student engagement, and so forth)" (Elmore, 1989, p. 20). Finally, teachers demonstrate more control over the supporting ingredients of schooling—such as budgets, personnel, and administration—that affect the way they carry out their responsibilities.

Advocates of transformational change also see teaching becoming a more collegial activity. Isolation, so deeply ingrained in the structure and culture of the profession, gives way to more collaborative efforts among teachers. At the macro level, teachers are redefining their roles to include collaborative management of the profession, especially providing direction for professional standards. At a more micro level, new organizational structures are being created to allow teachers to plan and teach together and to make important decisions about the nature of their roles.

New conceptions of teaching include other efforts to expand "teachers' roles and responsibilities beyond their regular classroom assignments" (Smylie & Denny, 1989, p. 4). The opening of decision-making forums historically closed to teachers is one example of this expansion. Thus, redefining teaching entails "acknowledging and institutionalizing the central managerial role of teachers" (Sykes & Elmore, 1989, p. 85)—a phenomenon that plays out in each individual teacher's expanded responsibility for the professionalization of colleagues and collectively in decision-making bodies such as school-site councils. As was the case with governance and organization, new views of learning and teaching call for quite different understandings of school leadership and the role of universities in preparing school administrators.

Consternation at Home: Meltdown of the Core

In addition to pressures from the environment, a good deal of internal soul searching also anchored calls for the reform of school administration. As has been the case in other major periods of change in the profession, these concerns were centered on the two core dimensions of the academy: (a) the intellectual infrastructure supporting the profession, including the research methods used as scaffolding in the construction process, and (b) the methods and procedures used to educate school leaders.

Questions About the Intellectual Infrastructure

In this section, we examine what appears to be an irreparable gash in the fabric of the profession that has acted as a catalyst for the rising turmoil in school administration as well as for the efforts to reshape the profession. We refer specifically to attacks from a variety of quarters on the administration-as-science intellectual foundations that grounded the profession from the mid-1950s through the mid-1980s.

Although, over the life of the theory movement, the profession "increased in formality, structure, and complexity, much as did the school system—from amateur to professional, from simple to complicated, and from intuitive to 'scientific'" (Cooper & Boyd, 1987, p. 7)—the outcomes of the quest for a science of administration were considerably less robust than had been anticipated. By the mid-1970s, this failure of the theory movement to deliver on its promises was brought to a head in a landmark paper delivered by Greenfield (1975) at the Third International Intervisitation program in Bristol, England (Griffiths, 1988a). Although other scholars had been drawing attention to the limitations of a near-exclusive emphasis on a scientific approach to training for some time, Greenfield unleashed the first systemic broadside attack on the central tenets of the theory movement, especially on its epistemological roots and guiding values. In a word, he found the scientific era of educational administration to be impoverished. Greenfield's paper went a long way toward galvanizing critique of the field that began to wash over the profession in the mid-1980s.

Over the past 20 years, other thoughtful analysts have joined the debate about the appropriate value structure and cognitive base for educational administration. On the knowledge base issue, there has been increasing agreement—although with noticeable differences in explanations—that "a body of dependable knowledge about educational administration" (Crowson & McPherson, 1987, p. 48) did not emerge during the behavioral science era. This condition means that exiting the behavioral science era, there was not much "conceptual unity" to the field (Erickson, 1979, p. 9). In practical terms, Erickson (1979) concluded that "the field consist[ed] of whatever scholars associated with university programs in 'educational administration' consider[ed] relevant. It is, to say the least, amorphous" (p. 9). In his review, Boyan (1988a) concurred, arguing that "the explanatory aspect of the study of administrator behavior in education over 30 years appears to be an incomplete anthology of short stories connected by no particular story line or major themes" (p. 93). Given this absence of conceptual unity, there has not been much common agreement about the appropriate foundation for the profession, either. Thus, as the behavioral science era drew to a close,

Goldhammer (1983) reported that although there were "general areas of concern that might dictate to preparatory institutions the names of courses that should be taught, . . . there [was] less agreement on what the content of such courses should actually be" (p. 269).

At the same time, a pattern of criticism was forming about both the definition of legitimate knowledge and the accepted ways in which it could be generated. As Crowson and McPherson (1987) reported, during this transition phase, critics "questioned with increasing vigor the appropriateness of traditional research methods and assumptions as a guide to an understanding of practice" (p. 48). Analysts called for both relegitimization of practice-based knowledge and the acceptance of

> an increasing diversity of research methods, including attempts at qualitative, ethnographic, naturalistic, phenomenological, and critical studies . . . [and] an *effort* to generate "theories of practice" that incorporate both objective and subjective ways of knowing, both fact and value considerations, both "is" and "ought" dimensions of education within integrated frameworks for practice. (Silver, 1982, pp. 53, 56)

Finally, there was a deepening recognition that the knowledge base employed in preparation programs had not been especially useful in solving real problems in the field. This questioning of the relevance of theory to practice can be traced to a number of causes. Deeply ingrained methods of working that assumed that one could discover theory that would automatically apply itself to situations of practice was the first. A second was the emergence of a "parochial view of science" (Halpin, 1960, p. 6)—one in which social scientists became "intent upon aping the more prestigious physical scientists in building highly abstract, theoretical models" (p. 6) at the expense of clinical science. A third was the proclivity of educational researchers employing social and behavioral sciences to contribute to the various disciplines rather than to administrative practice; administrative "structure and process were studied mostly as a way of adding to disciplinary domains" (Erickson, 1977, p. 136). Along these same lines, during this entire era, there was a lack of effort on the part of professors to distinguish systematically those aspects of the social and behavioral sciences that were most appropriate for practitioners (Gregg, 1969). Largely because of the overwhelming nature of the task (Culbertson, 1965), the weakness of the theory movement noted by the American Association of School Administrators (AASA) in 1960—the failure "to work out the essentials in the social sciences for school administrators and to develop a program containing these essentials" (p. 57)—was still a problem as the sun set on the behavioral science era.

A number of critics also have pointed out that regardless of its usefulness, the knowledge base constructed during the scientific era gave rise to a "narrowly defined concept of administration" (Greenfield, 1988, p. 147). This line of analysis spotlights the failure of the profession to include critical concepts, materials, and ideas. To begin with, by taking a "neutral posture on moral issues" (Culbertson, 1964, p. 311), the theory movement largely excluded value issues from preparation programs. When the term *value judgment* did surface, it was "frequently as an epithet indicating intellectual contempt" (Harlow, 1962, p. 66). Throughout the behavioral science era, there was "little serious, conscious effort to develop demonstrably in students the skills or behavioral propensities to act in ways that could be considered ethical" (Farquhar, 1981, p. 199). Attention to the "humanities as a body of 'aesthetic wisdom' capable of contributing its own unique enrichment to the preparation of school administrators" (Popper, 1982, p. 12) was conspicuous by its absence.

Also neglected during this period of administration qua administration were educational issues—a phenomenon exacerbated by efforts to professionalize administration and thereby distinguish it from teaching. What Anderson and Lonsdale reported in 1957—that "few items in the literature of educational administration . . . say much about the psychology of learning" (p. 429), and what Boyan concluded in 1963—that "the content of the advanced preparation tends to focus on the managerial and institutional dimensions as compared to teaching, the technical base of educational organizations" (pp. 3-4), were equally true in 1987.

In summary, by the early 1990s, a multifaceted assessment of the intellectual foundations of the profession had produced a good deal of disquiet in the profession. This unease, in turn, has continually fueled the turmoil that still characterizes the academic arm of the profession. It has also served, both directly and indirectly, as a springboard for many of the reform initiatives that have sprung up in the 10 years since the release of the NCEEA report.

Concerns About Preparation Programs

The current era of ferment is fueled not only by critique of the intellectual foundations of the profession but also by critical reviews of preparation programs for school leaders. Reviewers have chronicled a system of preparing school leaders that is seriously flawed and that has been found wanting in nearly every aspect. Specifically, critics have uncovered serious problems in (a) the ways students are recruited and selected into training programs; (b) the education they receive once there, including the content emphasized and the pedagogical strategies employed; (c) the methods used to assess academic fitness; and (d) the procedures developed to certify and select principals and superintendents.

Recruitment and selection. Analysts of the recruitment and selection processes employed in the mid-1980s by institutions in the administrator training business consistently found them lacking in rigor. Procedures were often informal, haphazard, and casual. Prospective candidates were often self-selected, and there were few leader recruitment programs (Murphy, 1992). Fewer than 10% of students reported that they were influenced by the recruitment activities of the training institutions. Despite well-documented, if commonsensical, reminders that training outcomes depended on the mix of program experiences and the quality of entering students, research on the recruitment of school administrators was quite anemic.

Standards for selecting students into preparation programs were often perfunctory: "Most programs ha[d] 'open admissions,' with a baccalaureate degree the only prerequisite" (Griffiths, Stout, & Forsyth, 1988b, p. 290); "for too many administrator preparation programs, *any body* is better than *no body*" (Jacobson, 1990, p. 35). The UCEA-sponsored study of the mid-1970s (Silver, 1978) discovered that the rejection rates in preparation programs were quite low—about 12% for master's students, 14% for sixth-year students, and 25% for doctoral students. In 1984, Gerritz, Koppich, and Guthrie found that only about 1 in 30 applicants was denied admission to certification programs in California. Part of the reason for this nonselectivity can be traced to the use of questionable methods and procedures and to poorly articulated standards for entry. If all one needed 50 years ago to enter a training program in educational administration was a "B.A. and the case to pay tuition" (Tyack & Cummings, 1977, p. 60), the situation was not much improved as the profession took stock of itself in the mid-1980s.

It is not surprising that the quality of applicants is, and has been for some time, rather low. In 1988, for instance, Griffiths (1988b) revealed that "of the 94 intended majors listed in [the] Guide to the Use of the Graduate Record Examination Program 1985-86 . . . educational administration is fourth from the bottom" (p. 12). This lack of rigorous recruitment and selection procedures and criteria has several negative effects:

First, it lowers the level of training and experience possible, since courses are often geared to the background and intelligence of the students.

Second, "eased entry downgrades the status of the students in the eyes of the populace." Third, the candidates themselves realize that anyone can get in and that nearly everyone will get the license if he or she just keeps paying for credits. In part, this lack of rigor at entry reflects a lack of clear criteria for training or clear vision of what candidates and graduates will look like, and the realization that the graduate school experience itself is not very demanding. (Cooper & Boyd, 1987, p. 14)

This lack of rigor was believed to be contributing to the serious oversupply of credentialed administrators in the United States.

Program content. Turning to the content of preparation programs at the time the ferment in the profession was beginning to warm up, critical reviews revealed the following problems: the indiscriminate adoption of practices untested and uninformed by educational values and purposes, serious fragmentation, the separation of the practice and academic arms of the profession, relatively nonrobust strategies for generating new knowledge, the neglect of ethics, an infatuation with the study of administration for its own sake, and the concomitant failure to address outcomes.

Critics averred that in many preparation programs, "course content [was] frequently banal" (Clark, 1988, p. 5). Nor did training programs exhibit much internal consistency. Students often confronted a "confusing melange of courses, without clear meaning, focus, or purpose" (Cooper & Boyd, 1987, p. 14). There was an absence of a "continuum of knowledge and skills that become more sophisticated as one progress[ed]" (Peterson & Finn, 1985, pp. 51-52). What all this meant was "that most administrators receiv[ed] fragmented, overlapping, and often useless courses that add[ed] up to very little" (Cooper & Boyd, 1987, p. 13).

One of the most serious problems with the cognitive base in school administration training programs in the mid-1980s was the fact that it did not reflect the realities of the workplace and therefore was, at best, "irrelevant to the jobs trainees assume" (Mulkeen & Cooper, 1989, p. 1) and, at worst, "dysfunctional in the actual world of practice" (Sergiovanni, 1989, p. 18). As we reported earlier, scholars of the behavioral science era attempted to develop a science of administration. One of the effects was an exacerbation of the natural tension between the practice and academic arms of the profession. The nurturance and development of the social sciences became ends in themselves. Professors, never very gifted at converting scientific knowledge to guide practice, had little motivation to improve. As a result, the theory and research borrowed from the behavioral sciences "never evolved into a unique knowledge base informing the practice of school administration" (Griffiths, 1988b, p. 19).

Mann (1975), Bridges (1977), Muth (1989), Sergiovanni (1989, 1991), and others have all written influential essays in which they describe how the processes and procedures stressed in university programs in the theory era were often diametrically opposed to conditions that characterize the workplace milieu of schools. Other thoughtful reviewers concluded that administrators-in-training were often "given a potpourri of theory, concepts, and ideas—unrelated to one another and rarely useful in either understanding schools or managing them" (Mulkeen & Cooper, 1989, p. 12). In their review of training programs at the end of the theory era, Crowson and McPherson (1987) argued that institutions "that had emphasized a solid grounding in theory, the social sciences, [and] rational decision making . . . were discovered to be well off the mark as effective preparation for the chaotic life of a principal or superintendent" (p. 49).

Evidence from nearly all fronts led to the conclusion that the focus on the behavioral sciences during the scientific era of training resulted in a glaring absence of consideration of the problems faced by practicing school administrators. The pervasive anti-recipe, anti-skill philosophy that characterized many programs of educational administration resulted in significant gaps in the prevailing knowledge base: an almost complete absence of performance-based program components, a lack of attention to practical problem-solving skills, "a neglect of practical intelligence" (Sergiovanni, 1989, p. 17), and a truncated conception of expertise. Administrators consistently reported that the best way to improve training in preparation programs would be to improve instruction of job-related skills (Erlandson & Witters-Churchill, 1988).

The clinical aspects of most preparation programs in educational administration at the time of the NCEEA report were notoriously weak. Despite an entrenched belief that supervised practice "could be the most critical phase of the administrator's preparation" (Griffiths, 1988b, p. 17) and a long history of efforts to make field-based learning an integral part of preparation programs, little progress has been made in this area. And despite concern over the impoverished nature of clinical experience for nearly 30 years, Pepper was still able to report as late as 1988 that "few, if any, university programs in school administration offer a thorough clinical experience for future school administrators" (p. 361). The field-based component continued to be infected with weaknesses that have been revisited on a regular basis since the first decade of the behavioral science revolution in administrative preparation: (a) unclear objectives; (b) inadequate number of clinical experiences; (c) activities arranged on the basis of convenience; (d) overemphasis on role-centered as opposed to problem-centered experiences; (e) lack of individualization; (f) poor planning, supervision, and follow-up; (g) absence of "connecting linkages between on-campus experiences and field-based experiences" (Milstein, 1990, p. 121); and (h) overemphasis on low-level (orientation and passive observation) activities.

Woven deeply into the fabric of "administration as an applied science" was the belief that there was a single best approach to educating prospective school leaders (Cooper & Boyd, 1987), including a dominant worldview of administration as an area of study (content) and method of acting (procedure). A number of thoughtful analysts maintained that this perspective has resulted in significant gaps in the knowledge base employed in training programs of the era. Missing was consideration of the diversity of perspectives that informed scholarship and practice. For example, in her review of the literature on women administrators, Shakeshaft (1988) discovered "differences between the ways men and women approach the tasks of administration" (p. 403). She concluded that, although "these differences have implications for administrative training programs . . . the female world of administrators has not been incorporated into the body of work in the field . . . [n]or are women's experiences carried into the literature on practice" (pp. 403-406). Similar conclusions were reached about racial minorities.

One of the most troubling aspects of preparation programs of the mid-1980s was that they had very little to do with education. Most programs showed "little interest in exploring the historical roots and social context of schooling" (Anderson, 1990, p. 53) and did "a very bad job of teaching . . . a wider vision of schools in society (Mulkeen & Cooper, 1989, p. 12). Furthermore, there was ample evidence that the content in training programs focused on managerial issues and largely ignored matters of teaching and learning, of pedagogy and curriculum. Most of the interest and scholarly activity of the behavioral science era heavily reinforced the "separation of problems in administration from problems in education" (Greenfield, 1988, p. 144) and the emphasis on noneducational issues in training programs. As Evans (1991) astutely chronicles, the era sponsored discourse and training primarily on "the administration of education" (p. 3), or administration qua administration—a major shift from its formative years when the emphasis "was upon the adjective 'educational' rather than upon the noun 'administration'" (Guba, 1960, p. 115). The separation of educational administration "from the phenomenon known as instruction" (Erickson, 1979, p. 10) meant that the typical graduate of a school administration training program could act only as "a mere spectator in relation to the instructional program" (Hills, 1975, p. 4).

By the early 1960s, the second major root of the field—values and ethics—like education before it, had atrophied. The result was reduced consideration of two issues: (a) organizational values, purpose, and ethics, and (b) organizational outcomes. According to Greenfield (1988), "the empirical study of administrators has eluded their *moral* dimensions and virtually all that lends significance to what they do" (p. 138). Despite some early notices that "educational administration requires a distinctive value framework" (Graff & Street, 1957, p. 120), pleas to reorient administration toward purposing (Harlow, 1962), and clear reminders that education is fundamentally a moral activity (Culbertson, 1963; Halpin, 1960), the issue of meaning in school administration as a profession and in its training programs had taken a back seat "to focus upon the personality traits of administrators— upon the mere characteristics of administrators rather than upon their character" (Greenfield, 1988, pp. 137-138). Thus, at the close of the theory era, administrators were exiting training programs unprepared to grapple with ethical issues or address openly the values deeply embedded in schools that often hide behind "a mask of objectivity and impartiality" (Greenfield, 1988, p. 150).

As early as 1960, Chase was pointing out what was to become an increasingly problematic situation in educational administration in general and in training programs in particular—a lack of concern for outcomes. Seventeen years later, Erickson (1977) reported that studies in the field "between 1954 and 1974 provided no adequate basis for outcome-oriented organizational strategy in education" (p. 128). Two years later, Erickson (1979) expanded on the ideas of his earlier essay. He documented "the tendency to neglect the careful tracing of connections between organizational variables and student outcomes" (p. 12). He decried the focus on the characteristics of administrators at the expense of more useful work. He laid out his now famous line of attack on the problem: "The current major *emphasis*, in studies of organizational consequences, should be on postulated causal networks in which student outcomes are the bottom line" (p. 12). At the time of the NCEEA report, preparation programs had yet to resonate to this idea.

Delivery system. The delivery system that shaped preparation programs in the mid-1980s was marked by a number of serious problems, most of which have a long history. Looking at the profession as a whole, it is clear that there are too many institutions involved in the training business. At the time of the

22

NCEEA (1987) report, there were 505 i[...]
educational leadership, with "less than [...]
commitment to provide the excellence call [...]
Many of these programs were cash cows [...]
kept open more for political and economic tnan for educational reasons. In 1983, Willower offered this assessment of the situation:

> [Many] offer graduate study in . . . name only. They seriously stint inquiry and survive by offering easy credentials and by working hard at legislative politics. Their faculties neither contribute to the ideas of the field nor are they actively engaged with them. (p. 194)

These institutions tended to be characterized by high student-faculty ratios and limited specialization among faculty.

A related problem was the framework in which students' educational experiences unfolded: "Administrator training . . . [was] most often a dilatory option, pursued on a convenience basis, part-time, on the margins of a workday" (Sykes & Elmore, 1989, p. 80). Programs had indeed drifted far from the traditional residency model: At the end of the 1970s, Silver (1978) reported that "the ideal of one or two years of full-time student life at the graduate level seems to be disappearing from our preparatory programs, and with it the notions of time for scholarly objectivity, student life, and colleague-like interaction between professors and students" (pp. 207-208). As many as 95% of all students were part-timers (Griffiths et al., 1988b), and "many students complet[ed] their training . . . without forming a professional relationship with a professor or student colleague" (Clark, 1988, p. 5).

By the mid-1980s, the arts and science model of education had become firmly entrenched in schools of education and departments of school administration, which the critics believed was to the detriment of the profession. According to them, this arts and science framework emerged more to help professors develop "greater academic sophistication through their professional roles in order to gain acceptance by their peers in other departments" (Goldhammer, 1983, p. 256) than in response to the needs of prospective administrators. Unfortunately, it was clear by 1985 that the model had neither furnished professors the status for which they had hoped nor provided graduates with the tools they needed to be successful practitioners. In addition, it had driven a wedge between professors and practitioners, creating what Goldhammer (1983) labeled the "university-field gap" (p. 265).

The emulation of the arts and science model had spawned a number of subproblems in preparation programs. One of the most serious was that education designed for practitioners (EdD programs) had been molded to parallel the training provided to researchers (PhD programs) in terms of both research requirements (Silver, 1978) and general coursework (Norton & Levan, 1987). This blurring of requirements and experiences for students pursuing quite distinct careers resulted in the development of ersatz research programs for prospective practitioners. Students, burdened with a variety of inappropriate activities, were being prepared to be neither first-rate researchers nor successful practitioners.

In attempting to address the need to develop intradepartmental balance between professor-scholars attuned to the disciplines and professor-practitioners oriented to the field, departments had generally produced the worst of both by the mid-1980s. Unclear about the proper mission of preparation programs, seeking to enhance the relatively low status afforded professors of school administration, and overburdened with multitudes of students, faculties in educational leadership were characterized by weak scholarship (McCarthy, Kuh, Newell, & Iacona, 1988) and problematic connections to the field (Willower, 1988). A number of reviewers concluded "that only a relatively small number of those in the field of educational administration [were] actively engag[ed] in scholarly activities" (Immegart, 1990, p. 11). Even more disheartening were the assessments of the quality of the scholarship at the time. According to Hawley (1988), because of serious limitations in their own training, many professors were not qualified to supervise research. Coupling this deficiency in ability with the previously noted lack of effort resulted in a situation in which "very little good research was being conducted by [educational administration] faculty and students" (Hawley, 1988, p. 85) and in which students developed a truncated, academic view of scholarly inquiry.

It is probably not surprising, although it is distressing, that inappropriate content that was ineffectively packaged was also being poorly delivered in many training institutions. "The dominant mode of instruction continu[ed] to be lecture and discussion in a classroom setting based on the use of a textbook" (Mulkeen & Tetenbaum, 1990, p. 20). Although some progress was made during the behavioral science era to infuse reality-oriented instructional strategies into preparation programs, the change was hardly revolutionary, and the use of innovative pedagogical methods was not prevalent by the mid-1980s. For example, in the Texas NASSP study (Erlandson & Witters-Churchill, 1988), principals reported "lecture and discussion" to be the primary instructional mode used for eight of nine skill areas examined—and the ninth skill, written communication, was a close second!

Standards. Thoughtful critique of preparation programs at the time of the NCEEA report revealed that the lack of rigorous standards was a serious problem that touched almost every aspect of educational administration. Previously, we noted the general absence of standards at the point of entry into preparation programs. According to critics, once students entered preparation programs, the situation did not improve: "The quality of [their] experiences [was] often abysmally low" (Mulkeen & Cooper, 1989, p. 1). They were not exposed to rigorous coursework: "Students mov[ed] through the program without ever seeing a current research study (other than a local dissertation), without ever having read an article in ASQ or EAQ or AJS [*Administrative Science Quarterly, Educational Administration Quarterly,* and *American Journal of Sociology,* respectively]. They [were] functionally illiterate in the basic knowledge of our field" (Clark, 1988, pp. 4-5). Because performance criteria were ill-defined, there was also very little monitoring of student progress (Hawley, 1988). Not surprisingly, very few entrants into certification programs failed to complete their programs for academic reasons. Most former students indicate that their graduate training was not very rigorous (Jacobson, 1990; Muth, 1989). The delivery system most commonly employed—part-time study in the evening or on weekends— resulted in students who came to their "studies worn-out, distracted, and harried" (Mann, 1975, p. 143) and contributed to the evolution and acceptance of low standards (Hawley, 1988). Exit requirements in turn were often "slack and unrelated to the work of the profession" (Peterson & Finn, 1985, p. 54). Compounding the lack of standards at almost every phase of preparation programs were university faculty who were unable or unwilling to improve the situation (Hawley, 1988; McCarthy et al., 1988). An even greater obstacle to improving standards were the bargains, compromises, and treaties that operated in preparation programs—the lowering of standards in exchange for high enrollments and compliant student behavior. The NCEEA (1987) and the National Policy Board for Educational Administration (1989) and other reviews also concluded that the time had come to elevate markedly standards in school administration.

Markers on the Path to Reform

Although it is impossible to prejudge what future historians of educational administration will designate as the major events that helped shape the profession for the post-theory era, certain events appear likely to receive considerable attention. All later chapters, but especially Chapters 2 through 4, provide thoughtful reviews of these markers. In this section, we provide an overview of significant events of the past decade as an introduction to that work.

One marker that will surely be singled out is the set of activities comprising the work of the NCEEA. Growing out of the deliberations of the Executive Council of the University Council for Educational Administration, the commission was formed in 1985 under the direction of Daniel E. Griffiths. Support for the commission came from funds contributed by a variety of foundations in response to concerted efforts on the part of the UCEA staff. The NCEEA has produced three influential documents that have promoted considerable discussion both within and outside educational administration: the 1987 report *Leaders for America's Schools*; Griffiths's highly influential address to the annual meeting of the American Educational Research Association (AERA; subsequently published as a UCEA paper— Griffiths, 1988b); and a UCEA-sponsored edited volume containing most of the background papers commissioned by the NCEEA (Griffiths et al., 1988a). These three documents helped to crystallize the sense of what is wrong with the profession, extend discussion about possible solutions, and, to a lesser extent, provide signposts for those engaged in redefining school administration.

Following up on these activities, the UCEA Executive Director, Patrick Forsyth, initiated discussions with foundations and set about mustering support for one of the NCEEA recommendations—the creation of the National Policy Board of Educational Administration (NPBEA). After considerable work on the part of UCEA to forge a union among the executive directors of 10 groups with a deep-seated interest in school administration, the NPBEA was created in 1988. Its care was entrusted to David L. Clark, then a professor of educational leadership at the University of Virginia. The NPBEA has undertaken a series of activities designed to provide direction for the reconstruction of the academic arm of the profession. After a year of work supported by the UCEA and chaired by its Executive Director, Patrick Forsyth, and facilitated by the NPBEA Executive Secretary, David L. Clark, the NPBEA released its first report, titled *Improving the Preparation of School Administrators: The Reform Agenda*, in May of 1989. The report outlines an extensive overhaul and strengthening of preparation programs. Its recommendations were later adopted in slightly modified form by the 50-plus universities comprising the UCEA. Following the release of *The Reform Agenda*, the NPBEA published a series of occasional papers that were designed to inform the reform debate in educational administration. It also sponsored, in conjunction with the Danforth Foundation, national conferences to help professors discover alternatives to deeply ingrained practices in training programs. Its 1992 conference on problem-based learning drew nearly 150 participants from universities throughout the United States and Canada.

Building on earlier noted documents, two national efforts to redefine the knowledge base of the field unfolded in the early 1990s. In 1990, the National Commission for the Principalship (NCP), under the leadership of Scott D. Thomson and funded by the National Associations of Elementary and Secondary School Principals, published a report titled *Principals for Our Changing Schools: Preparation and Certification*. The document represents an attempt to unpack the functional knowledge base required by principals. Working from this document, Thomson, under the aegis of the NPBEA—of which he was executive secretary at the time—assigned teams to flesh out each of the 21 knowledge domains identified in the report. The resulting document, *Principals for Our Changing Schools: The Knowledge and Skill Base* (NCP, 1993), provides a "comprehensive description of the core knowledge and skill base required of principals in contemporary settings" (Thomson, this volume's p. 101).

A year later, the UCEA authorized six writing teams under the overall direction of Wayne K. Hoy to update the knowledge bases in educational administration preparation programs. (See Forsyth, Chapter 3, for a full description.)

In addition to the reform reports described earlier, change efforts were shaped by a series of volumes devoted to the analysis and improvement of the academic arm of the profession. Each of these books helped focus attention on the problems of the field and provided alternative visions for a post-theory world as well as solution paths to guide the voyage. Some of the most important of these volumes are the first handbook of research in the field, an AERA–sponsored volume edited by Norman Boyan and published in 1988 (*The Handbook of Research on Educational Administration*); two volumes on the professoriate authored by Martha M. McCarthy and colleagues—a 1988 book entitled *Under Scrutiny: The Educational Administration Professoriate* and the 1997 follow-up volume, *Continuity and Change: The Educational Leadership Professoriate*; the edited volume growing out of the NCEEA project (*Leaders for America's Schools*, Griffiths et al., 1988a); the 1990 National Society for the Study of Education Yearbook (*Educational Leadership and Changing Contexts of Families, Communities, and Schools*, Mitchell & Cunningham, 1990); a volume resulting from the National Center for Educational Leadership conference on cognitive perspectives in school administration (*Cognitive Perspectives on Educational*

Leadership, Hallinger, Leithwood, & Murphy, 1993); and a volume on school administration published by the Politics of Education Association and edited by Hannaway and Crowson (*The Politics of Reforming School Administration,* 1989).

Other books devoted primarily to the reform of the academic arm of the profession include those edited by Murphy in 1993 (*Preparing Tomorrow's School Leaders: Alternative Designs*); by Mulkeen, Cambron-McCabe, and Anderson in 1994 (*Democratic Leadership: The Changing Context of Administrative Preparation*); and by Donmoyer, Imber, and Scheursch in 1995 (*The Knowledge Base in Educational Administration: Multiple Perspectives*); as well as those written by Beck in 1993 (*Reclaiming Educational Administration as a Caring Profession*); by Beck and Murphy in 1994 (*Ethics in Educational Leadership Programs*); by Milstein and Associates in 1993 (*Changing the Way We Prepare Educational Leaders: The Danforth Experience*); and by Murphy in 1992 (*The Landscape of Leadership Preparation: Reframing the Education of School Administrators*).

The initiatives of the Danforth Foundation will no doubt be seen as an important marker in this decade of reform. In addition to its sponsorship of the NCEEA and its core support for the NPBEA, Danforth has underwritten four significant efforts designed to assist self-analyses and improvement efforts in educational administration, all of which capture multiple elements from the various reform volumes and documents of the late 1980s: (a) a Principals' Program to improve preparation programs for prospective leaders; (b) a Professors' Program to enhance the capability of departments to respond to needed reforms; (c) research and development efforts, such as the Problem-Based Learning Project under the direction of Philip Hallinger at Vanderbilt University, that are designing alternative approaches to understanding the profession and educating tomorrow's leaders; and (d) a series of conferences and workshops created to help the professoriate grapple with important reform ideas in the area of preparing leaders for tomorrow's schools.

Two standards-defining activities are also likely to be heavily referenced in future reports of events shaping the evolution, and perhaps the transformation, of the profession as it moves into the 21st century. The first initiative was the development by the National Council for the Accreditation of Teacher Education of their curriculum guidelines for school administration. This work, completed under the aegis of the NPBEA over a 3-year period, brought the best thinking of the Policy Board—via *Principals for Our Changing Schools* (NCP, 1993)—and the various professional associations (e.g., National Association of Elementary School Principals, American

Association of School Administrators, Association for Supervision and Curriculum Development) into a comprehensive framework to reshape preparation programs for school leaders. A second initiative, conducted under the auspices of the Council of Chief State School Officers and in cooperation with the NPBEA—the Interstate School Leaders Licensure Consortium (ISLLC)—produced the first universal set of standards for school leaders (ISLLC, 1996). Approved in late 1996, *Standards for School Leaders* sets about strengthening the academic arm of the profession primarily through the manipulation of state controls over areas such as licensure, relicensure, and program approval.

Finally, it is likely that two additional triggering events from AERA and UCEA during this past decade will stand the test of time when the history of the profession is written. For AERA, the important event was the establishment of the Special Interest Group on Teaching in Educational Administration. For UCEA, it was the development of an annual convention. Both of these catalyzing initiatives have helped create sustained work in the service of reshaping the academic arm of the profession.

Summary

In this introductory chapter, we accomplished three objectives. We provided a brief overview of the volume, including a description of the design principles and snapshots of forthcoming chapters. We listed the major reform markers during the decade since the release of the NCEEA report, and we also analyzed the forces that have pushed and pulled school administration to reinvent itself. The bulk of the chapter was devoted to this third objective. We began by scanning the educational environment and found important changes under way in the economic, political, and social foundations of society— alterations that argue for rethinking the educational industry and the role of school leaders in that enterprise. We also observed that the infrastructure of the educational enterprise itself was being rebuilt—that our understanding of learning, organization, and governance for postindustrial schools was being reconstructed. We reported that internal pressures for change sprang from discontent with the way leaders were being prepared for administrative roles and from concern about the vitality and relevance of the knowledge base that currently undergirds those preparation efforts. We turn next to the story of recent reforms as chronicled by professors of educational administration.

Note

1. The material in this section is drawn primarily from recent work in the areas of school improvement (Murphy, in press; Murphy & Beck, 1995) and administrator preparation (Murphy, 1990a, 1992).

References

American Association of Colleges for Teacher Education. (1988). *School leadership preparation: A preface for action.* Washington, DC: Author.

American Association of School Administrators. (1960). *Professional administrators for America's schools* (Thirty-eighth American Association of School Administrators Yearbook). Washington, DC: National Educational Administration.

Anderson, G. L. (1990). Toward a critical constructionist approach to school administration: Invisibility, legitimation, and the study of non-events. *Educational Administration Quarterly, 26,* 38-59.

Anderson, W. A., & Lonsdale, R. C. (1957). Learning administrative behavior. In R. F. Campbell & R. T. Gregg (Eds.), *Administrative behavior in education* (pp. 426-463). New York: Harper.

Bailey, R. W. (1987). Uses and misuses of privatization. In S. H. Hanke (Ed.), *Proceedings of the Academy of Political Science: Vol. 36, No. 3. Prospects for privatization* (pp. 138-152). Montpelier, VT: Capital City Press.

Barber, B. R. (1984). *Strong democracy: Participatory politics for a new age.* Berkeley: University of California Press.

Barth, R. S. (1986). On sheep and goats and school reform. *Phi Delta Kappan, 68,* 293-296.

Bauman, P. C. (1996). Governing education in an antigovernment environment. *Journal of School Leadership, 6,* 625-643.

Beare, H. (1989, September). *Educational administration in the 1990s.* Paper presented at the national conference of the Australian Council for Educational Administration, Armidale, New South Wales, Australia.

Beck, L. (1993). *Reclaiming educational administration as a caring profession.* New York: Teachers College Press.

Beck, L. G., & Murphy, J. (1994). *Ethics in educational leadership programs: An expanding base.* Thousand Oaks, CA: Corwin.

Boyan, N. J. (1963). Common and specialized learnings for administrators and supervisors: Some problems and issues. In D. J. Leu & H. C. Rudman (Eds.), *Preparation programs for school administrators: Common and specialized learnings* (pp. 1-23). East Lansing: Michigan State University Press.

Boyan, N. J. (1988a). Describing and explaining administrator behavior. In N. J. Boyan (Ed.), *Handbook of research on educational administration* (pp. 77-97). New York: Longman.

Boyan, N. J. (Ed.). (1988b). *Handbook of research on educational administration.* New York: Longman.

Bridges, E. M. (1977). The nature of leadership. In L. L. Cunningham, W. G. Hack, & R. O. Nystrand (Eds.), *Educational administration: The developing decades* (pp. 202-230). Berkeley, CA: McCutchan.

Burke, C. (1992). Devolution of responsibility to Queensland schools: Clarifying the rhetoric, critiquing the reality. *Journal of Educational Administration, 30*(4), 33-52.

Campbell, R. F., Fleming, T., Newell, L., & Bennion, J. W. (1987). *A history of thought and practice in educational administration.* New York: Teachers College Press.

Candoli, I. C. (1991). *School system administration: A strategic plan for site-based management.* Lancaster, PA: Technomic.

Chase, F. S. (1960). The administrator as implementor of the goals of education for our time. In R. F. Campbell & J. M. Lipham (Eds.), *Administrative theory as a guide to action* (pp. 191-201). Chicago: University of Chicago, Midwest Administration Center.

Clark, D. L. (1988, June). *Charge to the study group of the National Policy Board for Educational Administration.* Unpublished manuscript.

Clark, D. L., & Meloy, J. M. (1989). Renouncing bureaucracy: A democratic structure for leadership in schools. In T. J. Sergiovanni & J. A. Moore (Eds.), *Schooling for tomorrow: Directing reform to issues that count* (pp. 272-294). Boston: Allyn & Bacon.

Cohen, D. K. (1988, September). *Teaching practice: Plus ca change . . .* (Issue Paper 88-3). East Lansing: Michigan State University, National Center for Research on Teacher Education.

Cooper, B. S., & Boyd, W. L. (1987). The evolution of training for school administrators. In J. Murphy & P. Hallinger (Eds.), *Approaches to administrative training* (pp. 3-27). Albany: State University of New York Press.

Crowson, R. L., & McPherson, R. B. (1987). The legacy of the theory movement: Learning from the new tradition. In J. Murphy & P. Hallinger

(Eds.), *Approaches to administrative training in education* (pp. 45-64). Albany: State University of New York Press.

Culbertson, J. A. (1963). Common and specialized content in the preparation of administrators. In D. J. Leu & H. C. Rudman (Eds.), *Preparation programs for administrators: Common and specialized learnings* (pp. 34-60). East Lansing: Michigan State University Press.

Culbertson, J. A. (1964). The preparation of administrators. In D. E. Griffiths (Ed.), *Behavioral science in educational administration* (Sixty-third National Society for the Study of Education Yearbook, Part II, pp. 303-330). Chicago: University of Chicago Press.

Culbertson, J. A. (1965). Trends and issues in the development of a science of administration. In Center for the Advanced Study of Educational Administration, *Perspectives on educational administration and the behavioral sciences* (pp. 3-22). Eugene: University of Oregon, Center for the Advanced Study of Educational Administration.

Dahrendorf, R. (1995, Summer). A precarious balance: Economic opportunity, civil society, and political liberty. *The Responsive Community,* pp. 13-39.

Dellar, G. B. (1992, April). *Connections between macro and micro implementation of educational policy: A study of school restructuring in Western Australia.* Paper presented at the annual meeting of the American Educational Research Association, San Francisco.

Donahue, J. D. (1989). *The privatization decision: Public ends, private means.* New York: Basic Books.

Donmoyer, R., Imber, M., & Scheursch, J. J. (Eds.). (1995). *The knowledge base in educational administration: Multiple perspectives.* Albany: State University of New York Press.

Elmore, R. F. (1989, April). *Models of restructured schools.* Paper presented at the annual meeting of the American Educational Research Association, San Francisco.

Elmore, R. F. (1993). School decentralization: Who gains? Who loses? In J. Hannaway & M. Carnoy (Eds.), *Decentralization and school improvement* (pp. 33-54). San Francisco: Jossey-Bass.

Elshtain, J. B. (1995). *Democracy on trial.* New York: Basic Books.

Erickson, D. A. (1977). An overdue paradigm shift in educational administration, or how can we get that idiot off the freeway. In L. L. Cunningham, W. G. Hack, & R. O. Nystrand (Eds.), *Educational administration: The developing decades* (pp. 114-143). Berkeley, CA: McCutchan.

Erickson, D. A. (1979). Research on educational administration: The state-of-the-art. *Educational Researcher, 8,* 9-14.

Erlandson, D. A., & Witters-Churchill, L. (1988, March). *Design of the Texas NASSP study.* Paper presented at the annual convention of the National Association of Secondary School Principals.

Evans, R. (1991, April). *Ministrative insight: Educational administration as pedagogic practice.* Paper presented at the annual meeting of the American Educational Research Association, Chicago.

Farquhar, R. H. (1981). Preparing educational administrators for ethical practice. *The Alberta Journal of Educational Research, 27,* 192-204.

Foster, W. (1988). Educational administration: A critical appraisal. In D. E. Griffiths, R. T. Stout, & R. B. Forsyth (Eds.), *Leaders for America's schools: The report and papers of the National Commission on Excellence in Educational Administration* (pp. 68-81). Berkeley, CA: McCutchan.

Gerritz, W., Koppich, J., & Guthrie, J. (1984). *Preparing California school leaders: An analysis of supply, demand, and training.* Berkeley: University of California, Policy Analysis for California Education.

Goldhammer, K. (1983). Evolution in the profession. *Educational Administration Quarterly, 19,* 249-272.

Gottfried, P. (1993). *The conservative movement* (rev. ed.). New York: Twayne.

Graff, O. B., & Street, C. M. (1957). Developing a value framework for educational administration. In R. F. Campbell & R. T. Gregg (Eds.), *Administrative behavior in education* (pp. 120-152). New York: Harper.

Greenfield, T. B. (1975). Theory about organization: A new perspective and its implications for schools. In M. G. Hughes (Ed.), *Administering education: International challenge* (pp. 71-99). London: Athlone.

Greenfield, T. B. (1988). The decline and fall of science in educational administration. In D. E. Griffith, R. T. Stout, & P. B. Forsyth (Eds.), *Leaders for America's schools: The report and papers of the National Commission on Excellence in Educational Administration* (pp. 131-159). Berkeley, CA: McCutchan.

Gregg, R. T. (1969). Preparation of administrators. In R. L. Ebel (Ed.), *Encyclopedia of educational research* (4th ed., pp. 993-1004). London: Macmillan.

Griffiths, D. E. (1988a). Administrative theory. In N. J. Boyan (Ed.), *Handbook of research on educational administration* (pp. 27-51). New York: Longman.

Griffiths, D. E. (1988b). *Educational administration: Reform PDQ or RIP* (Occasional paper, No. 8312). Tempe, AZ: University Council for Educational Administration.

Griffiths, D. E., Stout, R. T., & Forsyth, P. B. (Eds.). (1988a). *Leaders for America's schools: The report and papers of the National Commission on Excellence in Educational Administration.* Berkeley, CA: McCutchan.

Griffiths, D. E., Stout, R. T., & Forsyth, P. B. (1988b). The preparation of educational administrators. In D. E. Griffith, R. T. Stout, & P. B. Forsyth (Eds.), *Leaders for America's schools: The report and papers of the National Commission on Excellence in Educational Administration* (pp. 284-304). Berkeley, CA: McCutchan.

Guba, E. G. (1960). Research in internal administration—what do we know? In R. F. Campbell & J. M. Lipham (Eds.), *Administrative theory as a guide to action* (pp. 113-141). Chicago: University of Chicago, Midwest Administration Center.

Guthrie, J. W. (1986). School-based management: The next needed education reform. *Phi Delta Kappan, 68,* 305-309.

Hallinger, P., Leithwood, K., & Murphy, J. (Eds.). (1993). *A cognitive perspective on educational administration.* New York: Teachers College Press.

Halpin, A. W. (1960). Ways of knowing. In R. F. Campbell & J. M. Lipham (Eds.), *Administrative theory as a guide to action* (pp. 3-20). Chicago: University of Chicago, Midwest Administration Center.

Hannaway, J., & Crowson, R. (Eds.). (1989). *The politics of reforming school administration.* New York: Falmer.

Hanson, E. M. (1991). *School-based management and educational reform: Cases in the USA and Spain.* (ERIC Document Reproduction Service No. ED 336 832)

Hardin, H. (1989). *The privatization putsch.* Halifax, Nova Scotia: The Institute for Research on Public Policy.

Harlow, J. G. (1962). Purpose-defining: The central function of the school administrator. In J. A. Culbertson & S. P. Hencley (Eds.), *Preparing administrators: New perspectives* (pp. 61-71). Columbia, MO: University Council for Educational Administration.

Hawley, W. D. (1988). Universities and the improvement of school management. In D. E. Griffiths, R. T. Stout, & P. B. Forsyth (Eds.), *Leaders for America's schools: The report and papers of the National Commission on Excellence in Educational Administration* (pp. 82-88). Berkeley, CA: McCutchan.

Hawley, W. D. (1995). The false premises and false promises of the movement to privatize public education. *Teachers College Record, 96,* 735-742.

Hills, J. (1975). The preparation of administrators: Some observations from the "firing line." *Educational Administration Quarterly, 11,* 1-20.

Himmelstein, J. L. (1983). The New Right. In R. C. Liebman & R. Wuthrow (Eds.), *The New Christian Right: Mobilization and legitimation* (pp. 13-30). New York: Aldine.

Hirsch, W. Z. (1991). *Privatizing government services: An economic analysis of contracting out by local governments.* Los Angeles: University of California, Institute of Industrial Relations.

Hood, C. (1994). *Explaining economic policy reversals.* Buckingham, England: Open University Press.

Immegart, G. L. (1990). What is truly missing in advanced preparation in educational administration? *Journal of Educational Administration, 28*(3), 5-13.

Interstate School Leaders Licensure Consortium. (1996). *Standards for school leaders.* Washington, DC: Council of Chief State School Officers.

Jacobson, S. L. (1990). Reflections on the third wave of reform: Rethinking administrator preparation. In S. L. Jacobson & J. A. Conway (Eds.), *Educational leadership in an age of reform* (pp. 30-44). New York: Longman.

Katz, M. B. (1971). From voluntarism to bureaucracy in American education. *Sociology of Education, 44,* 297-332.

Lawton, S. B. (1991, September). *Why restructure?* Revision of paper presented at the annual meeting of the American Educational Research Association, Chicago.

Lewis, D. A. (1993). Deinstitutionalization and school decentralization: Making the same mistake twice. In J. Hannaway & M. Carnoy (Eds.), *Decentralization and school improvement* (pp. 84-101). San Francisco: Jossey-Bass.

Liebman, R. C. (1983a). Introduction. In R. C. Liebman & R. Wuthnow (Eds.), *The New Christian Right: Mobilization and legitimation* (pp. 1-9). New York: Aldine.

Liebman, R. C. (1983b). The making of the New Christian Right. In R. C. Liebman & R. Wuthnow (Eds.), *The New Christian Right: Mobilization and legitimation* (pp. 227-238). New York: Aldine.

Liebman, R. C., & Wuthnow, R. (Eds.). (1983). *The New Christian Right: Mobilization and legitimation.* New York: Aldine.

Mann, D. (1975, May). What peculiarities in educational administration make it difficult to profess: An essay. *The Journal of Educational Administration, 13,* 139-147.

Marshall, R., & Tucker, M. (1992). *Thinking for a living: Work, skills, and the future of the American economy.* New York: Basic Books.

Martin, B. (1993). *In the public interest? Privatization and public sector reform.* London: Zed.

Mayberry, M. (1991, April). *Conflict and social determinism: The reprivatization of education.* Paper presented at the annual meeting of the American Educational Research Association, Chicago.

McCarthy, M. M., & Kuh, G. D. (1997). *Continuity and change: The educational leadership professoriate.* Columbia, MO: University Council for Educational Administration.

McCarthy, M. M., Kuh, G. D., Newell, L. J., & Iacona, C. M. (1988). *Under scrutiny: The educational administration professoriate.* Tempe, AZ: University Council for Educational Administration.

Milstein, M. M. (1990). Rethinking the clinical aspects of preparation programs: From theory to practice. In S. L. Jacobson & J. A. Conway (Eds.), *Educational leadership in an age of reform* (pp. 119-130). New York: Longman.

Milstein, M., & Associates. (1993). *Changing the way we prepare educational leaders: The Danforth experience.* Newbury Park, CA: Corwin.

Mitchell, B., & Cunningham, L. L. (Eds.). (1990). *Educational leadership and changing contexts of families, communities, and schools* (Eighty-ninth National Society for the Study of Education Yearbook, Part II). Chicago: University of Chicago Press.

Mulkeen, T. A. (1990). *Reinventing school leadership.* Working memo prepared for the Reinventing School Leadership Conference. Cambridge, MA: The National Center for Educational Leadership.

Mulkeen, T. A., Cambron-McCabe, N. H., & Anderson, B. J. (Eds.). (1994). *Democratic leadership: The changing context of administrative preparation.* Norwood, NJ: Ablex.

Mulkeen, T. A., & Cooper, B. S. (1989, April). *Implications of preparing school administrators for knowledge-work organizations.* Paper presented at the annual meeting of the American Educational Research Association, San Francisco.

Mulkeen, T. A., & Tetenbaum, T. (1990). Teaching and learning in knowledge organizations: Implications for the preparation of school administrators. *Journal of Educational Administration, 28*(3), 14-22.

Murnane, R. J., & Levy, F. (1996). *Teaching the new basic skills: Principles for educating children to thrive in a changing economy.* New York: The Free Press.

Murphy, J. (1990). The educational reform movement of the 1980s: A comprehensive analysis. In J. Murphy (Ed.), *The reform of American public education in the 1980s: Perspectives and cases* (pp. 3-55). Berkeley, CA: McCutchan.

Murphy, J. (1992). *The landscape of leadership preparation: Reframing the education of school administrators.* Newbury Park, CA: Corwin.

Murphy, J. (Ed.). (1993). *Preparing tomorrow's school leaders: Alternative designs.* University Park, PA: University Council for Educational Administration.

Murphy, J. (in press). New consumerism: Evolving market dynamics in the institutional dimension of schooling. In J. Murphy & K. S. Louis (Eds.), *The handbook of research on educational administration* (2nd ed.). San Francisco: Jossey-Bass.

Murphy, J., & Beck, L. G. (1995). *School-based management as school reform: Taking stock.* Thousand Oaks, CA: Corwin.

Muth, R. (1989). *Reconceptualizing training for educational administrators and leaders: Focus on inquiry* (Notes on Reform, No. 2). Charlottesville, VA: National Policy Board for Educational Administration.

National Commission for the Principalship. (1990). *Principals for our changing schools: Preparation and certification.* Fairfax, VA: Author.

National Commission for the Principalship. (1993). *Principals for our changing schools: The knowledge and skill base.* Fairfax, VA: Author.

National Commission on Excellence in Educational Administration. (1987). *Leaders for America's schools.* Tempe, AZ: University Council for Educational Administration.

National Policy Board for Educational Administration. (1989). *Improving the preparation of school administrators: The reform agenda.* Charlottesville, VA: Author.

Norton, M. S., & Levan, F. D. (1987). Doctoral studies of students in educational administration programs in UCEA member institutions. *Educational Considerations, 14*(1), 21-24.

Olson, L. (1992). A matter of choice: Minnesota puts "charter schools" idea to test. *Educational Week, 12*(12), 10-11.

Pepper, J. B. (1988). Clinical education for school superintendents and principals: The missing link. In D. E. Griffiths, R. T. Stout, & P. B. Forsyth (Eds.), *Leaders for America's schools: The report and papers of the National Commission on Excellence in Educational Administration* (pp. 360-366). Berkeley, CA: McCutchan.

Peterson, K. D., & Finn, C. E. (1985). Principals, superintendents and the administrator's art. *The Public Interest, 79,* 42-62.

Popper, S. H. (1982). An advocate's case for the humanities in preparation programs for school administration. *Journal of Educational Administration, 20*(1), 12-22.

President's Commission on Privatization. (1988). *Privatization: Toward more effective government.* Washington, DC: Government Printing Office.

Putnam, R. D. (1995). Bowling alone: America's declining social capital. *Journal of Democracy, 6*(1), 65-77.

Rungeling, B., & Glover, R. W. (1991). Educational restructuring—The process for change? *Urban Education, 25,* 415-427.

Sackney, L. E., & Dibski, D. J. (1992, August). *School-based management: A critical perspective.* Paper presented at the Seventh Regional Conference of the Commonwealth Council for Educational Administration, Hong Kong.

Sergiovanni, T. J. (1989). Mystics, neats, and scruffies: Informing professional practice in educational administration. *Journal of Educational Administration, 27*(2), 7-21.

Sergiovanni, T. J. (1991). The dark side of professionalism in educational administration. *Phi Delta Kappan, 72,* 521-526.

Shakeshaft, C. (1988). Women in educational administration: Implications for training. In D. E. Griffiths, R. T. Stout, & P. B. Forsyth (Eds.), *Leaders for America's schools: The report and papers of the National Commission on Excellence in Educational Administration* (pp. 403-416). Berkeley, CA: McCutchan.

Silver, P. F. (1978). Trends in program development. In P. F. Silver & D. W. Spuck (Eds.), *Preparatory programs for educational administrators in the United States* (pp. 178-201). Columbus, OH: University Council for Educational Administration.

Silver, P. F. (1982). Administrator preparation. In H. E. Mitzel (Ed.), *Encyclopedia of educational research* (5th ed., Vol. 1, pp. 49-59). New York: Free Press.

Sizer, T. R. (1984). *Horace's compromise: The dilemma of the American high school.* Boston: Houghton Mifflin.

Smylie, M. A., & Denny, J. W. (1989, April). *Teacher leadership: Tension and ambiguities in organizational perspective.* Paper presented at the annual meeting of the American Educational Research Association, San Francisco.

Starr, P. (1991). The case for skepticism. In W. T. Gormley (Ed.), *Privatization and its alternatives* (pp. 25-36). Madison: University of Wisconsin Press.

Sykes, G., & Elmore, R. F. (1989). Making schools more manageable: Policy and administration for tomorrow's schools. In J. Hannaway & R. L. Crowson (Eds.), *The politics of reforming school administrations* (pp. 77-94). New York: Falmer.

Thayer, F. C. (1987). Privatization: Carnage, chaos, and corruption. In B. J. Carroll, R. W. Conant, & T. A. Easton (Eds.), *Private means, public ends: Private business in social service delivery* (pp. 146-170). New York: Praeger.

Tomlinson, J. (1986). Public education, public good. *Oxford Review of Education, 12,* 211-222.

Tyack, D. (1993). School governance in the United States: Historical puzzles and anomalies. In J. Hannaway & M. Carnoy (Eds.), *Decentralization and school improvement* (pp. 1-32). San Francisco: Jossey-Bass.

Tyack, D. B., & Cummings, R. (1977). Leadership in American public schools before 1954: Historical configurations and conjectures. In L. L. Cunningham, W. G. Hack, & R. O. Nystrand (Eds.), *Educational administration: The developing decades* (pp. 46-66). Berkeley, CA: McCutchan.

Whitty, G. (1984). The privatization of education. *Educational Leadership, 41*(7), 51-54.

Willower, D. J. (1983). Evolutions in the professorship: Past philosophy, future. *Educational Administration Quarterly, 19,* 179-200.

Willower, D. J. (1988). Synthesis and projection. In N. J. Boyan (Ed.), *Handbook of research on educational administration* (pp. 729-747). New York: Longman.

Wise, A. E. (1989). Professional teaching: A new paradigm for the management of education. In T. J. Sergiovanni & J. H. Moore (Eds.), *Schooling for tomorrow: Directing reforms to issues that count* (pp. 301-310). Boston: Allyn & Bacon.

2

The Reform of the Profession:
A Self-Portrait

JOSEPH MURPHY

A persistent dirge, plaintively crying "improve."

—ANONYMOUS RESPONDENT

As we discussed in the introductory chapter, the initial and ending sections of the book are designed to provide wide-angle perspectives on
changes in the profession of school administration. The middle part of the
volume highlights specific dimensions of this evolving landscape of educational leadership. We developed the broad outlines of the reform picture in
Chapter 1, where we laid out the forces that are pushing and pulling school
administration to reinvent itself. We continue that work in this chapter by
presenting a self-portrait of the profession, using as our palette the insights
contributed by 105 professors of school administration, who responded to our
queries between November 1996 and January 1997. This self-portrait is comprised of their perceptions of major events and trends occurring in the profession since the publication in 1987 of the NCEEA report *Leaders for
America's Schools.*

The opening section provides a description of the procedures employed
in the study. In the second section, we examine the thoughts of 19 members
of the profession who are especially knowledgeable about the academic arm
of school administration. The third part of the chapter unpacks insights about
changes in the profession offered by 86 regular members of the professoriate—57 UCEA professors and 29 non-UCEA professors. The chapter concludes with an analysis of common themes.

Procedures

Sample

Researchers Who Study the History and Development of Educational Administration

To develop a robust understanding of changes in the field over the past decade, we wanted to hear from two groups of professors. First, we wished to gather insights from those individuals who would be especially knowledgeable about the profession, its history, and its evolution. Faculty members who include the study of school administration in their research portfolios and who have occupied important roles in the organizations that shape the profession were the target audience here. Twenty-five professors were identified who met these criteria. All had written about the development of the profession, and all were or had been in formal leadership roles in professional organizations such as NCPEA, UCEA, and Division A of AERA. All were very well-known in the field, and not unexpectedly, almost all were senior scholars. Nineteen (76%) of these professors responded to our request for information. Demographic data of this group are contained in Table 2.1.

Regular Members of the Professoriate

Second, we desired to hear from colleagues whose understandings of alterations in the profession grew primarily from the changes they experienced as they performed their routine activities as faculty members—not from their research agendas or leadership activities. The large majority of professors are members of this group. They learn about changing curricula in preparation programs, not because the issue is a topic of research interest but rather because we are members of departments that are overhauling curricular expectations. To get a diverse sample of thinking, we collected input from professors in both UCEA and non-UCEA institutions.

UCEA professors. To identify professors at UCEA schools, we secured a master list of names from UCEA headquarters. From the original list of 230 names, we dropped 3 that we knew had relocated to non-UCEA schools or had retired. We then drew a random sample of one half (113) of the group. From that list, we deleted 7 colleagues already covered in our group of 25 researchers, as well as 8 others who wrote to tell us that they were not professors of educational administration (e.g., they were professors of higher education administration). From the 98 potential respondents, we received replies

TABLE 2.1 Professorial Experience and Gender of Sample—By Source

	Source																	
	Ed Admin Researchers[a]						UCEA Faculty[b]						Non-UCEA Faculty[c]					
	M		F		Total		M		F		Total		M		F		Total	
Experience (in years)	#	%	#	%	#	%	#	%	#	%	#	%	#	%	#	%	#	%
0-4		0.0		0.0		0.0	6	10.5	8	14.1	14	24.6	2	6.9		0.0	2	6.9
5-9							5	8.8	7	12.3	12	12.1	2	6.9	2	6.9	4	13.8
10-14	1	5.3	1	5.2	2	10.5	5	8.8	3	5.2	8	14.0	6	20.7	1	3.4	7	24.1
15-19	3	15.8	2	10.5	5	26.3	5	8.8	1	1.7	6	10.5	2	6.9			2	6.9
20-24	3	15.8	1	5.3	4	21.1	4	7.0			4	7.0	3	10.4			3	10.4
25-29	3	15.8			3	15.8	7	12.3			7	12.3	5	17.2			5	17.2
30+	5	26.3			5	26.3	6	10.5			6	10.5	4	13.8	1	3.4	5	17.2
Missing													1	3.5			1	3.5
Total	15	79.0	4	21.0	19	100.0	38	67.7	19	33.3	57	100.0	25	86.3	4	13.7	29	100.0

a. Nineteen of 25 = 76.0%.   b. Fifty-seven of 98 = 58.2%.   c. Twenty-nine of 90 = 32.2%.

from 57 individuals (58.2%). Information about gender and length of tenure in the professoriate for this group is contained in Table 2.1.

Non-UCEA professors. From a list of professors originally developed by Edward Lilley, we drew at random the names of 106 professors at non-UCEA schools. Four letters were returned as undeliverable, and 4 other names were deleted because they were covered in the group of 25 discussed previously. Eight other faculty members responded that they were not professors of educational administration. Of the 90 potential respondents, replies were received from 29 faculty members (32.2%).[1] Information about the gender and experience of members of this group is contained in Table 2.1.

Instrumentation

A questionnaire was developed for this study to gather information on changes in the professoriate over the past decade.[2] The protocol was shared with five colleagues. Based on feedback from four of these professors, revisions—primarily to clarify language—were made. The final protocol for the group of 25 researchers contained the following four open-ended questions, with 1, 10, 5, and 5 response options, respectively:

1. What is *the* most significant change that has occurred or trend that has emerged in departments of educational leadership and preparation programs in school administration in the last decade?

2. What are other significant changes/emerging trends in departments of educational leadership and preparation programs in school administration in the last decade?

3. What are the most important specific events that have occurred in the profession of educational leadership over the last decade (e.g., the beginning or end of an important activity; the publication of an important book, report, or special journal issue; the delivery of a major address)?

4. Focusing again on the academic arm of the profession—educational leadership departments and preparation programs in school administration—over the last decade, where have we fallen short in our quest for improvement? Where have we missed the mark—or taken the wrong path altogether?

The protocol sent to the random sample of UCEA and non-UCEA professors contained only the first three questions listed above, with 1, 7, and 5 response options, respectively.

Analysis

For the purposes of this chapter, questionnaires were analyzed to discern professors' perceptions of changes unfolding in departments of school administration and educational leadership preparation programs.

Coding

The questionnaire data—composed of phrases, sentences, and paragraphs in response to the open-ended probes—were coded (descriptively) like interview transcriptions. Material was coded both deductively and inductively (Miles & Huberman, 1984). To begin with, a "start list" of codes consistent with the research questions was applied (Miles & Huberman, 1984, p. 57). Next, an inductively derived set of codes grounded in the written responses was developed and applied separately. For example, based on the saliency of the issues in the professors' remarks, codes were created to help classify topics related to faculty composition and departmental mission.

Sense Making

To develop "a particular construction of the situation at hand" (Lincoln & Guba, 1985, p. 343), procedures described by Lincoln and Guba (1985), Miles and Huberman (1984), and Glaser and Strauss (1967) were employed. Pattern coding primarily by "themes" and secondarily "by relationships among people" (Miles & Huberman, 1984, p. 68) served as the basis for creating categories (Lincoln & Guba, 1985). The constant comparative method described by Glaser and Strauss (1967) and adopted for analysis with qualitative data by Lincoln and Guba (1985) was the specific strategy that guided the sensemaking process.

At the risk of creating some overlap, I present an analysis of the responses from each of the two groups separately.

Results: Professors Who Study Educational Administration

The Most Significant Change

From earlier work in the area of school improvement, especially studies that my colleague Philip Hallinger and I completed in the 1980s on effective schools, I have found it useful to ask respondents to cite the most important marker in the area under investigation. We employed this approach with Question 1 of the protocol developed for this study. Although two faculty members noted that there was no single "most important change," most respondents were comfortable addressing the question. Whereas three professors chronicled changes not corroborated by others (e.g., a focus on leadership as a collaborative activity rather than as the property of an individual), the answers provided by the others clustered into four groups.

The "feminization" of the field was one clearly defined theme. Professors who described this movement reported three related dimensions of the phenomenon: (a) a dramatic increase in the number of women in the professoriate, including the rise of women to positions of influence in professional organizations such as AERA, UCEA, and NCPEA; (b) an influx of women into certification and doctoral programs; and (c) the increasing presence of feminist perspectives in departments of school administration and in preparation programs for school leaders— "the infusion of the feminist perspective, feminist concerns, and feminist views of leadership, organization, and the role of education into educational leadership departments."

A second theme highlighted "challenges to positivism as the epistemological basis for educational administration as a field of study," the accompanying "downsizing and displacement of the theory movement," and "the incorporation of alternative perspectives . . . into preparation programs." A central aspect of this change is the legitimization of alternative and nontraditional research strategies. As one especially thoughtful respondent remarked:

> I do think that there is a significant methodological line emerging in educational administration, albeit slowly, painfully, and covered with warts. . . . It is difficult for me to give the line a name because it is not yet clearly defined. It can, however, be described as anti-positivist, nontraditional, and qualitative. . . . Rather than a line of inquiry, it should be called a movement. As far as ed admin is concerned, it started with Orin Graff with the support of Calvin Street, John Ramseyer, and Ralph Kimbrough. They, especially Graff and Ramseyer, were heavily influenced by Boyd Bode, a disciple of John Dewey.

Others who reflected on the decline of the theory movement turned their gaze less toward the development of alternative epistemological foundations and research designs than they did to yet another trend of the past decade—increased interest in problems of practice and in expanded connections to the field. One faculty member provided a particularly concise encapsulation of this dynamic: "I think the most significant change is a shift from a strong theory emphasis in ed admin to greater emphasis on the application of theory to practice—bridging the theory-practice chasm—more focus on addressing timely problems of practice." According to respondents, this shift is playing out at the macro level in an emerging understanding that a major function of preparation programs is to prepare practitioners. At the micro level, they described "a shift to a field-based focus, clinical internships, [and] action research," the incorporation of craft knowledge and field-based elements into training programs, and the employment of faculty who have worked as school administrators.

Finally, there was some support for the position that over the past decade, educational administration has been recast around issues of school improvement and that the floodlights are being redirected to children and youth. As one colleague argued, the most significant change afoot today is "the move from studying the administrator toward studying schooling and the lives of children in schools." Another put it more dramatically when he reported that the central purpose of school organization has been "rediscovered" by educational administration in the past decade.

Other Important Changes

According to this group of professors, whose members keep an especially close eye on the profession, educational administration experienced a variety of important changes over the past decade in addition to those just described. We review the most noteworthy of those shifts under the following headings: new patterns in the fabric of the profession, changes in the structure of departments and programs, reconfiguration of faculty, changes in the student population; the growth of reform efforts, alterations in program content and instruction, revisions to our understanding of scholarship, and the development of new connections with the field.

New Patterns in the Fabric of the Profession

The rebalancing of preparation programs was the featured issue in macrolevel discussions of the profession. Two dimensions of the issue were especially prominent. To begin with, reviewers identified a pattern that one analyst labeled the "de-eliting" of preparation programs. To some of these scholars, this meant that there was no longer "a group of 'elite' institutions carrying the field": "The decline and now death of the University of Chicago's once famous Midwest Administration Center; the closing of graduate programs at Yale, Johns Hopkins, and elsewhere—all signal a gradual decline in the prestigious universities and their Education Administration programs and the rise of the lesser-known, lower prestige, smaller colleges." Concomitantly, one faculty member saw a dispersal of talent: "With the use of doctoral programs at virtually every graduate school, the high scholarship, high productivity faculty have been dispersed."

Colleagues who study school administration also told of an increase in competition between suppliers of educational administration courses. There was a feeling among some that more institutions with less-well-staffed faculties were moving into the preparation business. Noted with concern were "the proliferation of vendors for quick, easy, pain-free administrator certification" and the expansion of executive-style programs with minimal residency requirements. Contrary to economic theory, individuals believed that this "competition" was lowering standards across educational administration programs in general and in the traditional quality institutions in particular.

Other new threads were also visible in the fabric of school administration, although none could be characterized as a theme. Among the most important were an increase in the amount of networking efforts across institutions and throughout the profession, the internationalization of the profession,[3] the reemergence of UCEA as a force and the strengthening of ties between UCEA and AERA, and the homogenization of programs across different types of institutions. With the exception of this last issue, increasing homogeneity, which has been confirmed by McCarthy and Kuh (1997), each of these issues merits further attention. (See also Chapter 3 of this volume by Forsyth for the story of the reemergence of UCEA.)

Changes in the Structure of Departments and Programs

The most developed line of discussion in this area centered on the topic of "reconfigured departments." A number of individuals made the point that departments of school administration were being reorganized in many colleges. Specifically, they were being merged with other programs to form larger departments or united with other departments to form larger divisions. Some colleagues maintained that these mergers influenced programs negatively, resulting in fewer faculty trained in educational leadership and in less focus on issues of school administration. On the other hand, the fact that mergers sometimes strengthen relationships between departments of educational administration and departments of curriculum was viewed favorably.

A second line of responses was characterized by one faculty member as "the doctoralization of education"—a heightened focus on the awarding of doctoral degrees in response to the need for leaders to secure this professional credential to secure employment in more and more jobs. Other individuals described changes in residency requirements, emphasizing primarily the growth of alternatives to full-time, on-campus residences. Finally, faculty members from the group of 25 explained that the basic structure of preparation programs had been reshaped by the rapid expansion of cohort programs over the past decade.

Reconfiguration of Faculty

There was a sense among this mostly quite-senior faculty group that a changing of the guard was under way in the profession. Looking backward, they saw significant faculty turnover during the 1987-1996 decade. Peering ahead, they foresaw the trend continuing unabated. They reported a trend that was difficult to miss—the increased representation of women and minorities in departments of school administration (see McCarthy & Kuh, 1997)—what one professor described as "more diversity all around." Beyond these two issues, however, there was little agreement. Some believed that the professoriate was getting older; others claimed that the opposite was true. Some argued that there was a decline in the number of professors with K-12 administrative experience; some reported the obverse. (See McCarthy, this volume.)

Three points that surfaced around the issue of retirement might merit further attention. One especially insightful colleague held that "aging faculty . . . have begun a relentless search for meaning, spirituality, and a sense of their own immortality." His conclusion is that the quest is having a not inconsequential pull on the research agenda of the profession. The same analyst expressed concern over the fact that

> many education administration programs have stopped hiring staff on tenure track and have begun to fill their ranks with "adjuncts," "clinical faculty," part-time faculty, professors on loan, and "visiting lines." These non-permanent, "on contract not tenure-line" staff create a three-tier profession: tenured faculty, untenured/tenure-track junior faculty, and now the off-track clinical and adjunct faculty. This tripartite staff structure has led to several real problems for the "regular" faculty.

Other faculty members questioned whether new professors are being adequately prepared in educational administration content and research methods and worried about how this dynamic might collide with the application of more rigorous standards for tenure and promotion.

Changes in the Student Population

In addition to changes in the way some students are grouped in their programs (e.g., the expansion of the cohort model described earlier), faculty members reported the following revisions in departments as regards students: a significant increase in the number of women in degree programs, meaningful attempts to strengthen the quality of candidates by enhancing recruitment practices, and a reduction in the number of full-time graduate students.

The Growth of Reform Efforts

A palpable sense of reform was evident in the questionnaire responses—the beliefs that "visibility and status" were being devoted to the reform of educational administration writ large and that within leadership departments, there was a discernible emphasis on "improving/reforming/updating" programs to prepare school leaders. At the macro level, three powerful forces in the reform initiatives were most evident to these reviewers: (a) the Danforth Foundation initiatives to strengthen the preparation of principals and the robustness of departments of educational leadership;[4] (b) the presence of highly visible reform agents, especially the task forces, commissions, and policy boards that were active over the past decade; and (c) the active pursuit of reform by key agencies in the profession, especially NPBEA and UCEA. (See chapters by Forsyth and Thomson, this volume, for a discussion of these last two points.)

Alterations in Program Content and Instruction

The 19 faculty members who include the study of the profession in their research portfolios believed that a variety of important changes began to occur in preparation programs over the past decade. On the instructional front, a renewed interest in teaching was an embedded message evident throughout the responses—a story line consistent with the recent formation of the AERA Special Interest Group (SIG) on Teaching in Educational Administration. The reviewers highlighted what they perceived to be a marked increase in the use of technology in instruction—in redefining the classroom (e.g., distance learning), in classroom activities (e.g., teaching simulations), and in building working relationships with students outside of class (e.g., e–mail). They chronicled greater stress on applied approaches and relevant materials in general and on the additional use of problem- and case-based materials specifically. Finally, they suggested that the emergent cognitive perspectives that are helping to redefine learning may be working their way into instruction in departments of educational administration. (See Chapter 5 by Hart and Pounder.)[5]

Although respondents placed a variety of topics on the curricular reform agenda, five issues stand out. To begin with, they perceived a greater interest on matters of learning and teaching, including connections between principals' actions and the core technology, than was the case a decade earlier. In addition to this extended focus on the core technology, professors chronicled the emergence and rise of ethics, values, and morals in preparation programs—"coursework related to the normative dimensions of educational leadership." They also narrated how issues of race and gender were being treated more thoroughly in 1996 than they were in the past. Closely related to this last focus, they believed that additional attention was being devoted to topics related to underserved children and their families—especially the issues of inequality and of integrated services for children. Finally, and consistent with the points raised above, there was some support for the claim that a shift from a discipline-based curriculum to more integrated or "generalized courses" was occurring.

Revisions to Our Understanding of Scholarship

Scholarship and research in an applied field such as school administration can be thought about in a number of ways. The two that capture the answers of these individuals are the intellectual foundations of the profession and the research perspectives that characterize the development of these foundations. On both of these issues, responses echo answers described in the preceding section of the chapter. On the first topic, these professors described a movement away from interest in theory, especially traditional behavioral science theory, as well as the growing influence of nonorthodox theory.[6] Shifting research perspectives, in turn, received considerably more attention than any other topic discussed by these senior scholars. One strand of the story they conveyed revolves around "the loss of a research paradigm," "the movement away from [a] strict positivist paradigm": "The old-style hypotheses testing, quantitative, positivist (scientific) approach to research in the field has given way." A second strand privileges "a diversity of underlying viewpoints" and accepts varied approaches to research. Of special importance in this emerging richness of approaches is the increased emphasis on qualitative methods.

The Development of New Connections With the Field

As outlined in the earlier discussion of the most significant change in the profession, many of these faculty members believed that the connections with the field that had grown threadbare over the past 30 years were being strengthened in some cases and rebuilt in others. They reported new efforts under way to link the academic and practice arms of the profession through partnerships. Preparation programs, in turn, they argued, were more likely now than a decade earlier to acknowledge the significance of field-based experiences for students and the importance of practice-based problems for shaping learning activities in classes. Throughout the responses, there was an underlying sense of greater willingness to acknowledge the applied nature of the profession and to share the spotlight with practitioner colleagues—a movement to what Clark (1997) calls "authentic educational leadership" (p.1).

Important Events

Question 3 focused respondents' attention on important events that marked the decade from 1987 through 1996. However, because discussions of "events" were found in answers to Question 2 as well, our report here is based on an analysis of both questions.

Two points became obvious as we progressed. First, a handful of professors did not limit themselves to "important specific events that . . . occurred in *the profession of educational leadership*" (emphasis added). Rather, they outlined significant events in education writ large (e.g., the development of Goals 2000 or the publication of *A Nation at Risk*). Because most members of the group did not provide such information, it is not particularly useful to search for patterns in the responses of those who did, even though their individual responses were quite thoughtful. Second, even though we specifically asked for information on important books, journal articles, and conference presentations, no piece of work other than commissioned reports and the *Handbook of Research on Educational Administration* (Boyan, 1988) was listed by more than one respondent. Most professors simply did not focus on this dimension of the question. Therefore, we do not include information on this aspect of the study.

Significant events identified by the group of faculty members that studies the profession are presented in Table 2.2. Four events are particularly noteworthy: (a) the founding of the National Policy Board for Educational Administration (NPBEA) and its development of a reform agenda for educational administration; (b) the formation of the annual UCEA convention and the activities that unfolded at those meetings; (c) the work of the National Commission on Excellence in Educational Administration and the release of its report, *Leaders for America's Schools*; and (d) the publication of the AERA–sponsored *Handbook of Research on Educational Administration* (Boyan, 1988).

Four other events were listed by at least two respondents: (a) the work of the NPBEA study group on the reform of preparation programs, including the publication of its 1989 report *Improving the Preparation of School*

TABLE 2.2 Significant Events in Educational Leadership, 1987-1996: Professors Who Study Educational Administration (N = 19)

Event	Number of Times Noted	Rank
National Policy Board for Educational Administration		
Creation of NPBEA	8	1
NPBEA preparation program reform project and Convocation of 100	3	5
Publication of *Principals for Our Changing Schools*	1	10
University Council for Educational Administration		
NCEEA work and publication of *Leaders for America's Schools*	7	3
Creation (and annual meeting) of UCEA Convention	8	1
UCEA knowledge base project	2	6
Primis project	1	10
Initiation of UCEA program centers	2	6
American Educational Research Association		
Publication of *Handbook of Research on Educational Administration*	5	4
Creation of SIG on teaching and learning in educational administration	1	9
Interstate School Leaders Licensure Consortium		
Work on *Standards for School Leaders*	2	6
Other		
Funding of *Journal of School Leadership*	2	6
Demise of Danforth funding	1	10
Adoption of nondiscriminatory guidelines by AERA	1	10
Michigan's decision not to require administration certification	1	10

Administrators: An Agenda for Reform and the accompanying Convocation of 100 in Charlottesville, Virginia; (b) the founding of the *Journal of School Leadership*; (c) the UCEA knowledge base project; and (d) the work of the Interstate School Leaders Licensure Consortium (ISLLC) and the publication of its final report, *Standards for School Leaders*, in 1996.[7]

Where We Have Fallen Short

Although it is our hope that efforts to redesign and strengthen programs and departments of school administration will produce improvements, it is always possible that different results will materialize. Reconstruction initiatives may uncover deeper structural problems than the ones we set out to repair. Change efforts may also reveal that pursuing alternative paths would have been a wiser strategy. Reforms may consume a good deal of financial and human capital yet leave the profession largely unaltered. To explore these types of issues in the context of the reform measures of the past decade, we asked our colleagues to reflect on where we may have fallen short in our quest for improvement—where we may have missed the mark or taken the wrong path altogether. Analyses of continuing deficiencies in the profession cluster into the five groupings outlined below.

A Too-Comfortable Bunker

There was a sense among these faculty members that the profession is still too insular. This theme played out in a variety of forms. As I discuss more fully below, it was evident in the predominant research model employed in the profession (i.e., the lone researcher working away in isolation). It was also seen in the belief of some respondents that the professoriate remains fairly complacent in the face of considerable problems. (See McCarthy, this volume.) Insularity was detected in our penchant to go our own way and in failing to be proactive in working with other groups, especially the practice arm of the profession. Finally, some faculty members voiced concern over what they would describe as the nonpermeable nature of the educational administration membrane. They commented on both an unwillingness to "attend sufficiently to the external environment in our preparation programs (e.g., implications of the privatization movement, impact of the agenda of conservative citizen groups)" as well as our failure to influence the environment. This final concern, however, was counterbalanced somewhat by colleagues who either credited the profession for adapting programs to environmental realities, such as poverty and underserved children, or critiqued it for importing untested ideas, such as assessment centers or Total Quality Management.

Sisyphus and Program Reform

The limitations of program reforms were as obvious to these faculty members as the gains. As one colleague proclaimed, "Despite the rhetoric to the contrary, we have not made significant changes in the structure or content of leadership preparation programs." Deficiencies in program content were raised by some individuals. Negative marks were given for our continued reliance on the university version of the Carnegie unit and on courses anchored in the disciplines and wrapped around certification requirements. Our inability to more successfully bridge the theory-practice gap was characterized as a continuing problem, as was "the failure to establish a culture of full-time study" and to significantly increase the number of minority graduate students. Two process issues also caused some concern: (a) our unwillingness to stay with reform initiatives for a sufficient length of time to permit them to become institutionalized across the profession, and (b) our "failure to work from a guiding, accepted premise that improvement is a process rather than a product (i.e., preparation reform sometimes is viewed as a completed activity rather than a process that is never ending)."

O Lost[8]

A number of problems cited go to the heart and soul of the profession. Most important was the feeling expressed by some that the profession was adrift, that it was ungrounded and fragmented—that "we have failed to define school administration in any credible way." As one colleague remarked, "It does not appear that we have found the needed focus. The theory movement gave EDA [educational administration] a rallying perspective that we do not have presently." Thus, the struggle "to achieve an accepted consensus regarding the primary focus of preparation content" continues despite a decade of reform efforts.

A few other, mostly structural issues were underscored as core problems as well. Among the most important were (a) a lack of success in developing (or even evolving toward) a professional school model for departments of educational administration and the colleges in which they are housed—and, relatedly, "attempting to implement program reform within existing guidelines of graduate schools rather than seriously challenging those guidelines"; (b) a lack of fortitude in scaling back the number of preparation programs that are ill-equipped to provide serious academic work; (c) allowing the doctoral degree to become the de facto credential for advancement in the profession, a purpose for which it is poorly suited; (d) a reluctance to incorporate the professional development of school leaders as a central pillar of our professional mission; and (e) the loss of many senior scholars whose wisdom is needed to help the profession right itself.

Trouble at the Core

Earlier, we described some of the research gains that have been mined during the past decade of reform. Many of the respondents reported the presence of problems in this tunnel as well. Consternation about the missing central dynamic for the profession, described previously, was coupled here with anxiety about a "failure to shape a research paradigm for the profession." Considerable concern was also expressed about the way research continued to be conducted and the quality of those efforts.[9] There was some worry that newer, younger professors were not receiving the training required to conduct rigorous research. A particular concern was that qualitative research training was "quite vague." The problem of isolated, noncoordinated research efforts was heavily underscored:

> We've missed the chance to work collegially with each other, our students, and the field. The "team approach" to education administration lags years behind the medical team model where doctors, epidemiologists, statisticians, and public health professionals obtain common grants and do common research (and publish together). It's not uncommon to see medical journal articles with six to ten authors, showing teamwork at work.

> Education administration professors still abide by the outdated, outmoded arts-and-sciences model of the lone researcher, occasionally writing with a co-author. But instead, we need to be engaged in real interdisciplinary teamwork, to solve real problems, and to improve the field of education administration and the training of school leaders for the 21st century.

> [There is] very little well-coordinated research effort to address the most important problems of practice—research is too fragmented and often has little (or weak) empirical evidence—thus conclusions are weak with few substantive recommendations for the improvement of practice. Given the complexity of most educational problems, we would be better to work in well-coordinated research teams so that we *push our knowledge farther faster*—versus this fragmented approach that often involves the use of little or weak empirical evidence.

> Our research programs lack coherence, are not in fact programmatic. We show little evidence of doing the kind of "normal science" that is crucial to developing a robust knowledge base.

Even when isolated research activities were assessed on their own terms, critics found them to be wanting. Research in educational administration was characterized as (a) "drifting off to esoteric, nonfundamental issues"; (b) failing to provide valid, useful information in some cases and offering up inconsequential findings in others; and (c) neglecting to document important outcomes, especially "to demonstrate in a convincing way that school leaders make a difference."

Strained Relations in the Family

Although acknowledging that new linkages between the two arms of the profession are being forged, there was a sense that progress has been measured—that many efforts to reform the partnership have been less robust than they could have been, that we are "still not working closely enough with the field." Two standards were especially relevant in reaching these conclusions—the level of cooperation found in the profession in the past and the potential for enhanced relations. On the first issue, it was argued that relations with professional associations have never returned to the level they were before the theory movement took hold in universities: "A separation continues to exist between AASA and UCEA—a separation that increases suspicion and reduces coordinated action by both groups." Using the second standard, one colleague remarked,

> We've lost great chances to work closely with the field leadership and become part of the latest practical reforms. We still sit in stolid classrooms, talking about real problems in the field, while schools a few blocks away need our help and the assistance of our students. Doctoral dissertations rarely lead to changes in practice and often fail even to reflect these realities.

Another faculty member summarized the situation as follows: "Universities have not sold themselves well to the field."

Results: Regular Faculty Members

For purposes of analysis, we organize the responses of faculty members in this group into two clusters—changes and events.

Changes

As we were engaged in our analysis of this group, it became clear that combining the responses to Questions 1 and 2 to craft an integrated storyline about important activities afoot in departments of school administration was the appropriate path to follow. The resulting narrative is comprised of three tales of change: in the structure of departments, in educational administration as a profession and a field of study, and in preparation programs.

Department Structure

As might be expected, remarks here covered a good deal of ground. Yet two patterns of ideas are discernable in the data, one dealing with the nature of departments themselves and one focusing on the composition of the faculty. On the first issue, nine respondents noted a consolidation trend in departments—a trend for programs of school administration to be merged with other units. (For a similar story, see McCarthy & Kuh, 1997, p. 35.) In this study, mergers most often occurred with higher education units, although curriculum and instruction units and policy units were also mentioned. It was somewhat surprising that seven of the respondents were silent on the issue of whether such mergers were beneficial or harmful, with one colleague commenting on the loss of identity and the other reporting gains that might accrue from working with other "human service professionals." Less neutral was an accompanying assessment by seven professors that departments of school administration were suffering from reduced institutional support, in terms of both fiscal resources and lines for academic positions.

In terms of faculty composition, one theme dominated the responses: the increase in women and, to a lesser extent, minorities in the professoriate—a message contained in 18 of the replies. The other important change seen by these 86 professors was an expansion in the variety of experiences of faculty members in departments of educational administration, in particular an increase in the number of professors with K-12 administrative experience. (See McCarthy & Kuh, 1997, pp. 45 and 237, for confirming evidence.)

Educational Administration as a Profession and as a Field of Study

Faculty members in this study made a case that the foundations of educational administration have been undergoing important changes over the past decade. In particular, they described efforts to reshape the definition of school administration as a profession and to redefine educational administration as an area of study. On the first issue, there was considerable agreement that our conception of the school administrator role was being reconstructed around central ideas of leadership. For these professors, at the most basic level, this meant a movement away from a century-long preoccupation with management ideology and with the dominant metaphor of principal as manager.

Leadership, to these colleagues, conveyed specific images, images perhaps best captured by one person's claim that "leadership is an intellectual and moral craft." The dominant element of this emerging vision, these professors maintained, was a deeper understanding of the centrality of learning and teaching and school improvement within the role of the school administrator— "a shift in focus *from* educational administration as management *to* educational administration primarily concerned with teaching and learning." Although other qualities of this new school administrator were less clear, the respondents did provide clues about what they might be: (a) an understanding of caring and humanistic concerns as a key to effective leadership, (b) knowledge of the transformational and change dynamics of the principalship, (c) an appreciation of the collegial and collaborative foundations of school administration, and (d) an emphasis on the ethical and reflective dimensions of leadership.

At the same time that these faculty members outlined the redefined role of tomorrow's schools, they also portrayed shifts under way in the prevailing conceptions of educational administration as a field of study. Three issues dominate the landscape here: (a) the search for a post-theory-movement knowledge base, (b) the emergence of alternative methods of investigation, and (c) a rebalancing of the academic-practitioner scale. On the first issue, respondents echoed what reviewers have been arguing for more than a decade—that the infrastructure supporting the knowledge base for the past 40 years has weakened considerably, and that we have been witnessing "the loss of an intellectual foundation" for our profession. Consistent with the reform literature in this area, some of these professors observed a reduction in emphasis on the social science disciplines at their institutions. Although it would be inaccurate to suggest that there was an emerging consensus among respondents about the defining elements of a developing knowledge base, those who did address the issue suggested that it would be more critical and more general in nature than it has been in the past and that it would be marked by postmodern and feminist theories. As I discuss below in the treatment of curricular changes in preparation programs, faculty respondents argued that a post-theory-movement knowledge base would likely feature educational issues, ethics and values, and social conditions of children and their families and communities.

Concomitantly, respondents claimed that new forms of research have started to be privileged during the past decade. The consensus among the large number of those who addressed the issue was that ethnographic and other qualitative methods have gained considerable legitimacy since the NCEEA report was released in 1987. They also stated that they expected this trend to continue into the future.

The professors in this investigation also reported that educational administration as a field of study was moving toward better integration of—or developing more powerful linkages between—theory and practice. They stated that this was being accomplished in part by (a) placing more emphasis on constructing the knowledge base from the raw material of practice, (b) highlighting "theory in action/practice" in research and preparation programs, (c) recognizing practitioners as legitimate contributors to the development of knowledge, and (d) legitimizing discourse about practice in educational leadership departments.

Preparation Programs

Changes in training programs cluster into three groups: alterations in the curriculum, new pedagogical approaches to instruction, and revisions of program structure.

Curriculum. According to the sample faculty in this study, the curriculum in preparation programs has been evolving in discernible ways over the past decade. Most noticeably, there has been an increase in attention provided to the *core technology* of schooling—a "tighter connection of leadership to learning," or what one respondent characterized as a "refocus on student learning and curriculum as major content/skill areas for administrators." The prevailing metaphor was "school administrator as instructional leader." The overall feeling was that the program curriculum was being configured "to facilitate instructional improvement." At the macro level, our colleagues averred, this has meant more consideration being devoted to unpacking and examining the purposes of education and the appropriate missions for schools. It has also led to the pursuit of deeper understandings of and commitment to school reform, educational change, and school improvement. At the micro level, throwing the spotlight on the core technology has underscored the importance of theories of learning and teaching in preparation programs and promoted increased "legitimacy for studying effective teaching." It has also enhanced the saliency of student outcomes in assessing organizational effectiveness.

According to the respondents in this study, over the past decade, preparation programs have been awakening to the need to attend more forcefully to the *moral and ethical dimensions* of schooling and the *political aspects* of education. Although there was a shortage of specificity in their responses on these topics, some ideas did emerge. In the ethics area, the moral context of leadership and the moral dimensions of the administrator's role were noted; so, too, was the importance of values and the growing recognition of the ethic of caring in good schools. In the policy domain, there was a sense that the curriculum in preparation programs has been evolving to reflect the "ecology of organizations"; that is, the use of policy not as a managerial tool but as a vehicle for leaders to guide organizations with increasingly permeable boundaries.

Our colleagues in this sample also reported increased attention to the *social fabric of education* in program curriculum over the past decade. Although this concept covers a good deal of ground, for these colleagues it unpacks into at least three clusters of ideas, all of which are anchored in what one respondent labeled "the human factors in school leadership." To begin with, expanded emphasis on the social aspects of education has meant more attention devoted to the relationships between school and community—to a new "focus on education as part of the larger society" and to preparing leaders to operate from this perspective. The social dimension of the curriculum also includes greater attention to issues of diversity and its impact on schooling and school leaders. Diversity, in turn, was defined by respondents primarily in terms of race, income, gender, other cultures, and internationalization. It also was suggested that more consideration is being given to collaborative organizational processes in preparation programs today than was the case a decade ago. Learning experiences designed to help future school leaders understand the importance of empowerment and to develop skills in the exercise of shared decision making/leadership were the central topics highlighted in this area. Related ideas included nurturing teacher professionalism, learning to lead from the center rather than the apex of the organization, and developing schools as learning communities and collaborative cultures.

Other curricular changes also were noted but with less frequency than the attention devoted to the educational, moral, and social dimensions of preparation programs. Three concepts define this second-tier grouping of curriculum revisions: (a) the continuing trend to emphasize qualitative research methods in research courses and in assignments completed in other classes; (b) a focus on technology in coursework, primarily as a tool for better organizational management (i.e., technology applied to administration); and (c) renewed attention to curricula grounded in "successful corporate practice" and "business management tools and techniques."

Instruction. The professors in this study also told an interesting story of pedagogical changes afoot in preparation programs over the past decade. They provided examples of "growing interest/concern about graduate-level instruction in educational administration programs." They saw "more creative approaches to instruction," more "interest in diverse teaching strategies," "the use of alternative methods and strategies," and a "trend toward active learning experiences." They also suggested that the role of the professor in the instructional process may be changing. At the heart of this change, our colleagues maintained, is greater cooperation among faculty members in the instructional program.

Overall, five themes (one major and four minor) dominate the narrative on instruction constructed from the responses of these faculty members. Turning to the major theme first, there was a widespread sentiment among respondents that instruction has become grounded much more firmly in issues of practice than was the case only a decade before. They characterized a variety of defining elements of practice-anchored instruction. For programs as a whole, they described a willingness for institutions to base their classes in schools and an "increased cooperation with area schools." They chronicled a renewed eagerness to engage "field-based people to deliver programs and services"—what one professor called "close integration of preparation programs with field personnel and sites." They told of the increased involvement of their students in schools and in school improvement activities. Finally, they portrayed the development of important partnerships between universities and local educational agencies in the preparation of school leaders.

They spoke forcefully and repeatedly of a "renewed appreciation of the clinical setting in which school leaders work." They described a growing emphasis on more sophisticated field-based preparation experiences, including (a) revitalized clinical aspects of preparation programs; (b) more authentic, thoughtfully integrated, and relevant practicums; and (c) much more rigorous internships. Across all three, they reported an expanded use of field-based mentors in the learning activities.

Respondents lavished considerable attention on the instructional strategy of problem-based learning (PBL). In particular, they noted the influence during the decade of the contributions of pioneers in the area of PBL, such as Bridges and Hallinger (1995)—scholars who significantly increased both our understanding of practice-anchored instruction and the supply of tools available to assist professors in using PBL in their classes.

Four minor instructional themes—technology, interdisciplinary instruction, assessment, and competency-based training—were discussed in considerably less detail than the topic of practice-anchored leadership. A number of respondents argued that technology had made inroads into instructional delivery systems. Distance learning, in particular, was noted as one area where there had been change over the past decade, especially "the greater use of technology to deliver off-campus instruction." Although not particularly well-specified, respondents also saw some seepage of technology into coursework and field experiences during this time. Integrated or interdisciplinary instruction was noted by a few colleagues, but only in very general terms. On the issue of assessment, some colleagues maintained that preparation programs were placing more emphasis on student testing in 1996 than they did in 1987. In addition, these faculty members reported "more emphasis on diagnostic procedures to determine what students need" and the development of alternative (e.g., performance-based and other authentic) forms of assessment. Finally, some professors stated that there was a movement toward competency-based instructional formats.

Structure. In the area of program structure, the surveys feature three changes that have occurred over the past decade. The first addresses the composition of the students in preparation programs. Specifically, respondents stated that there are many more women in their programs today than were there a decade earlier. They also reported an increase in the number of minority members in preparation programs. A second change has been the widespread implementation of cohort programs in universities throughout the nation, a model that, according to the respondents in this study, has moved to center stage in the play known as educational administration reform. According to respondents, the cohort model has helped create programs that are more integrated, focused, and sequential than those that dotted the landscape in 1987. The third change has been an increase in the number of alternative delivery structures (e.g., executive doctoral programs) over the past decade—a phenomenon that they believe has continued to erode the traditional residency requirement in preparation programs.

Events

Activities

Significant events that were identified by at least two respondents from the 86 faculty members in this group are presented in Table 2.3. Five clusters of events are particularly noteworthy. To begin with, as was the case with the group of 19, the establishment of the NPBEA and its early forays into reform was seen as an important event for these professors. Second, and unlike the group of 19, these colleagues highlighted the importance of the K-12 educational reform movement and its impact on the academic arm of school

TABLE 2.3 Significant Events in Educational Leadership, 1987-1996: Regular Professors (N = 86)

Event	Number of Times Cited		
	Non-UCEA	UCEA	Total
Establishment and activities of NPBEA	6	13	19
Educational reform movement in K-12	8	8	16
Development of standards for the profession	8	7	15
Danforth programs to restructure educational administration	3	10	13
UCEA convention established and convention activities	0	9	9
The use and impact of technology	0	3	3
Rise of state interest in school administration programs	0	2	2
Creation of SIG on teaching and learning in educational administration	0	2	2
Growth in importance of UCEA in reform of educational administration	0	2	2

NOTE: Of the 86 respondents, 29 were from non-UCEA and 57 were from UCEA institutions.

leadership. Initiatives at the national level, such as Goals 2000, and at the state level, such as charter schools, were spotlighted, as were more general topics, such as the standards and accountability movements.

Whereas there was a diffuse sense of attention to the issue of standards for educational administration departments in the replies of the earlier group, the respondents here addressed the issue directly. They spoke mostly about standards in a general sense, such as the emphasis on new standards, the rising question of national certification, and the move toward performance standards. However, they also addressed specifics, especially the new work of professional groups such as NPBEA, UCEA, and NCATE and what they perceived to be an enhanced role for state certification and accrediting agencies in the standards movement in educational administration.

The programs of the Danforth Foundation to strengthen leadership preparation programs and faculties in departments of school administration were listed by 13 professors. Interesting, if perhaps not surprising, is the fact that nine of the respondents from UCEA institutions and none from non-UCEA institutions considered the creation and subsequent activities of the UCEA annual convention as a significant marker in the decade of reform. In addition, although the issue is not treated in this section, to provide comparable data, we should note that six professors (all from UCEA institutions) characterized the publication of the *Handbook of Research on Educational Administration* (Boyan, 1988) as an important historical occurrence.

Publications

Because many respondents did not address the topic of publications and presentations, the analysis here should be treated with some caution. Nevertheless, there is enough information to develop a feel for what these professors saw as important written markers in the decade of reform that we are exploring in this volume.[10] Under the topic of "commissioned works," six publications were cited by multiple respondents: *The Handbook of Research on Educational Administration* (6); *A Nation at Risk* (6); the UCEA knowledge base document (5); the Carnegie report on teaching (2); Goals 2000 (2); and Boyer's *Scholarship Revisited* (2). Important publications in education, but not specifically in educational administration, included the following: the work of Senge, especially *The Fifth Discipline* (6); *The Manufactured Crisis* by Berliner and Biddle (5); Wheatley's *Leadership and the New Science* (4); and Covey's work, especially his volume on *The 7 Habits of Highly Effective People* (2). Publications and presentations within the field of educational leadership covered a good deal of ground, with some respondents noting specific works and others highlighting lines of work by various authors. A complete picture of those responses is contained in Table 2.4 under the headings of educational reform, organizations/leadership, ethics, and reform of educational administration programs/departments.

TABLE 2.4 Important Publications and Presentations Within
　　　　　　Educational Administration

Authors	Work Cited	Number of Cites
Educational Reform		
Sergiovanni	Work on community	2
Fullan	*What's Worth Fighting For*	1
Murphy & Hallinger	Work on the core technology of schooling	1
Newmann	Work on restructuring	1
Elmore, Peterson, & McCarthey	*Restructuring* book	1
Murphy	*Restructuring Schools*	1
Barth	*Improving Schools From Within*	1
Sizer	Coalition-based books	1
Brown	*Schools of Thought*	1
Goodlad	*A Place Called School*	1
Glatthorn	*Outcome-Based Education: Reform and Curriculum Processes*	1
Organizations/ Leadership		
Bolman & Deal	Writings of, including *Reframing Organizations* and *Leading With Soul*	5
Greenfield, T.	Work of, including 1974 address	2
Foster	*Paradigms and Promises*	1
Shakeshaft	Work of	1
Weick	UCEA address on *Fighting Fires*	1
Hoy & Miskel	*Educational Administration: Theory, Research, and Practice*	1
Leithwood	Work on transformational leadership	1
English	Curriculum audit work	1

(continued)

TABLE 2.4 Continued

Authors	Work Cited	Number of Cites
Ethics		
Starratt	Work on building an ethical school, and *EAQ* article	2
Strike, Haller, & Soltis	*The Ethics of School Administration*	1
Beck	Work on ethic of caring	1
Reform of Educational Administration Programs/Departments		
Murphy	*Landscape of Leadership Preparation*, and related publications	5
Bridges & Hallinger	Work on problem-based learning	3
Forsyth	Critique of educational administration programs	1
Journal of School Leadership	Special issue on teaching and learning in educational administration	1
Griffiths	*Reform PDQ or RIP* address at AERA	1
Pitner	Critique of educational administration programs	1
Achilles	Critique of educational administration programs	1

Conclusion

This chapter has been devoted to an analysis of important activities and events unfolding in the service of reforming the academic arm of educational administration from 1987 through 1996. It was not my intention to assess the implementation of reforms, nor do I make any claims in this profile chapter about either the vitality of these reforms or their impacts on departments of leadership or on preparation programs for prospective school administrators. The goal here was more modest—to help map the landscape of improvement initiatives during a decade of considerable reform energy. The map itself was constructed from the insights of 105 colleagues in the profession—19 who devote at least some of their research agenda to studying the profession and 86 others whose knowledge derives primarily from the fact that they are active players in departments of school administration.

Notes

1. The more we worked with the names from the non-UCEA schools, the less confidence we had in the accuracy of the list.

2. The questionnaire for the group of 25 was originally designed as an interview protocol. However, after conducting three interviews at the 1996 UCEA convention, it became clear that respondents needed more time to reflect than the interview format permitted.

3. For a good treatment of the international issue, see Chapman, Sackney, and Aspin (in press).

4. For discussions of the Danforth initiatives, see especially Leithwood, Jantzi, and Coffin (1995) and Milstein and Associates (1993).

5. For a thoughtful analysis of the introduction of cognitive science perspectives into educational administration, see Hallinger, Leithwood, and Murphy (1993).

6. A good starting point on nontraditional theory is the 1991 special issue of *Educational Administration Quarterly* titled "Nontraditional Theory and Research" and edited by Daniel E. Griffiths.

7. The ISLLC project to develop standards is a very recent activity. The standards were not approved until November 1996—a month after the questionnaire for this study was distributed. For it to be included on any list of important events, therefore, is surprising.

8. With acknowledgement to Thomas Wolfe.

9. Philip Hallinger and Ronald Heck (1996) have recently provided some evidence on this topic.

10. Respondents stretched the decade to include work presented and published before 1987.

References

Boyan, N. J. (Ed.). (1988). *Handbook of research on educational adminis-tration.* New York: Longman.

Bridges, E. M., & Hallinger, P. (1995). *Implementing problem-based learn-ing in leadership development.* Eugene: University of Oregon, ERIC Clearinghouse on Educational Management.

Chapman, J. D., Sackney, L., & Aspin, D. N. (in press). Internationalization in educational administration: Policy and practice, theory and research. In J. Murphy & K. S. Louis (Eds.), *Handbook of research on educational administration* (2nd ed.). San Francisco: Jossey-Bass.

Clark, D. L. (1997, March). *Searching for authentic educational leadership in university graduate programs and with public school colleagues.* In-vited presentation at the annual meeting of the American Educational Re-search Association, Chicago.

Glaser, B. G., & Strauss, A. L. (1967). *The discovery of grounded theory: Strategies for qualitative research.* Chicago: Aldine.

Griffiths, D. E. (Ed.). (1991). Nontraditional theory and research [Special issue]. *Educational Administration Quarterly, 27*(3).

Hallinger, P., & Heck, R. (1996). Reassessing the principal's role in school effectiveness. *Educational Administration Quarterly, 32,* 5-44.

Hallinger, P., Leithwood, K., & Murphy, J. (Eds.). (1993). *Cognitive perspec-tives on educational leadership.* New York: Teachers College Press.

Interstate School Leaders Licensure Consortium. (1996). *Standards for school leaders.* Washington, DC: Council of Chief State School Officers.

Leithwood, K., Jantzi, D., & Coffin, G. (1995). Preparing school leaders: What works. *Connections, 3*(3), 1-7.

Lincoln, Y. S., & Guba, F. G. (1985). *Naturalistic inquiry.* Beverly Hills, CA: Sage.

McCarthy, M. M., & Kuh, G. D. (1997). *Continuity and change: The educa-tional leadership professoriate.* Columbia, MO: The University Coun-cil for Educational Administration.

Miles, M. B., & Huberman, A. M. (1984). *Qualitative data analysis: A source book of methods.* Beverly Hills, CA: Sage.

Milstein, M., & Associates. (1993). *Changing the way we prepare educa-tional leaders: The Danforth experience.* Newbury Park, CA: Corwin.

National Commission on Excellence in Educational Administration. (1987).
    Leaders for America's schools. Tempe, AZ: The University Council for
    Educational Administration.
National Policy Board for Educational Administration. (1989). *Improving the
    preparation of school administrators: An agenda for reform.*
    Charlottesville, VA: Author.

PART II

Tracking Change

3

The Work of UCEA

Patrick B. Forsyth

The mission of UCEA has not changed significantly since the consortium was founded in 1956. As Culbertson (1995) points out, its beginnings were influenced by the leaders of AASA and the Kellogg Foundation in the late 1940s, who believed that the quality of school leadership was in need of improvement, that the key to quality school leadership was improving professional preparation, and that a cooperative approach would be needed, especially among the nation's great universities (p. 26). These ideas constitute the essence of UCEA. The decade under scrutiny here can be characterized as especially turbulent for UCEA because it has pursued its mission in a highly politicized environment. Yet this decade has been a decidedly active one for the UCEA, which, despite its sometimes stodgy image, has made the reform of educational leadership its focal work.

To capture the reform efforts of UCEA (the Council) from 1987-1997, three themes are examined: (a) leader preparation, (b) knowledge, and (c) practice. Although the Council's work is difficult to summarize because it is fragmented, collaborative, and intermittent, these three themes, and the sample of initiatives considered under each, capture the primary thrusts and arguably the most significant work undertaken by the Council in this period.

Campbell and colleagues rightly characterize the years prior to the focus of this book as "a decade of drift and introspection" for UCEA (Campbell, Fleming, Newell, & Bennion, 1987, p. 183). They attribute this situation to the fragmentation of scholarship, the emergence of subspecialties, a decline

in federal funds available to the Council, and the departure of some prestigious universities from the membership roster. Indeed, in the mid-1980s,
UCEA had no external funding, was losing membership, had no palpable
program, and was consuming its endowment at an alarming rate. By the
1990s, a different view was emerging. In 1992, Sergiovanni, Burlingame,
Coombs, and Thurston proclaimed that "UCEA appears to have been reju-
venated as both a community of scholars committed to building up the knowledge base of educational administration and as a potent voice in the reform
of the profession" (p. 90).

UCEA and School Leader Preparation

The theme of leader preparation improvement has taken various shapes
and forms in UCEA's 40 years. The papers of incorporation drafted in 1958
designate UCEA as "a voluntary association of universities in which the
member institutions will seek bases for improving their own programs for
the professional preparation of administrative personnel in the field of education" (UCEA Papers of Incorporation, 1958). It might be argued that the
Council sometimes strayed from this purpose, but clearly, focus on preparation was restored during the years after 1985. A sample of initiatives demonstrates this renewed attention to school leader preparation: The National
Commission on Excellence in Educational Administration, the establishment of UCEA's convention, and a series of reform publications.

The National Commission on
Excellence in Educational Administration

In 1984, Daniel E. Griffiths was named interim executive director of
UCEA following the resignation of Charles Willis. Griffiths proposed to the
Plenum that it cease using its endowment to cover UCEA's operating ex-
penses, thus holding at bay the fiscal crisis. Following the appointment of
Patrick B. Forsyth as executive director, effective 1985, Forsyth committed
UCEA to return to its narrower focus of earlier years on the preparation of
school leaders. Forsyth's view was that the resources of the Council were
too few to support the expanded interests related to higher education and
international education. To restore UCEA to leadership and regain the capacity to improve the profession, Forsyth and the elected leadership of UCEA
decided that a single project flowing directly from UCEA's mission and
involving large numbers of individuals would be the way to restore vitality

while making the most of limited resources. These two actions—a mandated balanced budget and the conscious decision to narrow the focus of the Council—were responsive to the elements of crisis alluded to previously by Campbell.

Fortuitously, in his presidential address, Michael J. Murphy, then professor at the University of Utah, sounded an alarm about the condition of educational administration, calling for the better use of social science, the reduction of the number of administrator training programs, and a new efficiency based on cooperation among UCEA member universities (Murphy, 1984). Forsyth, with UCEA's new president, Richard Rossmiller, and outgoing interim executive director Griffiths, determined that the mechanism for revitalizing UCEA and addressing the issues pointed to by Murphy should be some sort of blue-ribbon commission. And so, at his first executive committee meeting as UCEA's executive director (at AERA in Chicago, April 1985), Forsyth proposed that UCEA establish a commission to study and make recommendations concerning the preparation of school administrators for the future. This motion was unanimously adopted, and an interim committee was established to name the commission chair and commissioners. On April 30, the entire UCEA Plenum approved the commission. In May, Griffiths was asked to serve as chair of the Commission, and during the summer of 1985, the 26 members of the Commission were invited and secured, including outspoken critics of the status quo, such as then-Governor Bill Clinton, Roland Barth, Judith Lanier, Thomas Payzant, and Al Shanker. The Commission staff, in addition to Griffiths, was made up of Robert T. Stout as director of studies, Forsyth as coordinator, and special assistants Joyce McGuiness and Terrence A. Weninger.

Forsyth and Griffiths were successful in raising funds from a wide variety of agencies, including the Danforth, MacArthur, Spring Hill, Johnson, and Ford Foundations, as well as UCEA and the Association of Colleges and Schools of Education in State Universities and Land Grant Colleges. Additionally, regional hearings were sponsored and supported by Arizona State University, University of Oregon, Georgia State University, University of Houston, Texas A&M University, The Ohio State University, and New York University.

In December 1985, the Commission had its first meeting in Wayzata, Minnesota at the Spring Hill Center. Discussion focused on a series of questions:

1. How should the roles of principals and superintendents be conceptualized to meet present and future challenges?

2. How should public elementary and secondary schools be organized for more effective education?
3. What should be the components of a high-quality, professional preparation program for educational administrators?
4. How can we make certain that educational administrators continue to stay competent?
5. What is the proper role of the professor of educational administration?
6. How can professors of educational administration be kept up-to-date?

The Commission staff kept an exhausting travel schedule during the next year and a half, seeking the ideas of deans of education, meeting with the commissioners, and holding six regional hearings. Twenty-six papers were commissioned by the staff during this time period to inform the Commissioners and to produce successive drafts of its report.

In June 1986, the Commission met at Wingspread in Racine, Wisconsin to debate the merits of the first draft. On the first day of the meeting, the Commissioners discussed and debated each section of the report. Heated discussion surrounded several dilemmas: How can the Commission report emphasize the urgent need for reform and still recognize what is positive in the profession? How can the tone of the report mobilize the profession to action without demoralizing it? A similar dilemma also appeared during debate on an appropriate image for school leadership. Two images had been introduced in the draft report: culture builder and manager. The Commissioners rejected both. The appropriate academic degree for beginning to practice school leadership was also debated.

There was disagreement on the status of administrator licensure. Some thought the draft excessively harsh on the subject; others thought the draft understated the reprehensible situation. Commissioners were anxious to establish a specific implementation strategy. It was agreed that the purpose of the Commission was to do more than create an awareness of the current situation; it was also to provide a blueprint for change—to revitalize and take the profession into the next century. Griffiths adjourned the group on June 21, armed with ideas to shape the next draft.

At its fall 1986 Plenum, representatives from UCEA's member universities debated another draft of the Commission report. The Plenum urged articulation of recommendations with other reform reports. It suggested that the recommendations be specific and include an agenda for action for the various stakeholders in school administration (UCEA Review, 1997).

Drafts 1 through 3 were written by staff, and it was generally agreed that they looked as though they had been written by a professor of education (Griffiths & Forsyth, 1987). Recommendations in the fourth draft were written by commission members at their previous meeting, and Griffiths mused that it looked as though it were written by 27 professors of education. Ann Lewis was hired to write the fifth draft, and this version was again reworked by the staff.

The National Commission process and report suffered from the same inadequacies that Peterson points to as common in such work (Peterson, 1983). For example, interesting language was struck down as provocative. Griffiths, in arguing for higher GRE scores for admission to graduate programs in educational leadership, wrote, "There are no recorded examples of good dumb principals or successful stupid superintendents" (Griffiths & Forsyth, 1987, p. 11). The Commissioners removed this language and substituted bland and nonconfrontational language.

The Commissioners met again at Wingspread on November 13-14, 1996, to debate and vote on what was believed at the time to be the final draft report and recommendations (it was actually the fourth draft). By the sixth draft, two prominent members of the Commission had decided not to sign the final report. Judith Lanier (then president of the Holmes Group) and Al Shanker both found the report too tepid for their tastes. In the spring of 1987, after more than a year of study, the preparation of more than 30 research papers, six regional hearings, and the participation of 1,300 people, the National Commission announced eight major recommendations calling for the redefinition of educational leadership; the establishment of a national board to shape policy related to school administration; the modeling of administrator preparation programs after other professional schools; a reduction in the number of preparation programs; the increased recruitment, preparation, and placement of ethnic minorities and women; the establishment of partnerships with the public schools in the preparation of school administrators; increased emphasis on professional development for practicing administrators; and the reform of licensure and certification.

Lanier and Shanker were not the only ones who disliked the NCEEA report. Most notable was Gibboney's infamous assertion decrying its conventionality, saying, "This is not even old wine in new bottles; it is more like Mississippi River water in tin cans" (Gibboney, 1987, p. 28). But probably the most objections were raised by those who read the Commission's recommendations as a plot to monopolize educational administration by prestigious research universities (Jacobson, 1990, p. 37). The authors of the

Commission's report would at least agree that NCEEA was a conspiracy, one aimed at improving the profession.

There were not only critics of the Commission's work. The report was very widely distributed to the nation's governors, education leaders, and policymakers, and it clearly influenced thinking about school leadership across the country. In the years since the NCEEA report was issued, most of the recommendations gained endorsement, but few have been unambiguously achieved. For the most part, the work of school leaders continues to be defined by tradition and the problems that surface each day in the chaotic world of practice. Some would argue that school administrators have more responsibility now than a decade ago, but they have less control as a result of efforts to empower everyone. The workday of school administrators approaches the inhumane, precluding an outside life, and has become, by its overwhelming capacity to consume its incumbents, an unattractive career, even for many who are drawn to it by disposition. Efforts that had some promise, such as defining the principal as an instructional leader, appeared to have little ultimate effect.

A National Policy Board (see Chapter 4) was established a short time after the Commission's report was released with the support of the Danforth Foundation. The Board, which meets quarterly, has brought together the national associations having an interest in school leadership and has played a key role in forging national standards, cooperating with the Council of Chief State School Officers on the development of an interstate licensure examination, collaborating with NCATE to improve accreditation procedures, and, in general, urging improvement of the profession. In recent years, the NPBEA has formed a Policy Circle, which is a cluster of education policy centers from around the nation that serves as the research arm of the Board. The Policy Circle's first charge is to determine why many individuals licensed to practice school leadership either choose not to or are not given the opportunity to practice.

It is not clear that educational administration preparation looks more like preparation in other professional schools now than it did 10 years ago. Generally, there has been an increase in the use of internships as a required part of administrator preparation. But recruitment and selection continue to be poorly tended to, and programs still suffer from the problems associated with part-time graduate study. For the most part, the curriculum in preparation programs still looks like an interdisciplinary smorgasbord, with little integrity or direct relevance to practice.

Rather than closing down preparation programs as recommended, there has been a proliferation of them since the Commission report. Moreover, regional and proprietary colleges have taken an increasingly significant role in school administrator preparation. The Commissioners feared that convenience and lack of rigor were winning out over quality in the delivery of professional preparation. There are no data that would substantiate a claim that the general quality of preparation has increased or decreased following the Commission's report.

The recommended recruitment and placement of minorities has simply not happened. Although women have been in the majority of those who complete school leadership preparation for more than a decade, they are inexplicably absent from the levels of executive school management. Advanced-degree educational leadership programs continue to admit almost everyone who shows up at their doorstep, as if there were an inalienable right to a doctorate in educational administration. In an age when universities are competing for the best students in engineering, medicine, economics, and many other fields, the tradition of recruitment has never been integrated into schools of education.

Generally, the public schools have not become full partners in the preparation of school administrators, certainly not to the extent that they have in the preparation of teachers. In the early 1990s, the Holmes Group and others were advocating the use of professional development schools (PDSs) as centers for the training of fledgling educators and the professional development of experienced educators. PDSs were conceived as centers for the study of teaching and learning, with participation by university faculty and researchers, preservice educators, and seasoned educators. The notion of having preservice administrators learn collaborative school improvement in this type of school setting was promising but never did catch on. There seemed to be a lack of enthusiasm for this approach by school university faculty.

A recommendation that professional development for professors and administrators be improved is nearly impossible to evaluate. However, school leadership–related professional associations have been building stronger programs of professional development as a service to their members in recent years. Development for professors continues to be driven by personal choice and indirectly by the promotion and tenure criteria of universities. Stated differently, it has everything to do with publication and very little to do with other professorial responsibilities.

Finally, with respect to licensure, there has been some movement. The National Policy Board, especially in its joint venture with the Council of Chief State School Officers, has helped to raise the bar, develop common standards across many states, and deliver a licensure assessment tool that has credibility. There is movement, too, in the other quality assurance mechanisms of the profession, namely, accreditation and certification. NCATE is attempting to bring a greater number of the nation's schools of education under its wing, and at the same time, it is possible that a new teacher education accreditation group (TEAC) may effectively challenge NCATE's monopoly. Additionally, there is some interest in developing national voluntary certification systems for both principals and superintendents paralleling the project in teacher certification.

It is obvious that the process and recommendations of the NCEEA did shape significantly the activity of UCEA over the past decade. Moreover, through this important activity, UCEA regained visibility and began to exert some influence on the reform efforts of its member universities and on the work of other professional associations interested in school leadership. The entire profession, and especially administrator preparation, has embraced reform slowly and with some hesitation.

Other Influences on Preparation

Other activities of the Council can be pointed to as having been successfully directed to the reform of educational leadership preparation during this decade as well. Most important was the UCEA Convention, which has served as a forum for stimulating discussion and debate on reform issues related to education and educational leadership, as well as reporting research on those topics. During her UCEA presidency in 1986, Martha M. McCarthy proposed the idea of a UCEA Convention. Somewhat skeptical at first, the Executive Committee and executive director decided to experiment with it in the fall of 1987 as part of a celebration of UCEA's 30th Anniversary. The officers and staff were impressed with the first convention, cosponsored with the University of Virginia, and quickly understood the potential of this activity to involve greater numbers of faculty from member universities. Prior to the convention, a university's membership in UCEA was, in effect, the purview of one individual, the plenum representative, who attended annual governance meetings. The convention provided an opportunity for many faculty from member universities to attend a UCEA–sponsored activity. Through the papers and symposia planned for the convention, UCEA faculty, and the hundreds of non–UCEA faculty who attended, became more engaged in current reform ideas being debated.

The UCEA Convention has been very successful, attracting between 400 and 500 participants annually, most of whom are professors of educational administration from North America. It regularly draws participants from

Great Britain, Australia, Israel, Canada, and Russia as well. In its 12 years of existence, it has quickly become the largest conference specifically dedicated to educational administration held in the world. Despite its growth, it has retained the aura of a relatively small community of scholars who have in common their interest in professional and self-improvement.

During this decade, in addition to an extensive monograph series, UCEA has produced a number of influential books focusing on strengthening school leader preparation, starting with *Leaders for America's Schools: The Report and Papers of the National Commission on Excellence in Educational Administration* (Griffiths, Stout, & Forsyth, 1988). That volume included all of the commissioned papers on reform and is an often-cited volume in the educational administration reform literature. Several editions of Samuel H. Popper's *Pathways to the Humanities in Administrative Leadership* were published by UCEA during this decade (Popper, 1994). This work represents an enduring interest of some within the UCEA family. Forsyth suggested, in his note to the fourth edition, that "the questions and issues that are raised by the legacy of the humanities are often of greater import, more honest, and more relevant to the current human condition than are the combined scholarly corpus of all the professions" (Forsyth, 1994, p. iii). Through most of its history, the Council has balanced its advocacy of scientific research and systematic inquiry with a parallel emphasis on values and the humanities.

Two studies of the educational administration professoriate, with an eye to reform, were undertaken by Martha M. McCarthy and colleagues (McCarthy & Kuh, 1997; McCarthy, Kuh, Newell, & Iacona, 1988). These reports have been extremely useful in monitoring progress in the areas of equity, changes in the demographic profile and values of the professoriate, uncovering professorial complacence, and changes in commitment to research, as well as program changes in the structure and job satisfaction of professors. In 1993, UCEA published *Preparing Tomorrow's School Leaders: Alternative Designs*, edited by Joseph Murphy, which contained descriptions of program innovations at nine universities and an analysis and critique of emergent reform designs. Also in 1993, *City Schools: Leading the Way* (Forsyth & Tallerico) was published and widely distributed. It was aimed at making the preparation of urban school leaders more relevant and stimulating research in the area of urban leadership, topics that have historically been underemphasized in the school administration literature. Lynn G. Beck and Joseph Murphy wrote two volumes on ethics in educational leadership programs (Beck & Murphy, 1994, 1997). Some of these publication projects were undertaken in cooperation with Sage Publications and Corwin Press, with whom UCEA has had close ties since 1985. Most recently, UCEA, the Holmes Partnership, and a team of scholars from SUNY—Buffalo have cooperated to produce *Transforming Schools and Schools of Education: A New Vision for Preparing Educators*, which examines the reform efforts of one institution (Jacobson, Emihovich, Helfrich, Petrie, & Stevenson, 1998).

In 1987, through the NCEEA, UCEA was able to jump-start a reform discussion within a relatively complacent professoriate. Over the ensuing decade, with its annual convention and publications, the Council provided a forum in which emerging reform strategies and ideas about leadership preparation could be debated. Despite these grand efforts, it is hazardous to take credit for specific improvements in school leader preparation programs. Clearly, UCEA has been a player; less clear is how many goals it has scored.

UCEA and Knowledge

The theme of professional knowledge for school leadership is one that has been a notable focus of UCEA since its beginnings. Moore, discussing the earliest days of UCEA, noted in his 1964 description that "A research approach has characterized the UCEA endeavors. Career-development seminars concentrate on relevant topics. 'Position papers' prepared for the UCEA seminars are among the most thoughtful and provocative publications in the field of educational administration" (Moore, 1964, p. 31). It could have been expected that a consortium made up primarily of research universities would focus a good deal of its attention on knowledge. In its early days, UCEA and its member universities were largely concerned with developing a credible theoretical and empirical knowledge base for the field. This was seen to be a goal sharply in contrast with the focus of the profession from 1900 to 1946 (Murphy, 1992). Here, the discussion will focus on UCEA's direct effort in this decade to shape knowledge in the field through the Steering Committee project; however, other initiatives, such as UCEA's commitment to publishing quality scholarship, will also be mentioned.

The Steering Committee on Knowledge and Research in Educational Administration

UCEA's recent interest in the professional knowledge base took root as it became clear that the National Commission would not be able to address the controversial issue of curriculum content for administrator preparation. The most ambitious and controversial project related to professional knowledge in school administration to take place in this decade of reform was the Project on Knowledge and Research. In the spring of 1991, the UCEA Executive Committee was concluding its long-term planning effort under the leadership of President Gail T. Schneider. Several perceived needs resolved themselves into a commitment of Council resources to develop a professional knowledge base and curriculum initiative. At its New Orleans meeting, the executive committee outlined the two central tasks of a steering committee—to plan a series of events and activities aimed at defining the knowledge base, and to propose curriculum goals for the field of school administration (*UCEA Review*, 1991a, p. 1). At that time, UCEA was also participating in a collaborative curriculum reform project with the Holmes Group. These two efforts were envisioned to go hand in hand, but the partnership with Holmes fell apart when it chose to focus exclusively on teacher education.

President Schneider appointed a steering committee whose members were Terry A. Astuto, Muriel Mackett, Rodney J. Reed, Pedro Reyes, Patrick Forsyth, and herself, with Wayne K. Hoy as chair. The committee elected to use the knowledge domains identified in the National Policy Board for Educational Administration's report (National Policy Board for Educational Administration, 1989) as an initial framework for the project. It voted to establish seven study teams, one for each of the knowledge domains, and to ask a prominent scholar to chair each team and organize formal inquiry within that domain (i.e., its theory, research, and practice).

The committee asked the teams to carry out their charge with a great deal of autonomy; however, some general guidelines were identified. Each team was to (a) identify both the process and content components of the knowledge base; (b) use knowledge that had been acquired through both empirical and interpretive perspectives; (c) incorporate the wisdom of both practice and scholarship; (d) include multicultural, emergent, and traditional perspectives; (e) identify areas within the knowledge domains that need to be expanded; and (f) create a series of products that communicates the professional knowledge base for use in reforming curriculum, guiding research and development, and informing educational policies related to preparation of educational administrators (*UCEA Review*, 1991b, p. 6). The steering committee chose Kofi Lomotey (Societal & Cultural Influences on Schooling), Brian Rowan (Teaching and Learning Processes), David L. Clark (Organizational Studies), Robert O. Slater (Leadership and Management Processes), William L. Boyd (Policy and Political Studies), Martha M. McCarthy (Legal, Moral, and Ethical Dimensions of Schooling), and James

G. Cibulka (Economic and Financial Dimensions of Schooling) to chair the domain teams.

In October 1991, Hoy presented the project to the plenum (UCEA's representative governing body) in Baltimore. Later, plenum representatives met with the study teams of their choosing. During these sessions, some important concerns were brought to the attention of the steering committee. One question was whether the seven-domain structure predetermined the outcome of the project. A second concern expressed was whether the domains suffered from conventionality, and finally, a question was raised as to how broad involvement and voice might be provided to a large group of participants.

The steering committee pondered these critical questions and discussed them at length at its next meeting in April 1992. It adopted a tentative three-phase plan to guide the immediate future of the project. Phase 1 would involve gathering information, securing resources, and increasing involvement. Phase 2 was to consist of preliminary reporting, feedback, and opportunities to redirect the project. Phase 3 would conclude with descriptions of the knowledge domains; presentation to the plenum and convention, and development of a variety of products, including instructional materials.

During this time, UCEA President Terry Astuto became acquainted with a representative of McGraw-Hill Publishers, who was very intrigued with the steering committee project. McGraw-Hill officials came to believe that the Knowledge and Research Project could serve as the basis for a new technology—flexible textbooks—which they called *Primis*. It enabled professors to build their own textbooks by selecting works from a document base holding a corpus of selected writings with copyright agreements already in place. Several university teams had agreed to provide the document bases for other education-related areas and psychology. By the April meeting, Astuto, Forsyth, and Hoy had already met with McGraw-Hill representatives in Philadelphia and New York to craft an agreement for presentation to the steering committee.

In San Francisco, Forsyth outlined some of the benefits related to an agreement with McGraw-Hill. The proposed agreement brought with it the financial support that would cover costs associated with the project. This was key, because the objectives of the steering committee were far too esoteric to enlist support from private foundations, and UCEA had no funds to cover the costs of such a massive undertaking. Moreover, the agreement would provide study teams with immediate objectives on which to focus. *Primis* would also provide additional visibility to the work and make it more available to scholars and students. Finally, *Primis* would provide a continuing forum for updating the knowledge base long after the steering committee had completed its work. The steering committee, study teams, and UCEA Executive Committee all urged participation in the *Primis* experiment.

The 36 members of the study teams began their work during a week-long retreat at Penn State in July 1992, where they were specifically charged with preparing five draft documents: (a) a domain taxonomy, (b) a narrative overview of domain content, (c) an annotated bibliography, (d) a selected list of 10 key illustrative articles or book chapters, and (e) a case reflecting important contemporary issues relevant to the domains. Teams agreed to have nearly completed draft documents by November 15, 1992.

The project moved slowly after that, and it was not until the spring of 1994 that Phase 1 was completed with the announcement of the availability of *Educational Administration: The UCEA Documents Base*. At this point, the project began to fall apart. McGraw-Hill was in the midst of a series of corporate reorganizations. Symptomatic was the move of *Primis* management from Boston to New York, back to Boston, and finally to St. Louis. As a consequence, *Primis* was not marketed very successfully by McGraw-Hill. UCEA was caught in a Catch-22 as McGraw-Hill refused to load new articles and chapters into the system unless sales increased. UCEA argued that sales would not increase unless the system was as diverse and comprehensive as originally planned.

The project also encountered difficulties related to copyright and the emergent publishing technology of flexible textbooks. Lawyers for the publishing houses holding copyright on material that UCEA wanted to place into the *Primis* system refused even generous copyright agreements. This was especially true in reference to book chapters. Fewer than half of the documents selected by the Teaching and Learning Processes team were able to be included for this reason.

These were not the only problems that plagued the project. This was a high-visibility effort, and there were many who wanted to participate at the highest levels and were unable to do so. Culbertson summarized the problem succinctly:

> In the years ahead I would encounter the anger of individual professors and even of staffs who had felt the pain of exclusion from projects in which they wanted to participate. UCEA's elite status enhanced the perceived value of participation, at the same time that it added to the discontent of those excluded from circles in which they wanted to sit. Limited time and resources, incomplete information, and the press for

mission attainment would make it difficult always to hold high the ideal of equity. (Culbertson, 1995, p. 59)

Epistemological disagreements were also introduced into the deliberations and criticisms of the steering committee's work. Although the project leadership did everything it could to accommodate the variety of perspectives, ultimately, it became clear that those who believed the world can be known and described in abstract terms could not appease those who believed that knowledge is socially constructed in the most literal sense. The efforts to compromise may have produced a Phase 1 set of documents that pleased very few.

In 1995, a monograph was published that captured many of the concerns some had with the project (Donmoyer, Imber, & Scheurich, 1995), although the book both claims and does, in fact, raise questions broader in focus than the shortcomings of the UCEA project. The book's ostensible purposes were

> to alert readers to problems or positions that have not been sufficiently addressed and to make sure voices that have traditionally not been heard . . . are presented and . . . heard. More fundamentally, we want to open up a debate about what the notion of professionalism should mean in a field such as ours and what role knowledge can legitimately play in grounding and legitimating professional expertise. (p. 12)

Unfortunately, on the important latter question, the book's chapters seem incoherent and unsophisticated.

The second phase of the project had seven objectives: (a) review the completeness of the seven domain structures, making adjustments and additions where necessary; (b) expand the knowledge in each domain; (c) analyze each knowledge domain for adequacy; (d) modify the content of each domain; (e) articulate the knowledge of each domain; (f) identify appropriate media for each domain; and (g) search for ways to integrate knowledge across domains. Funding for this phase was never found, and the spirit to move the project forward had waned. There was a final effort to carry the project forward through a series of articles published in *Educational Administration Quarterly*, providing an update and critique of each domain. Harsh criticisms of the project were partly responsible for its demise after completion of its critical, but potentially its least significant phase, outlining what we think we know.

What has been learned through this effort to identify the professional knowledge of school administration is that our profession continues without agreement. As argued elsewhere, the consequences of failing to come to consensus about the requisite knowledge and skill for school administration may be the demise of professional schools of education and the establishment of alternative delivery systems, such as apprenticeship programs for the training of educators (Forsyth, 1992, p. 32). Not everyone is opposed to this possibility. For the time being, in the academy, underlying differences about professionalism and an appropriate, common paradigm for discovering knowledge appear to divide us irreconcilably.

Others Initiatives to Enhance Knowledge

With its first issue in 1964, UCEA's *Educational Administration Quarterly* became the first journal in North America dedicated exclusively to scholarship in this field. For almost 35 years, the journal has published the finest scholarship available and has had an impressive array of editors: Roald Campbell, Van Miller, F. Don Carver, Daniel E. Griffiths, Glenn L. Immegart, Jerome P. Lysaught, Cecil G. Miskel, Steven T. Bossert, Ann W. Hart, James G. Cibulka, and Gail T. Schneider. The journal has upheld high standards of quality, generally publishing fewer than 10% of submissions.

In the past decade or so, the journal has instituted a number of changes worthy of note. First, the editorial board has been expanded to 35, including as many as 10 non–UCEA and international scholars. There has been a concerted effort to seat an editorial board that is both methodologically and demographically diverse while retaining a preference for experts in empirical inquiry. Editorial policy, while continuing to hold high standards of scholarship, has become more "user friendly" by mentoring the work of junior scholars, cutting back lengthy review time, and expanding its volume length to accommodate a greater variety of research methods and longer articles.

Throughout its history, UCEA has found the means to promote scholarship—whether through its "career development seminars," journals, books, monographs, conventions, or task forces. Commitment to scholarship seems to be the most enduring commonality among an increasingly diverse set of member universities, and this commitment is likely to be the motivation driving UCEA's future.

UCEA and Practice

The theme of professional practice for school leadership has been important from the very beginning of the Council as well. Some of UCEA's first initiatives were related to the uses of case studies. Most notable was the Monroe City Simulation, launched in 1969 in response to the membership's call for improved training for urban school administrators (Culbertson, 1995, pp. 209-210). The UCEA Partnership with school districts, introduced in the late 1970s, was also aimed at improving professional practice by creating theory-practice bridges and increasing the chances of knowledge utilization in practice (Culbertson, 1995, pp. 239-267).

In the most recent decade, three major initiatives were aimed directly at improving practice: the Urban Initiative, APEX, and IESLP. APEX was tried unsuccessfully, the Urban Initiative continues to influence subsequent preparation of urban school leaders, and IESLP is just about to be launched.

The Urban Initiative

On December 28, 1989, the Danforth Foundation announced an award to UCEA for a proposed Urban Initiative aimed at improving the preparation of urban school principals. The purposes of the project were, first, to designate key "problems of practice" appropriate for the work of city school administrators; second, to collect, organize, and integrate existing knowledge and intervention techniques around these problems; and third, to initiate the reshaping of future curricula for urban administrator preparation by creating a network of education deans and professors sensitive and committed to the critical needs of city schools (*UCEA Review*, 1989).

The approach was to be inductive, seeking the criteria for organizing professional knowledge from the field of practice rather than from the traditions of academic disciplines. The intent was to cluster the activity of principals under problems of practice at a middle-range level of abstraction. This approach was used to produce a language and set of functional concepts of mutual interest to practitioners and researchers.

In April of 1989, the Urban Initiative held a select conference in Arizona to identify the critical problems of urban administrative practice. Ten highly successful principals from cities spanning the nation were the primary participants. They were joined by a variety of youth-serving professionals and members of the Urban Initiative task force. The conference employed Nominal Group Technique to identify the problems of urban practice from hundreds of descriptions of principal work. By examining transcriptions of conversations of these expert practitioners, task force members distilled a final set of moderately abstract problems of practice.

Nine problems of practice were extracted: (1) understanding the urban context and conditions of practice; (2) using urban resources; (3) collecting and managing information for decision making; (4) building open climates in urban schools; (5) effecting change in urban schools; (6) governing the urban school; (7) managing instructional diversity; (8) motivating urban children to learn; and (9) establishing the mission, vision, and goals.

In 1993, the task force published its work in a volume called *City Schools: Leading the Way* (Forsyth & Tallerico, 1993). The task force's book had some palpable effect on the preparation of urban school leaders; for example, the recently unveiled University of Cincinnati program, exclusively designed to prepare urban principals, was influenced by ideas developed through the Urban Initiative. The Cincinnati program starts with the assumption, as does the Urban Initiative, that the curriculum of preparation programs for urban school leadership must be unique and obviously relevant to the particular leadership challenges presented by life and schooling in today's American cities.

The project's second phase was never funded. It was to involve a series of summer institutes, bringing together scholars interested in urban education to outline research agendas related to urban school administration and encouraging scholars to develop specialties in urban administration related to the problems of practice. This network of specialists, in turn, was to influence future curriculum development in universities, complete research, teach courses, lend technical assistance to urban schools, and focus greater attention on the issues of urban school leadership for decades to come.

Advancing Principalship Excellence (APEX)

Paula Silver, a professor at the University of Illinois and former UCEA Associate Director, had developed a system for recording the problem-framing and intervention strategies of principals. It involved a format and series of questions that practicing principals could use to document their cognitive processes and actions. At the time of her death in 1987, Silver had built a growing network of principals from all over North America, and her center was accumulating a growing set of problem case descriptions (more than 1,000). A professional problem taxonomy and corpus of best professional practice was beginning to emerge.

Silver's estate made a bequest to UCEA for purposes of continuing the APEX project, and UCEA issued a request to its member universities for proposals to host the APEX Center. Hofstra University's proposal was selected by the Executive Committee, and Karen F. Osterman was named project director. Initially, the center maintained the goals of APEX to enhance the development of educational leadership in the principalship by generating and sharing information about administrative practice. This was done by the development and use of case records as an integral component of administrator preparation and development. Some of the ideas and approaches inherent in the APEX approach ultimately proved unworkable. After 2 years of funding, the Silver family informed the Center Board of Directors that the project had diverged too far from Paula's original concepts for them to continue its support, and the center was discontinued.

Silver's notions of reflection and efforts to catalog best practice are unparalleled in this field. Her early work on professionalization in educational administration, although some of the best informed and coherent, have been largely and unfortunately ignored by contemporary treatises on the same subject (see Silver, 1983). Her enduring contributions to this field may be her insistence that practitioners must have a way of contributing to our knowledge, as well as her efforts to find ways of making this happen.

The Information Environment
for School Leader Preparation (IESLP)

The basic concepts of IESLP had emerged already in the late 1980s when it became apparent that the simulation materials that UCEA had developed in the 1970s were outdated and no longer used. At the same time, staff and others participating in the early discussions of IESLP began to think that "in-basket" approaches to school administration training were inherently wrong-minded and simplistic. It was decided to develop something quite different from a simulation. The idea was to put in place an environment that would combine the information resources of several existing school districts with those of a university research library to serve as a backdrop for a set of "catalysts," or stage setters, for various investigations and activities. Learners would work in groups to discover both problems and opportunities to improve schools. The process was designed to emphasize inquiry and collaborative approaches to the work of school leadership.

Intense, early efforts to fund IESLP were not successful, although several major foundations found the ideas and approach innovative. In 1993, an IESLP meeting that included more than 35 UCEA faculty members was convened at the University of Wisconsin—Madison to introduce the basic concepts of IESLP, with the intent of engaging them in the preparation of problem exercises. Several teams continued to work on the project, even during the years when there was no funding. Ed and Patti Chance worked to collect comprehensive rural school district data. Paula Short and Patrick Forsyth reworked the funding proposal with the assistance of technical and instructional design consultants at Penn State. Then, in 1996, the Danforth Foundation agreed to fund part of the project, contingent on a matching arrangement with the University of Missouri.

In the summer of 1997, another work group was convened for a week in St. Louis to complete a set of exercises for IESLP, and UCEA and the University of Missouri entered into a contractual relationship to roll out the project during 1998. In some ways, the delays in project development were fortunate, because technological advances have made a net-based approach possible, adding new advantages and capacity to the IESLP system. At this writing, it is anticipated that IESLP will be ready for use in preparation programs and professional development environments by early 1999.

All three of these initiatives—APEX, the Urban Initiative, and IESLP—are aimed directly at improving the knowledge and skill of principals. APEX was an effort to build habits of reflection; the Urban Initiative was designed to organize ideas about best practice, theory, and empirical findings around urban problems of practice in a more useful way; and IESLP prepares decision makers who use information and work collegially. These initiatives also provide the basis for a very different kind of leadership preparation than the subdiscipline approach still in place in most programs. The approach is integrated and more directly relevant to the day-to-day work of school leaders.

Conclusion

Interuniversity cooperation, although the keystone of UCEA's existence, is fraught with peril. Universities are proud institutions designed to compete rather than cooperate. Nevertheless, the university members of the Council have accomplished a great deal in the past decade, provoking themselves to programmatic reform, examining every facet of what they do, how they prepare school leaders, and what kind of knowledge will make schools better and more effective places for children. These universities have often disagreed, but they continue to commit themselves in growing numbers to the ideal of cooperative improvement. Most important, they can lay claim to having provided national leadership in the careful scrutiny of the field of educational administration.

The scrutiny is not complete, however, and it has revealed some potentially life-threatening dilemmas for the future of educational administration within the research university. As with other professions across the campus, the stresses of operating in a research environment while holding a mission of preparing practitioners seem intractable. In the current volatile environment, consequent ambiguity of purpose can make university preparation of school administrators a noncompetitor in the marketplace. These uncertainties are exacerbated by continuing paradigm chaos, that is, radical disagreement about the legitimate means for knowledge discovery in the academy.

References

Beck, L.G., & Murphy, J. (1994). *Ethics in educational leadership programs: An expanding role.* Thousand Oaks, CA: Corwin.

Beck, L.G., & Murphy, J. (1997). *Ethics in educational leadership programs: Emerging models.* Columbia, MO: The University Council for Educational Administration.

Campbell, R., Fleming, T., Newell, J., & Bennion, J. (1987). *A history of thought and practice in educational administration.* New York: Teachers College Press.

Culbertson, J. (1995). *Building bridges: UCEA's first two decades.* University Park, PA: The University Council for Educational Administration.

Donmoyer, R., Imber, M., & Scheurich, J. J. (Eds.). (1995). *The knowledge base in educational administration: Multiple perspectives.* Albany: SUNY Press.

Forsyth, P. B. (1992). Redesigning the preparation of school administrators: Toward consensus. In S. Thomson (Ed.), *School leadership: A blueprint for change* (pp. 23-33). Newbury Park, CA: Corwin.

Forsyth, P. B. (1994). Publisher's note. In S. H. Popper, *Pathways to the humanities in administrative leadership* (4th ed.). University Park, PA: The University Council for Educational Administration.

Forsyth, P. B., & Tallerico, M. (Eds.). (1993). *City schools: Leading the way.* Newbury Park, CA: Corwin.

Gibboney, R. (1987, April 15). Education of administrators: "An American tragedy." *Education Week*, p. 28.

Griffiths, D. E., & Forsyth, P. B. (1987). *Lessons learned while commissioning.* Unpublished manuscript.

Griffiths, D. E., Stout, R. T., & Forsyth, P. B. (Eds.). (1998). *Leaders for America's schools: The report and papers of the National Commission on Excellence in Educational Administration.* Berkeley, CA: McCutchan.

Jacobson, S. (1990). Reflections on the third wave of reform: Rethinking administrator preparation. In S. Jacobson & J. Conway (Eds.), *Educational leadership in an age of reform* (pp. 30-44). White Plains, NY: Longman.

Jacobson, S. L., Emihovich, C., Helfrich, J., Petrie, H., & Stevenson, R. B. (1998). *Transforming schools and schools of education: A new vision for preparing educators.* Thousand Oaks, CA: Corwin.

McCarthy, M. M., & Kuh, G. D. (1997). *Continuity and change: The educational leadership professoriate.* Columbia, MO: The University Council for Educational Administration.

McCarthy, M. M., Kuh, G. D., Newell, L. J., & Iacona, C. M. (1988). *Under scrutiny: The educational administration professoriate.* Tempe, AZ: The University Council for Educational Administration.

Moore, H. (1964). The ferment in school administration. In D. E. Griffiths (Ed.), *Behavioral science and educational administration: The sixty-third yearbook of the National Society for the Study of Education, Part II* (pp. 11-32). Chicago: The National Society for the Study of Education.

Murphy, J. (1992). *The landscape of leadership preparation: Reframing the education of school administrators.* Newbury Park, CA: Corwin.

Murphy, J. (Ed.). (1993). *Preparing tomorrow's school leaders: Alternative designs.* University Park, PA: The University Council for Educational Administration.

Murphy, M. J. (1984, October). Presidential address at UCEA annual conference, Indianapolis, IN.

National Policy Board for Educational Administration. (1989). *Improving the preparation of school administrators: An agenda for reform.* Charlottesville, VA: Author.

Peterson, P. E. (1983, Winter). Did the educational commissions say anything? *The Brookings Review,* pp. 3-11.

Popper, S. H. (1994). *Pathways to the humanities in administrative leadership* (4th ed.). University Park, PA: The University Council for Educational Administration.

Sergiovanni, T. J., Burlingame, M., Coombs, F. S., & Thurston, P. W. (1992). *Educational governance and administration* (3rd ed.). Boston: Allyn & Bacon.

Silver, P. F. (1983). *Professionalism in educational administration.* Victoria, Australia: Deakin University Press.

UCEA Papers of Incorporation. (1958). Unpublished corporate documents.

UCEA Review. (1989). Vol. 30 (1), p. 1.

UCEA Review. (1991a). Vol. 32 (2), p. 1.

UCEA Review. (1991b). Vol. 32 (3), p. 6.

UCEA Review. (1997). Vol. 38 (3), pp. 1, 9 .

4

Causing Change:
The National Policy Board
for Educational Administration

Scott D. Thomson

The purpose of this chapter is to describe the formation of the National Policy Board for Educational Administration (NPBEA) and to identify various initiatives launched by the NPBEA to reform programs in educational leadership during the decade 1988-1997. Initially, the chapter focuses on chronological events as the NPBEA is founded. This approach provides a baseline for the players and developments that follow. Later, the chapter becomes more topical, describing program initiatives and publications aimed at revitalizing the profession of educational leadership during the 1990s. The chapter concludes with a brief analysis of the contributions of the NPBEA to reform in the field of educational leadership during the period as viewed by the author.

A Charter for Action

The key implementing recommendation of the National Commission on Excellence in Educational Administration's report, *Leaders for America's Schools* (1987), was "to establish a National Policy Board on Educational Administration." Chaired by Daniel E. Griffiths and sponsored by the University Council for Educational Administration, the Commission's 27 prominent educators and lay people included Governor Bill Clinton of Arkansas.

Tasks for the NPBEA to address, as conceived by the Commission, included conducting periodic national reviews of preparation programs for educational administrators and professors, encouraging the development of quality preparation programs for educational administrators, holding forums to discuss issues in educational administration, creating a national certification board for advanced professional standing, and publishing papers on critical national policy issues (Griffiths, Stout, & Forsyth, 1988).

Meanwhile, several people familiar with the Commission's draft reports began to discuss the early formation of a National Policy Board on Educational Administration. These participants included David Clark of the University of Virginia, Tom Shannon of the National School Boards Association (NSBA), Patrick Forsyth of the University Council for Educational Administration (UCEA), and Bruce Anderson of the Danforth Foundation. Developments moved ahead rapidly, resulting in the establishment of a "Planning Board for Policy on Educational Administration" that incorporated several national educational associations, UCEA, Danforth, and the University of Virginia. Subsequently, on July 14, 1987, the planning board met with Scott Thomson of the National Association of Secondary School Principals (NASSP) as chair and David Clark as executive secretary.

Planning board members, in addition to Forsyth, Clark, Anderson, Shannon, and Thomson, included Rich Miller of the American Association of School Administrators (AASA), Sam Sava of the National Association of Elementary School Principals (NAESP), Bob St. Clair of NASSP, Lloyd McCleary of the University of Utah, and Jim Esposito of the University of Virginia. The board, after discussion, endorsed founding the NPBEA, voted to support it with member dues, and scheduled a second meeting to consider (a) additional members, (b) initial issues to address, and (c) bylaws and other organizational matters (minutes of Planning Board of National Policy Board, July 14, 1987).

Concurrently, a formal proposal to fund the NPBEA was presented to the Danforth Foundation by Clark and Forsyth. A 3-year grant for $179,000 in support of the NPBEA was then awarded by Danforth for 1988-1990. These funds were supplemented by annual dues from member organizations and support from the University of Virginia.

Having been fathered by three groups—the National Commission on Excellence in Educational Administration, an ad hoc initiating body, and the planning board—the NPBEA was ready to begin serious work at its initial meeting on January 20, 1988. Joining as additional members then were the

American Association of Colleges for Teacher Education (AACTE) and the Association for Supervision and Curriculum Development (ASCD). Later, the Council of Chief State School Officers (CCSSO), the National Council of Professors of Educational Administration (NCPEA), and the Association of School Business Officials (ASBO) also became members, creating an NPBEA membership of 10 national associations—three from higher education, six from elementary and secondary education, and one governance body (the National School Boards Association). A representative of the Danforth Foundation served as an ad hoc board member as well. Scott Thomson of NASSP was elected chair of the NPBEA Board of Directors for 1988, and David Clark of the University of Virginia continued as executive secretary.[1]

Major business conducted at the first and second formal meetings of the board of directors of the NPBEA in January and May 1988 included approval of the bylaws, which defined three core purposes for the National Policy Board:

1. Develop, disseminate, and implement professional models for the preparation and inservice training of educational leaders.
2. Increase the recruitment and placement of women and minorities in positions of educational leadership.
3. Establish a national certifying board for educational administrators.

In addition, three program areas were agreed upon for the executive staff to address: (a) improving the preparation of school leaders, (b) redefining roles for school leaders, and (c) raising certification and accreditation standards for school leaders. Other organizational business conducted included establishing the annual dues of members and approving the budget (minutes of the January 20 and May 11, 1988 meetings of the NPBEA Board of Directors).

Following this agenda, actual program initiatives launched in 1988 included the following:

1. The appointment of a National Study Group "to draft a set of proposals for action and models of preparation to improve the education of school leaders. . . . The action agenda will focus specifically on *how* reform will occur" (NPBEA minutes, July 22, 1988). These proposals, after review by the NPBEA, would be considered by a larger body, the Convocation of 100, at a national meeting in 1989. The study group met initially on October 1-3, 1988. Participants were James Guthrie (UC Berkeley), Wayne Hoy (Rutgers), Karen Seashore Louis (Uni-

versity of Minnesota), Joseph Murphy (Vanderbilt), Charol Shakeshaft (Hofstra), David Clark (Virginia), and Patrick Forsyth (UCEA) as chair. The study group was considered essential for several reasons, including the observation that *Leaders for America's Schools* was not perceived generally as an agenda for reform, and

> the first crucial step in [our] reform effort is to create a platform, a set of distinguishing features or characteristics, that are understandable, achievable and directed toward the endemic characteristics of our field that have driven us to the point where our professional model of preparation is recognizable by its weaknesses rather than its strengths. (NPBEA, 1988)

The Study Group's recommendations were reviewed, modified, and approved by the Board of Directors prior to their publication in early 1989.

2. A proposal to establish a National Task Force on the Recruitment and Placement of Minority Groups and Women in Educational Leadership was not successfully funded.

3. A Working Committee on certification and accreditation was established. A short policy paper was prepared and forwarded to the National Council for the Accreditation of Teacher Education (NCATE) summarizing the work done to date by each of the member associations in developing curriculum guidelines for accrediting programs in educational leadership, and in coordinating these recommendations for NCATE.

In addition, David Clark, representing NPBEA, advised and consulted with several universities and organizations, including the Holmes Group, on the purpose and plans of the NPBEA. Likewise, the NPBEA sponsoring organizations briefed their boards of directors, carried articles in association publications, and spoke at association meetings about the NPBEA.

Initial Sponsored Activities

Completing the National Study Group's work, circulating its findings, and organizing the Convocation of 100 to discuss the working group's recommendations was the first major national initiative of the NPBEA.

The Convocation, by invitation only, included professors of educational leadership, state commissioners, association executives, deans, superintendents, principals, foundation officials, and lay people interested in reforming the field of educational leadership. Held at the Boar's Head Inn in Charlottesville, Virginia, on May 30-31, 1989, the program focused on recommendations found in the NPBEA's (1989) published report *Improving the Preparation of School Administration: An Agenda for Reform.*

The intention of this report was to guide improvement efforts in educational leadership at the state and local levels by applying the nine major initiatives outlined in the publication: (1) launching vigorous recruitment strategies to attract bright and capable candidates; (2) raising entrance standards for administrator preparation programs; (3) improving the quality of faculty and maintaining a minimum of five full-time faculty in university departments; (4) making an EdD the only path to certification and licensure in educational leadership, with a master's degree and 6-year programs being abolished; (5) requiring 1 year of full-time academic residency and 1 year of full-time field residency in precertification programs; (6) revising the common core of knowledge of skills to ground them in practice and to focus on school improvement, the teaching and learning process, organizational studies, management processes, inquiry, the ethical and moral dimensions of schooling, and cultural factors; (7) organizing permanent cooperative relationships between universities and school districts; (8) establishing a national professional standards board to manage a program of advanced professional standing; and (9) withholding national accreditation for programs failing to meet the standards just outlined.

The outcome of the convocation was mixed. Although some questions arose about several of the major recommendations, the discussion guides focused primarily on implementation issues (Clark & Astuto, 1989). Participants appeared to be uncertain about the central purpose of the convocation; was it to debate the recommendations and possibly revise them, or was it to discuss implementation strategies for the nine core recommendations? No consensus was reached by conferees on this point. Major points raised, however, were summarized and circulated to conferees.

Following the Convocation of 100, the executive staff made several presentations to state, regional, and national groups interested in reform. In addition, more than 1,000 copies of *Improving the Preparation of School Administration: An Agenda for Reform* were requested and mailed.

Additional early activities of the NPBEA included the publication of four newsletters through a supplementary grant from the Danforth Foundation. Seven *Notes on Reform*—white papers that addressed specific topics such as "The Importance of Being Pluralistic," "Educational Administration Programs: The Cash Cow of the University," "The North Carolina Story," "State Certification Requirements for Superintendents," and "Integrating Knowledge in Educational Administration: Moving Beyond Content"—also were published and distributed widely. In addition, a task force was established to examine the potential role of a National Professional Standards Board for Educational Administration.

Reflection and Redirection

David Clark resigned as executive secretary effective December 31, 1989, citing the unanticipated time demands of the position. Also resigning was Terry Astuto, his chief assistant. However, in his letter of resignation, Clark remained hopeful about reforming the field of educational administration in the immediate future.

The board of directors, after discussion, voted to continue the NPBEA and its present mission but to focus primarily on strengthening preparation programs for school leaders. To advance this goal, it was agreed that a new "Statement of Beliefs" should be developed to clarify the intentions of the board. Scott Thomson, recently retired executive director of the NASSP, was appointed as executive secretary effective January 1990 with offices at George Mason University in Fairfax, Virginia. The Danforth Foundation agreed to continue its funding support for the calendar year 1990, accepting the changes in staff and location.

Subsequently, the board of directors reviewed and approved in March 1990 a "Statement of Purpose" for the NPBEA. The statement declared that the central aim of preparation programs for educational administrators "is to develop school leaders who will actively shape organizational cultures that promote high performance and provide for individual creativity." Furthermore, graduates should be able to demonstrate the application of professional knowledge in a school environment and be fully prepared to improve instructional programs as their prime responsibility to students.

The statement calls for a strong program of professional certification at the entry and advanced levels of practice, including the formation of an independent certification body to determine professional standards. It also describes the architecture of effective preparation programs, declaring that "connections between the knowledge base and professional skills necessary for success as a school administrator are essential, as are clear linkages between these (proficiencies) and tasks performed in the workplace" (NPBEA, 1990b).

The recommended knowledge base included eight areas, many of which had been proposed jointly by the UCEA, the AASA, and the AACTE:

- Social, cultural, and developmental influences on schooling
- Legal, political, and economic relationships to education
- Learning environments, including teaching and learning, diagnostic processes, applications of technology, and supervision of instruction
- Leadership and management functions and processes, including applications of technology
- Theories of organization and methods of organizational change and development
- Policy studies and methodologies of policy analysis
- Assessment and evaluation processes
- Moral and ethical factors in schooling

In addition, the NPBEA statement incorporated a strong emphasis on critical leadership capabilities, including communication skills, interpersonal skills, and decision-making procedures. Another NPBEA declaration was for extensive clinical and fieldwork to provide opportunities for candidates to apply knowledge and skills in working environments.

The statement also addressed a need for school/university partnerships to provide sites for clinical programs and applied research, the importance of "vigorous and systematic recruitment programs" to attract promising candidates, and the significance of maintaining full-time faculty who are clinically oriented as well as research oriented.

Also at this time, a new NPBEA logo, letterhead, and quarterly newsletter, *DESIGN for Leadership,* were approved, with Bob Beach of Memphis State University appointed as editor. Six regional correspondents were selected to provide articles on innovative preparation programs in their geographical areas.

Responding to movements in several states to eliminate certification requirements for school administrators or to develop alternative certification procedures, the NPBEA published in 1990 the policy document *Alternative Certification for School Leaders* as a guideline for states considering nontraditional routes to the principalship or superintendency. The publication argues, in sum, that although alternative routes to certification are acceptable for exceptional candidates, this alternative route must meet the same criteria for demonstrated professional knowledge and skills as does the regular route. "The criteria for substantial equivalency are essential to maintaining the quality of professional service and for protecting the public interest" (NPBEA, 1990a).

The policy statement also refers to certification procedures in other professions, noting that while avenues to alternative certification are open in many professions, standards of admission are carefully controlled by specific procedures, including peer review, which confirm acceptable levels of professional performance. This prevents the scrambling of criteria for admission to a profession. (NPBEA, 1990a, p. 7)

The document then defines six guidelines to determine the qualifications of candidates for an alternative credential: (1) knowledge of teaching and learning; (2) leadership experience; (3) postbaccalaureate preparation; (4) certain personal attributes, including adequate written and oral communication abilities; (5) familiarity with current social and economic issues related to education; and (6) an understanding of the procedures and process by which school districts and schools are governed, develop policies, and deliver programs for students.

Alternative Certification for School Leaders proved to be popular. A reprint was required, and 2,500 copies were distributed nationally. The NPBEA had begun to act where politics and the profession intersect rather than confining its initiatives to the profession alone.

Turning directly to address the question of improving the education of school leaders, the NPBEA published *School Leadership: A Blueprint for Change* (Thomson, 1991). This 52-page paperback addressed six key issues central to the preparation of school leaders: (1) the nature of leadership, (2) leadership in schools, (3) the knowledge base for school leaders, (4) gaining consensus in the preparation of school leaders, (5) professional certification standards, and (6) ethics of professionalism. The book was conceived as a platform for planning specific initiatives to improve preparation programs for school leaders, and for responding to growing expectations for educators from the public and from the profession itself. It aimed at moving the conversation beyond an analysis of shortcomings to a plan of action for the NPBEA.

Following the NPBEA work plan of focusing first on national certification standards for principals, the NPBEA Board voted to use a publication by the National Commission for the Principalship (1990) titled *Principals for Our Changing Schools: Preparation and Certification* as the framework for developing a description of the core knowledge and skills, and the performance standards, to certify principals. The commission, chaired by former U.S. Education Secretary Terrel H. Bell, was organized in 1988 by the NAESP and the NASSP.

The commission's report, developed over 2 years and funded by the Danforth and Geraldine Rockefeller Dodge Foundations, addressed the question, "What must principals know and be able to do for successful school leadership today?" To answer this question, a developmental process was launched that resulted in the identification of 21 domains or areas of knowledge and skill considered essential to the principalship.

The developmental process involved several steps to identify the domains:

- Conducting a task analysis of the principalship
- Convening focus groups of principals, assistant principals, and assistant superintendents to identify the knowledge and skills necessary to perform these tasks; these groups used a list of knowledge and skills consolidated from several sources for their initial reference
- Using a conceptual model and "Taxonomy of Standards" for the principalship developed with the Principals' Center at Texas A&M University to identify the knowledge and skills theoretically applicable to the role
- Integrating the outcomes of the two approaches, one inductive and task driven and the other deductive and theoretically driven, to develop an initial list of performance domains
- Distributing the initial list of domains to a national "Jury of 50," which included prominent educators and a nominated group of principals, superintendents, and professors, for their review and comment
- Consolidating the recommendations of the Jury of 50 to develop a revised list of performance domains
- Receiving comment on the revised list from the Jury and making minor adjustments for the final definition of performance domains

The 21 domains, organized under four broad fields, blend the traditional, content-driven curriculum with leadership and process skills to create a new architecture for preparing principals. This framework recognizes the leadership skills and interpersonal competencies required of principals to succeed in today's school environment as well as the central responsibility of principals for the instructional program.

Using the Principals Commission structure, NPBEA staff planned and organized a second publication that provided a comprehensive description of the core knowledge and skill base required of principals in contemporary settings. This document was authored by 21 teams, one for each of the domains, and included 107 professors of educational leadership, elementary school and secondary school principals, and central office staff. Titled *Principals for Our Changing Schools: The Knowledge and Skill Base* (Thomson, 1993), this publication described performance standards for each of the domains and identified the specific knowledge areas and skills central to these domains. By 1997, more than 8,200 copies of the book had been purchased in the United States, Canada, and Europe, in addition to separate licensing agreements.

The book proved to be influential—it was used by groups setting standards for state certification, by faculties revamping educational leadership programs, by school districts for professional development programs, as a college text, as the framework for a textbook series on educational leadership, and as the basis for a nationally published professional development handbook. Its creation was funded by the Lilly Endowment, by the Danforth and Geraldine Rockefeller Dodge Foundations, and by an anonymous donor from the Northeast.

Two other initiatives of the NPBEA were stillborn because of unsuccessful funding efforts. A data collection and intervention project designed to increase the participation of minorities in preparation programs for school administrators failed to attract funding. Also, a proposal to establish a national certification board with the instruments and processes for voluntary professional certification could not attract funding from the 30 foundations contacted.

Other initiatives were more successful, including well-attended national forums on school district/university partnerships and on problem-based instruction conducted just prior to UCEA and American Educational Research Association (AERA) annual meetings; continuous interaction with the two federally funded educational leadership centers at Harvard and Illinois; and staff presentations at national conventions, LEAD Centers, state associations, and so on. Meanwhile, the quarterly newsletter *DESIGN for Leadership* was transferred to NPBEA headquarters, and Scott Thomson became editor. The newsletter began focusing on interesting and innovative new preparation programs and state certification standards for school leaders around the nation and in Canada. Also, an editorial board was established that included Joe Beckham from the University of Florida, Bob Beach from Memphis State, Nelda Cambron-McCabe from Miami University of Ohio, Tom Mulkeen from Fordham, Stan Landis from the East Penn School District, and Peter Wilson from the Danforth Foundation.

Two national test development firms indicated separately a strong interest in forming a partnership with the NPBEA to develop assessments for national certification. The board of directors voted to pursue this possibility should funding be found to establish a national certification board.

An Evolving Agenda

Given the foundation world's lack of support for a national professional certification system, a grant application was prepared to develop with states common content and technical standards for the licensure of principals and to organize an examination board of state licensing authorities that would develop a common assessment package for licensing principals. The grant application was presented to the Pew Trusts, the Annenberg Foundation, and to 12 other foundations. Pew and Annenberg both indicated serious interest, and staff met with Pew Trusts officers in Philadelphia.

Meanwhile, with strong encouragement from the Danforth Foundation, board members decided to organize a retreat to develop a revised mission and work plan for the NPBEA. A 2-day "Board Futures" planning meeting was then held at the Lansdowne Conference Center near Leesburg, Virginia, in July 1993.

The outcome of this retreat involving all 10 NPBEA sponsors was agreement on a new core mission statement and five central goals:

1. Define a set of outcomes for candidates in educational leadership preparing for state licensure, both the generic requirements and for specific roles. Implementation strategies will depend upon the priorities of individual states.

2. Agree on common accreditation standards for programs preparing school leaders for implementation by the NCATE.

3. Develop model policies for recruiting, selecting, and supporting candidates for administrative positions, with emphasis on women and people of color.

4. Develop an integrated, synergistic model of leadership for schools, beginning with teacher leaders.

5. Envision and define the tasks, performance expectations, and attributes of school leaders for the year 2000, with a focus on improving student outcomes.

Implementation of Goals 1 and 2 began immediately with the formation of an NCATE Working Group, cochaired by David Imig of AACTE and Ed Keller of NAESP, to develop common curriculum guidelines for the accreditation of departments of educational leadership, and with plans for an early National Convocation of States to consider designing common and higher standards for the state licensure of principals.

Developing Accreditation Guidelines

NPBEA staff had met earlier with Arthur Wise, president of the NCATE, to discuss converting the principalship domain materials to their format. Meanwhile, Wise and several members of the NPBEA expressed concern that educational leadership organizations had been working individually with NCATE on a piecemeal basis, and that these separate initiatives were failing to provide a cohesive framework for the field of educational leadership with which NCATE and NCATE–accredited universities could work. From this discussion evolved the Lansdowne decision for all NPBEA organizations to cooperate on a single set of NCATE Curriculum Guidelines for programs in educational leadership. As a result, an NCATE Working Group was appointed, including participants from four dues-paying NCATE members—AASA, ASCD, NAESP, and NASSP—plus three representatives from higher education—AACTE, NCPEA, and UCEA.[2]

In addition to the usual start-up agenda, the working group commissioned Joe Mathews, from the University of Utah, to develop a matrix of knowledge and skills from the recent publications of seven national groups that had independently formulated their own descriptions of the knowledge and skill base necessary for educational leaders to practice at high performance levels. The seven publications analyzed included—in addition to NPBEA's *Principals for Our Changing Schools* (Thomson, 1993)—NAESP's *Proficiencies for Principals* (1991), AASA's *Professional Standards for the Superintendency* (1993), ASCD's *Proposed NCATE Curriculum Guidelines for the Specialty Area of Educational Leadership* (1993), and the Northeast States/Region I DOE document *Framework for the Continual Professional Development of Administrators* (1993). Also incorporated in the matrix was *Principals Assessment Center,* developed by NASSP in 1975, and *Administrator Diagnostics Inventory,* implemented by NAESP in 1994.

Initial draft curriculum guidelines were developed from this matrix and then further refined in subsequent meetings of the working group. During this effort, working group members considered several broad shifts in the knowledge and skills required of educational leaders today compared to traditional roles. These include the following: (a) an increase in the importance of interpersonal skills as compared to technical skills, (b) a movement toward consensus building and motivational skills and away from issuing directives, (c) a responsibility for learning processes and outcomes rather than simply allocating resources, (d) the need to integrate community and campus resources rather than administering on-campus resources alone, and (e) the importance of becoming a policy participant rather than simply a policy recipient. Beyond these changing expectations, the working group addressed the importance of applied knowledge as well as analytical and conceptual competence.

Draft guidelines were presented to the NPBEA Board of Directors in April 1994 and, after feedback, were redrafted and presented again to the board of directors and a small sample of universities. Based on this feedback, third and fourth drafts were developed and presented in September 1994 to NCATE's Specialty Areas Studies Board (SASB) for preliminary review and comment. Using the SASB's responses, a fifth draft was approved by the NPBEA Board of Directors and circulated nationally by NCATE. Again, applying new feedback, the sixth draft was accepted by NCATE effective in autumn 1996 (Educational Leadership Constituent Council, 1995). Administration of the guidelines is by the Educational Leadership Constituent Council, which is composed of four national associations that hold membership in the NCATE—AASA, ASCD, NAESP, and NASSP. Offices of the constituent council are located initially at ASCD headquarters in Alexandria.

The new curriculum guidelines apply to institutions seeking NCATE accreditation for master's degrees through 6-year and specialist programs in educational leadership. These guidelines differ in five fundamental ways from earlier versions sponsored by individual associations:

1. The revised knowledge and skills are integrated and are generic for all school leaders.
2. They emphasize outcomes rather than simply providing a listing of courses and descriptions of content. To this end, the working group and ASCD sponsored the development and pilot-testing of program performance evaluation in six universities using the new curriculum guidelines.
3. Folios will require some evidence of content learned and applied.
4. Folios will be examined by teams of reviewers that include university professors, district administrators, and school-based personnel.
5. A robust internship is required.

The new guidelines include 11 knowledge and skill domains integrated under four broad areas and one process domain (the internship). The four broad areas are (a) strategic leadership, (b) instructional leadership, (c) organizational leadership, and (d) political and community leadership. The internship is defined as a variety of substantial experiences in diverse settings planned and supervised cooperatively by university and school district personnel.

NPBEA members assert that all preparation programs for educational leaders should be NCATE approved and should agree to advance that goal. Currently, only two thirds of these programs meet NCATE standards. In taking this position, the NPBEA noted that in all major professions except education, people cannot be licensed to practice unless they graduate from an accredited institution. The NPBEA believes that the current situation weakens the professions of teaching and school leadership and provides unnecessary opportunities for criticism of the profession and public education.

Common Standards for Licensing Administrators

Acting on its agenda generated at the Lansdowne conference, the NPBEA in 1993 appointed a steering committee on "Common and Higher Standards for State Licensure." Committee members representing the 10 NPBEA sponsors decided to convene all states interested in discussing the question of common standards as a basis for licensing school leaders.

Based on this decision, invitations were sent to the departments of public education in all 50 states and the District of Columbia to attend a "National Convocation on Common Standards for the State Licensure of Principals." The Convocation, held in January 1994 and funded by three foundations, was attended by representatives of 37 states and 10 national associations.

After 2 days of structured meetings, the participants voted for several recommendations: (a) Stakeholders will use and benefit from the development of common standards, (b) coherent standards should be developed and implemented, (c) a broad group of stakeholders should be involved in developing the standards, (d) intent as to purpose and process must be widely communicated, and (e) a steering committee should be formed to plan the next steps in the development of entry-level standards for the principalship.

Meanwhile, the CCSSO Board of Directors voted in mid-January to establish an "Interstate Principals Licensure Consortium" as a parallel to their national program to develop common standards for entry-level teachers. After discussion of several issues and the CCSSO plans, the NPBEA Board of Directors agreed that competing initiatives would be counterproductive to achieving the professional goal of common and higher licensing standards for school leaders. Therefore, the NPBEA voted to revise its mission from being the primary advocate of common standards for licensing principals to that of a working partner with CCSSO. The board of directors also voted to continue pursuing funding for the project with leads already established, as

· the goal remained the same as previously defined. Therefore, the original NPBEA grant request to the Pew Trusts to develop common and higher standards for the state licensure of principals was amended to designate CCSSO as assuming the primary responsibility for this work. The NPBEA remained the grant recipient for technical reasons. A 2-year grant for $300,000 was then received from the Pew Trusts for the 1995 and 1996 calendar years to develop common state standards as proposed. The Danforth Foundation also contributed almost $50,000 to the effort.

The initial meeting of the new Interstate School Leaders Licensure Consortium (ISLLC) was held in August 1994 and attended by 27 state representatives. The agenda had been planned by Ramsay Selden of CCSSO, Joseph Murphy of Vanderbilt University (appointed as chair of the Consortium), and Scott Thomson of the NPBEA. Most of the states involved with the CCSSO initiative to develop common standards for teacher licensure joined ISLLC.

The ISLLC crafted over 2 years, from 1994 to 1996, models standards and indicators for school leaders. Forged from research on productive educational leadership and from effective practice, the standards were drafted by representatives of 24 state education agencies and several professional associations. The final work was published as a monograph (ISLLC, 1996).

The document is organized by six broad standards, each with the lead phrase, "A school administrator is an educational leader who promotes the success of all students by . . ." The standards are (a) facilitating the development, articulation, implementation, and stewardship of a vision of learning that is shared and supported by the school community; (b) advocating, nurturing, and sustaining a school culture and instructional program conducive to student learning and professional growth; (c) ensuring management of the organization, operations, and resources for a safe, efficient, and effective learning environment; (d) collaborating with families and community members, responding to diverse community interests and needs, and mobilizing community resources; (e) acting with integrity, fairness, and in an ethical manner; and (f) understanding, responding to, and influencing the larger political, social, economic, legal, and cultural context.

As an introduction to the monograph, Joseph Murphy, Chair, and Neil Shipman, Director of ISLLC, noted that

> the standards present a common core of knowledge, dispositions, and performances that will help link leadership more forcefully to productive schools and enhanced educational outcomes. Although developed to serve a different purpose, the standards were designed to be compatible with the new National Council for the Accreditation of Teacher

Education (NCATE) *Curriculum Guidelines* for school administration—as well as with the major national reports on reinventing leadership for tomorrow's schools. As such, they represent another part of a concerted effort to enhance the skills of school leaders and to couple leadership with effective educational processes and valued outcomes.

One intent of the document was to stimulate vigorous thought and dialogue about quality educational leadership among stakeholders in the area of school administration. A second intent was to provide raw material that will help stakeholders across the education landscape (e.g., state agencies, professional associations, institutions of higher education) enhance the quality of educational leadership throughout the nation's schools.

Since the publication of these standards, the CCSSO and several states have formed a partnership with the Educational Testing Service to create new assessments based on the standards to be used for the initial licensure of candidates in participating states. The test will become available nationally in the fall of 1998.

National Networks

From 1991 to 1996, the NPBEA sponsored a series of national forums funded by Danforth, commissioned several publications on issues considered critical to the national conversation on educational leadership and schooling, and developed a national resource bank for programs in educational leadership.

The national forums were scheduled to precede UCEA and AERA annual meetings and included these four topics in addition to the themes cited earlier in this chapter: (a) developing and using clinical materials in preparation programs; (b) integrating services for students and families: implications for the preparation and development of school leaders; (c) transformational leadership for school, family, and community partnerships; and (d) using technologies in the preparation of school leaders. Each forum attracted 120 to 200 participants. Several were cosponsored by UCEA.

The NPBEA also commissioned, published, and distributed nationally several monographs. The initial monograph, *Gender and Politics at Work: Why Women Exit the Superintendency* (1993) was authored by Marilyn Tallerico, Joan N. Burstyn, and Wendy Poole. Subsequent monographs included *Building a Career: Fulfilling the Lifetime Professional Needs of Principals* (1994) by David A. Erlandson, and *Educating Democracy: The Role of Systemic Leadership* (1996) by Gary M. Crow and Robert O. Slater. Copies of the monographs were mailed to all chairs of departments of educational leadership nationally as well as being marketed generally.

With funding from the Danforth Foundation and in cooperation with UCEA, the NPBEA initiated the development of an international resource bank of exemplary programs for preparing educational leaders. A panel of educators appointed by the NPBEA and UCEA, and chaired by Joseph Murphy, developed a framework for the resource bank that included 12 main areas of preparation and development, ranging from recruitment and selection, to program content, to teaching and learning strategies, to internships, to student and program assessment. Documents were mailed by the NPBEA to all institutions preparing educational administrators in the United States, Canada, and Australia, inviting them to participate in building the resource bank. The completed materials were collected and assembled into hardcover and on-line formats for use by professors of educational leadership. UCEA assumed responsibility for managing the resource bank in early 1996.

In the continuing search for new foundations for educational leadership, the NPBEA and the Danforth Foundation organized in 1995 an invitational conference of 80 professors, school administrators, and representatives from six nationally based school improvement programs (Accelerated Schools, The League of Professional Schools, The Coalition of Essential Schools, Foxfire, Impact II, and The Center for Educational Renewal).

The conference, facilitated by Hunter Moorman of the U.S. Department of Education and Joseph Murphy of Vanderbilt University, grappled with this question: How can an understanding of school improvement inform our conception of educational leadership and our understanding of the preparation needed for tomorrow's school leaders? A report of the conference findings, summarized in the September 1995 issue of *DESIGN for Leadership*, outlines these major points:

1. Common elements and principles found in the six school improvement initiatives include the following: (a) Each group was able to articulate where it was coming from philosophically, (b) the efforts represented powerful communities engaging in a powerful dialogue, and (c) all stakeholders assumed responsibility for learning.

2. The foundations of educational leadership identified were that leaders need to focus on student learning and teaching, that leaders must operate on a set of moral imperatives, and that the leaders must demonstrate a passion for people.

3. The dimensions of leadership distilled from conference proceedings emphasize that leaders are "the builders of dreams, keepers of the vision, and translators of ideas"; that leaders must have a passion for student and teacher learning; and that leaders must promote consensus building and shared decisions based on purpose.

4. The implications for leadership preparation include the need to anchor programs well by attending to belief, attitude, and philosophy; programs should be constructed from problems of practice; and professional learning communities involving schools and universities should develop around preparation programs. These findings affirm the general thrust of efforts to reform and strengthen preparation programs during the 1990s.

The NPBEA quarterly newsletter *DESIGN for Leadership*, an eight-page publication, provided a consistent source of information on interesting and innovative preparation programs, the development of professional standards for school leaders, and the evolution of state licensure policies. Mailed to a national and Canadian audience of 2,000 educators and policymakers, each issue of *DESIGN* typically included five articles describing new or revised preparation programs or state licensure standards together with announcements of new publications or conferences in the field of educational leadership. Over the period 1991 to 1996, *DESIGN* articles described program revision or reform in 72 universities (Beach & Thomson, 1991-1996). This information, provided by six regional correspondents, created a catalyst for a continuing appraisal and recasting of preparation programs in departments of educational leadership nationally. It also offered, prior to the development of on-line networks, a ready reference to new activities in preparation and licensure nationally for the field.

Other networking activities by NPBEA staff included consulting directly with 20 states on standards for the principalship, consulting with universities on preparation programs, speaking at national meetings on NPBEA programs, and participating in national organizations such as the Holmes Group.

The Evolution Continues

Following the retirement of Scott Thomson as executive secretary in September 1996, the board of directors voted to move NPBEA offices to UCEA headquarters at the University of Missouri—Columbia. Patrick Forsyth was appointed corporate secretary, and a reappraisal of the priorities of the NPBEA began a new cycle.

The NPBEA and Reform: An Analysis

Although several organizations[3] and many individuals participated in constructing new foundations for the field of educational leadership during the 1990s, the NPBEA contributed some unique elements to this widespread effort.

1. Never before had all of the national associations representing higher education and elementary and secondary education in educational leadership worked together in one organization to address current issues and create new programs in the field. Initially, the professors and the school administrators were cautious, even suspicious, of one another's agenda. After several meetings, however, board members representing the 10 sponsoring organizations forged a common purpose and comfortable working relationship.[4] This development brought considerable weight to programs agreed upon and completed. The field became more unified, and the chasm between the professoriate and school practitioners narrowed appreciably. Educational leadership became less fragmented and more unified as to purpose, program, and process.

2. The incorporation of applied knowledge and professional skills to programs in educational leadership, a movement already under way, was enhanced by NPBEA initiatives. These initiatives stemmed from the conviction that the theory-based movement launched in the 1950s was threadbare and approaching obsolescence, and that it required a major makeover to accommodate contemporary requirements.

3. Similarly, the integration of clinical activities and robust field experiences into preparation programs—an NPBEA priority—although already used by some universities, clearly benefited from NPBEA advocacy.

4. The national dialogue on developing common standards for the state licensure of educational leaders was materially influenced by NPBEA publications, conferences, newsletters, and consultancies.

5. The development of new curriculum guidelines for the accreditation of programs in educational leadership by NCATE was initiated and completed. These guidelines incorporated a contemporary knowledge

and skill base and required program performance appraisal as part of the accreditation process. NPBEA members have agreed, as a continuing campaign, to advocate that all university programs preparing school leaders be accredited.

6. The initial national meeting to develop common professional standards for the state licensure of school leaders was sponsored by NPBEA. The NPBEA then contributed to, and supported, the CCSSO effort to develop and gain approval of these standards by the 24 participating states.

7. The NPBEA consciously chose specific program initiatives such as program accreditation and professional standards rather than confining its efforts to policy development or issue analysis in the belief that program changes "on the ground," if thoughtfully conceived and executed, affect a larger number of people in the long run than does a narrow adherence to analytical work. The NPBEA focused on integrating the conceptual and applied approaches to advance the profession.

8. The NPBEA gave priority to selected concepts to improve the field. For example, the notion of "educational leadership" was consciously applied, replacing "educational administration" to differentiate from old stereotypes and as an accurate descriptor of the role actually required of school leaders today. Leadership was viewed by NPBEA members as the core responsibility of principals and superintendents. A concept that had fallen on hard times among academics because no overarching theory proved adequate, leadership was becoming ever more critical to the success of individual schools. Therefore the NPBEA became an active advocate of the notion that the core skills, attributes, and processes of effective leadership are understood and can be taught and practiced apart from a general theory of leadership.

9. The NPBEA offices served as a national catalyst for universities and state associations interested in revising preparation programs, for states and professional associations planning new and higher standards of practice for licensing principals and superintendents, and for school districts seeking progressive and effective professional development curricula. Correspondence and calls from across the nation flowed into the NPBEA headquarters seeking information and advice. In addition, staff consulted directly with 20 states planning to revise standards of practice, and on-site with almost 50 universities nationally, ranging from Arizona to Connecticut and from Washington State to North Carolina.

10. By advocating that departments of educational leadership give priority to preparing practitioners and to applied research, the NPBEA acknowledged the natural tension between theory and academic research, on one hand, and professional practice and applied research on the other. Additional pressure on universities to differentiate between professional schools and schools of arts and science in their criteria for promotion may evolve from this position, allowing schools of education to reward clinical activities equally with more traditional academic routines as do other professional schools, such as architecture or engineering or pharmacy.

Final Word

Looking ahead, the NPBEA must continue to evaluate and reshape its activities and programs as contemporary priorities and research dictate. However, one central purpose should remain inviolate. Never again can the profession be divided and unfocused as it has been periodically in the past. The presence of the major national associations working together, analyzing issues and initiating activities as NPBEA colleagues, can preclude damaging fragmentation and nourish the strength of a unified and rising profession.

Notes

1. Other chairs of NPBEA were David Imig of AACTE (1989, 1990); Sam Sava of NAESP (1991); Pat Forsyth of UCEA (1992); Rich Miller of AASA (1993); Don McCarty of NCPEA (1994); Gene Carter of ASCD (1995, 1996); and Paul Houston of AASA (1997).

2. In addition to cochairs Imig (AACTE) and Keller (NAESP), NCATE working group members were Mary Reese (AASA); David Sperry (NCPEA); James Keefe (NASSP); Barbara Jackson (UCEA); Michele Terry and Susan Nicholas (ASCD); and Scott Thomson, secretary (NPBEA).

3. Chief among foundations supporting the reform of educational leadership was the Danforth Foundation; its president, Bruce Anderson; and staff members Gary Wright and Peter Wilson. Major financial contributions also came from the Pew Trusts, the Geraldine Rockefeller Dodge Foundation, and the Lilly Endowment.

4. The ASBO resigned from the NPBEA in 1995, leaving nine members. ASBO has developed a separate set of professional standards.

References

Beach, R. H., and Thomson, S. D. (Eds.). (1991-1996). *DESIGN for leader-ship*, Volumes I-VI. Fairfax, VA: National Policy Board for Educational Administration.

Clark, D. L., & Astuto, T. A. (1989). *Final report to the Danforth Foundation from the National Policy Board for Educational Administration.* Unpublished report.

Crow, G. M., & Slater, R.O. (1996). *Educating democracy: The role of systemic leadership.* Fairfax, VA: NPBEA.

Educational Leadership Constituent Council. (1995). *Curriculum guidelines for advanced programs in educational leadership.* Alexandria, VA: Association for Supervision and Curriculum Development.

Erlandson, D. A. (1994). *Building a career: Fulfilling the lifetime professional needs of principals.* Fairfax, VA: NPBEA.

Griffiths, D. E., Stout, R. T., & Forsyth, P. B. (Eds.). (1988). *Leaders for America's schools: The report and papers of the National Commission on Excellence in Educational Administration.* Berkeley, CA: McCutchan.

Interstate School Leaders Licensure Consortium. (1996). *Standards for school leaders.* Washington, DC: Council of Chief State School Officers.

National Commission for the Principalship. (1990). *Principals for our changing schools: Preparation and certification.* Fairfax, VA: National Association of Elementary School Principals and National Association of Secondary School Principals.

National Policy Board for Educational Administration. (1988). *Charge to the study group.* Unpublished report.

National Policy Board for Educational Administration. (1989). *Improving the preparation of school administrators: An agenda for reform.* Charlottesville, VA: Author.

National Policy Board for Educational Administration. (1990a). *Alternative certification for school leaders.* Fairfax, VA: Author.

National Policy Board for Educational Administration. (1990b). *The preparation of school administrators: A statement of purpose.* Fairfax, VA: Author.

Tallerico, M., Burstyn, J. N., & Poole, W. (1993). *Gender and politics at work: Why women exit the superintendency.* Fairfax, VA: NPBEA.

Thomson, S. D. (Ed.). (1991). *School leadership: A blueprint for change.* Newbury Park, CA: Corwin.

Thomson, S. D. (Ed.). (1993). *Principals for our changing schools: The knowledge and skill base.* Fairfax, VA: NPBEA.

5

Reinventing Preparation Programs: A Decade of Activity

ANN WEAVER HART
DIANA G. POUNDER

The structure and content of preparation programs for school leaders in the United States reflect the intellectual ferment of the past decade in educational administration. Although variety and experimentation took many forms, three themes dominated the reinvention of preparation programs. The first theme was a renewed effort to strengthen and clarify the knowledge base for educational leadership, accompanied by innovations in instructional delivery methods congruent with new knowledge approaches or capitalizing on new technologies. The second theme was professional practice—practice-based reforms of advanced professional degrees, such as the EdD, and practical experiences for new leaders, such as internships (many of which rely on cohort structures and some of which attempt to merge preparation and professional development for teachers and administrators). The third theme was the development of new licensure, certification, and accreditation standards and assessment techniques for school leaders.

In many ways, these three themes represent very different views of educational administration. The first seeks insight into leadership through a greater understanding of the way leaders think, what they think about, and ways in which they tie their thinking to their actions. The second is grounded in a pragmatic, action-based view of leadership preparation relying on high-quality experiential knowledge as a basis for improving leadership preparation.

Finally, the third theme reflects a movement toward more authentic standards and assessment for leadership licensure, certification, and accreditation—an oversight perspective—with an emphasis on the integration of cognitive and experiential knowledge and the application of that knowledge to authentic leadership situations.

This chapter presents an overview of the reinvention of educational administration programs during the past decade, responses to the criticisms that policymakers were not paying sufficient attention to leadership preparation programs (Clark & Clark, 1996), and the way in which the three themes of professional preparation are reflected in the changes that have taken place. Although these themes do not encompass all of the interesting ideas included in the discourse surrounding educational leadership and, thus, preparation programs, excluding such things as visionary leadership (Norris, 1990) and transformational leadership (Bass, 1985), they do reflect the primary organizing concepts that have had the greatest influence on preparation program reform. Additionally, we found scant evidence of the broad implementation of the reforms discussed in this chapter. The research that we found on implementation is reported, but data on the adoption of these innovations beyond their initial settings are not extensive.

The Knowledge Base

Building on the theory movement in educational administration from the 1960s and 1970s, the decade from the mid-1980s to mid-1990s saw changes in the intellectual approaches to educational leadership research and related preparation programs. These approaches especially shaped an expanded (and for some a redefined) knowledge base, including the application of cognition theory and problem-based pedagogies to research and preparation program reform in educational administration. Writers and practitioners emphasized the development and application of expertise; thinking and action connections; a renewed emphasis on professional practice; and critical approaches to analyzing the personal, school, and community.

Changes in approaches to educational leadership placed new demands on the knowledge base in educational leadership. To teach expertise, for example, the knowledge domain was hard-pressed to meet certain characteristics.

> Ill-structured [knowledge] domains present a . . . characterization of the problem-solving activity [in which] "surety about right action does not

exist, [and] the choice of a sensible solution strategy for a problem is a more complex task than is solving a problem in well-structured domains."
. . . [P]roblems remain stubbornly ill-defined and messy; solutions are elusive and uncertain; routinized or a priori identified knowledge structures and processes are either lacking or insufficient for the problem-solving activity; and the context is complex, ambiguous, and in constant flux. Achievement of expertise in ill-structured domains is difficult to ascertain as its development remains relatively uncharted and examination of the route to success in one problem-solving activity will not necessarily provide reliable markers applicable to attaining success in the next. (Prestine, 1993, pp. 195-196)

Additionally, at the end of the behavioral science and dialectic eras identified by Murphy (1992), many scholars and practitioners alike had little positive to say about the knowledge base. Immegart (1990) called the cognitive foundations of school administration "shaky" (p. 8). Murphy (1992), citing prominent scholars in the field, included a litany of reasons for this shaky foundation:

our ardor to borrow ideas before they are tested; the lack of theory upon which to ground research efforts; a failure to focus on educational administration as an area worthy of study in and of itself; poor scholarship habits within the field; and an absence of a sense of vision about the profession. (p. 87)

Furthermore, Murphy identified fragmented programs for administrator preparation with required but disconnected courses, a lack of attention to practice, and a lack of attention to education and ethics as contributing factors to the malaise. Others have added a reluctance, even an unwillingness, to critically analyze the state of the field, of schools, and of society at large in relation to education as components of the weak status of the knowledge base (Bates, 1987; Foster, 1986, 1994). McCleary (1992) emphasized that even if the deficiencies in formal knowledge identified by critics were rectified, "the leader must understand the nature and uses of knowledge appropriate to a given set of circumstances" (p. 17).

The nature of the knowledge base on which educational administration and leadership draw remained a focus of debate and lively discussion. Several perspectives on this debate dominated the past decade. First, those committed to an increased emphasis on practice in reaction to the perceived neglect emerging from the social sciences emphasis of the preceding two decades

sought to include more experiential knowledge drawn from practicing administrators into formal administrator preparation programs. In addition to fic-
tionalized case studies employed as part of formal preparation, members of
the field worked to accumulate a knowledge base of actual cases on which
teachers and students alike could draw. This emphasis also resulted in changes
in program structure discussed later in this chapter. Second, the cognitive
knowledge base—empirical and theoretical knowledge—was subject to increased scrutiny and criticism. Epistemologies other than those dominating
quantitative and psychological approaches to inquiry and theory drove much
of this criticism and ferment. One example of the result of this ferment is the
UCEA's knowledge base project and subsequent document base (see Chapter 3, this volume).

The field responded to this new pressure on the knowledge base in a
number of ways.

1. A new knowledge base project was initiated by UCEA, and expanded
   views of the knowledge base to include experiential as well as empirical and theoretical knowledge were explored.
2. Existing efforts to use case studies to systematize a knowledge base
   of practice for the field were intensified, and the use of case method
   pedagogy was expanded.
3. Efforts to capitalize on technology to acquire, systematize, and use
   the knowledge base were redoubled.

The Knowledge Base Project

The knowledge base project at UCEA grew from the recommendations
of the National Policy Board for Educational Administration's 1988 national
report on preparing school leaders. It includes seven major domains: (1) societal and cultural influences on schooling, (2) teaching and learning processes,
(3) organizational studies, (4) leadership and management processes,
(5) policy and political studies, (6) legal and ethical dimensions of schooling, and (7) economic and financial dimensions of schooling (UCEA, 1997).
The approach taken is limited almost exclusively to the United States in the
policy/political, legal/ethical, and economic/financial domains of the project.

Throughout most of the domains, and in the readings and resources to
which a user of the UCEA document base is referred, the knowledge base is
conceptualized in ways traditional to the educational administration field in
the decades preceding the 1980s. However, the project raised some interest-

ing questions that point to shifts in the field and changes that are no longer nascent. One of the first indicators of this shift was the choice of authors leading the societal and cultural influences domain—Henry Giroux and Kofi Lomotey among them. Giroux and Lomotey are vocal social critics whose critical theory perspectives on societal values and impacts on children, schools, and schooling are widely read and known. Echoing a long-standing debate in sociology, Scheurich and Laible (1995) argued that the perspective offered by Lomotey in readings offered through the document base, and Lomotey's discussion of the social and cultural influences domain, undermined the entire knowledge base project by reproducing the long-established structure already in place in educational administration programs and by replicating existing race, gender, and class differences. A further perusal of the literature offered in this revolutionary section that Scheurich and Laible found undermined the rest of the document base reveals reading after reading critical of the power, culture, and democratic failures of education interspersed with some more traditional historians' (such as David Tyack) perspectives.

Other indicators of more "critical" shifts in "cognate" and basic literatures emerged in the illustrative writings on issues in educational measurement that critique both behaviorist foundations of curriculum and testing practices and standardized testing practices in the United States. Furthermore, the literature was far more inclusive of alternative and critical voices in organizational studies (e.g., Richard J. Bates, Thomas B. Greenfield, William Foster), although it was dominated by traditional organizational theorists within and outside of education. Finally, the domain on ethical dimensions included illustrative writings universally critical of the ethical performance of schools because they embrace value neutrality, business models, and bureaucratic control; they fail to promote a moral ethic that encompasses justice, caring, and critique; and they embrace standard political and sociological conceptions of leadership rather than leadership that is critical, transformative, educative, and ethical.

Another new perspective on the knowledge base relied on the increased use of practitioners as a learning resource. Cases based on actual events in schools provided the core of the experience-based knowledge efforts of the decade, although many variations on the theme emerged in actual preparation programs.

Case Studies

In addition to their long-established use in business, professional, and social science teaching, case studies emerged in the past 10 to 15 years as both a component of the professional knowledge base and a teaching method. Over the decades, case methods have gained popularity in many professional fields, and many books of cases have been published as reference materials for professors and professional development consultants (Kowalski, 1991; Norris, 1990; Wendel, 1990b).

The case method is so widely used that it requires little discussion in this context. More interesting is the implication of efforts to establish a systematic, high-quality collection of cases as part of the professional knowledge base in educational administration, much as law has done (UCEA, 1997). Professor Gary M. Crow leads a UCEA effort to get the long-languishing case project, begun with a donation from the Paula Silver estate (the APEX Project), back on track and onto the Internet. The goal of this effort was to "create an electronic case set to be expanded annually" (UCEA, 1997, p. 12). This presented a tremendous challenge. Not only does the field lack a tradition of rigorous case-style analysis of professional problems and a commitment to cases as part of the "authority" to which the field would appeal for future decisions, but it also lacks a professional and intellectual nature and standards by which the cases themselves can be evaluated.

Among the questions the case approach to the knowledge base raised are the following:

1. How are users to judge whether a case's outcome was "positive" or "negative" in the professional or teaching context to which one would like to apply it?
2. Should the users employ only the material in which the "problem" is laid out, or should they include the outcome/solution as part of the professional development or teaching experience?
3. How might the custodians of such a case data bank solicit, review, select, and catalogue cases for the variety of purposes to which they might be put?
4. Can cases ever rise to the level of a truly professional facet of a cognitive knowledge base?

Although the past decade has only begun to explore this debate (after getting off to a slow start), case-based, experience-based contributions to the knowledge base in educational administration preparation programs continue to spark some interest.

Technology

Technology gets so much attention as a major influence on scholarly and information environments that we hesitated to include it in this discussion. However, some technological innovations that were developed recently may have major impacts on instructional delivery methods in educational leadership programs and are relevant to a discussion of reinvented preparation programs. We will emphasize here innovations that sought to create virtual schools in which budding and growing leaders could practice leadership and decision making. Simulations are not new to the field, but they have been woefully lacking in salience, vividness, and immediacy of feedback (Bridges & Hallinger, 1993). A number of programs were designed to provide virtual schools in which a variety of problematic situations can be posed and decision-tree alternatives pursued with multiple implications. These have been available for some time in a variety of commercially available platforms.

Within the profession, UCEA moved toward the development of an Information Environment for School Leader Preparation (IESLP). IESLP is a virtual rural school district on which administrators can practice their decision-making and leadership knowledge and skills and receive immediate feedback on the outcome of decisions. UCEA describes IESLP as an "on-line" innovation that has its own URL on the World Wide Web (UCEA, 1997). The site remains under construction. However, 23 just-completed exercises were presented to the UCEA Executive Committee at their meeting in October 1997. Perhaps this is the future that preparation programs face, as technology changes so quickly that available data must be changed dramatically and frequently.

IESLP's planners described it as containing six important elements (UCEA, 1993):

1. Information analysis (including data manipulation platform, quantitative analysis tools, display tools, comprehensive school district data sets, CD file drawers)
2. Research access system on-line, including full search capacity
3. A navigation and reporting system that includes conceptual, analytical, and problem identification systems; reporting templates; historical and "expert" solution files; and what its designers describe as "work-style monitory systems"
4. Problem-finding exercises
5. Problem-provided exercises that include interfaces with the available databases
6. A training system

On one front, this is a new view indeed of the professional knowledge base with a delivery to learners through simulations grounded more deeply in "reality." On the other front, it is a highly linear view grounded in the belief that "truth," or some version of it, is obtainable and usable. The case project may be one development in perspectives on the knowledge base that remains grounded in traditional approaches to the disciplines, especially in the social and behavioral sciences, and to knowledge in general.

Cognition

Cognitive perspectives on educational leadership combined

wise practice, reflection, and context as critical elements in revising mainstream assumptions [about educational administration and leadership]. By clearly focusing on the individual's intentions, knowledge, beliefs, and actions within a unique setting, cognitive perspectives sought to resolve long-standing disagreements about the relationship of knowledge (theoretical, empirical, and experiential) to action. They asked why, when, and where administrators act as they do and how they think about it along the way. (Cuban, 1993, p. xi)

"Cognitive approaches [to educational leadership] tend by nature to focus explicitly on the thinking processes of individuals" (Hallinger, Leithwood, & Murphy, 1993, p. 1). They addressed the core functions of problem finding and problem solving seen as central to decision making by educational leaders. Although scholars and preparation program reformers focused their attention differentially on problem finding, problem solving, and decision making, all are important to this approach. At the same time, attention was more on the everyday activities of educational leaders than on the "bigger matters" that arise in extensive, organization-based, and top-level decisions. For example, Kerchner (1993) argued that the decisions that administrators need to learn to make well are seldom the large, strategic decisions that shape the organization at large. Rather, he divided strategic decisions that educational leaders need to make into discrete and incremental categories along external and internal dimensions. Additionally, he found that internal decisions can be separated into group and individual levels. Because organizational decisions come rarely in administrative life, Kerchner argued that preparation programs probably "overeducate for the unusual and fail to teach students to recognize the strategic potential in everyday activities" (p. 17).

Because cognitive perspectives applied to administrator preparation programs required that proponents accept the responsibility to develop expertise in students, questions about the nature of administrative expertise and its acquisition became more important within formal preparation programs. Students in educational leadership programs were expected to change their thinking and decision-making processes from those characteristic of novices to those characteristic of experts. And preparation programs accepted the challenge of structuring learning experiences that facilitated that process. Features that characterize experts and have been integrated into these preparation programs include the following:

1. An expert within a specific domain will have amassed a large yet well-organized knowledge base.
2. This extensive body of knowledge allows experts to classify problems according to principles, laws, or major rules rather than surface features found within the problem.
3. The knowledge base is highly organized, allowing experts to quickly and accurately identify patterns and configurations. This ability reduces cognitive load and permits the expert to attend to other variables within the problem.
4. The problem-solving strategies of experts are proceduralized. Experts can automatically invoke these skills whereas novices often struggle with the problem-solving process.
5. The acquisition of this complex knowledge base takes a long time. Expertise within a domain is linked to years of practice, experience, or study. (Ohde & Murphy, 1993, pp. 75-76)

Cognitive psychologists provide some insight into how expertise develops. First, the novice acquires declarative knowledge that is used to direct performance and gradually is organized by the learner to reduce heavy demands on the working memory. Second, knowledge is compiled, routines are established, and demands on memory are reduced. Finally, as problem-solving procedures are refined, "insight and selectivity" replace trial and error and "domain-specific knowledge becomes directly embedded within the procedures for performing the skill" (Ohde & Murphy, 1993, p. 78). This organization requires the use of schemata, or abstract mental structures through which people organize knowledge and that allow connections to be drawn within that knowledge with minimal pressure on memory. Expert actions drawn from expert schemas are flexible and sensitive to the unique demands of each professional decision opportunity.

One immediate implication of this knowledge about the nature of expertise for the preparation of educational leaders was the general assessment of the vigor and clarity of the knowledge base that experts are called upon to apply (addressed later in this chapter). Another was the relationship of this knowledge to the expert's field of practice. Barnett and his colleagues (1992a) argued, for example, that instead of simply certifying administrators, the preparation program at the University of Northern Colorado was transforming its focus from managerial skills to leadership development. They argued that this constituted a new knowledge base for future administrators that stressed self-understanding, using inquiry, shaping organizations, and understanding people and environmental influences. They assessed this new knowledge base using the analysis of educational platforms and portfolios.

In many ways, the cognition movement in preparation programs appeared to have two seemingly opposite effects. It returned to the deliberate contemplation of apprenticeship models of skill and expertise acquisition. At the same time, scholars intrigued by the implication of cognition constructs hoped that it would lead the field to apply complex psychological and social-psychological theories in cognition, thinking-action linkages, and expertise to the preparation of school leaders. The first of these effects—the deliberate contemplation of apprenticeship models—was by far the most influential. In order to act on the basis of knowledge with increasing flexibility, effectiveness, and efficiency, as experts do, scholars examining this apprenticeship model pointed out that the challenge for cognition-based reforms in educational leadership preparation programs was to structure experiences that

1. Facilitate the acquisition of an extensive and well-organized knowledge base

2. Teach new educational leaders how to establish a context for problems to promote expert problem finding, problem solving, and decision making

3. Promote the development of forward thinking and reasoning skills that draw on an analysis of the actual facts present in a situation rather than on preestablished hypotheses about the problem that encourage one to fit facts into quickly reached judgments about the problem (Prestine, 1993)

As cognition-based changes in preparation programs were implemented during the decade, scholars studying the outcomes of these initiatives found evidence that supports optimism that these methods may be more effective in building expertise than are more traditional methods of pedagogy. For example, problem-finding and problem-solving processes were emphasized.

Hart (1993), observing students in a studio learning experience based on problem-finding and problem-solving activities and the development of action plans, found that the most common problem-solving errors (Barrows, 1988) made by students were related to backward mapping and thinking based on experiences that preceded their advanced studies in leadership preparation programs. Students were most likely to bring the process to premature closure and selectively ignore important information that did not fit their early diagnoses of problems. These patterns would have remained unaddressed in more traditional course and seminar activities.

One of the most important aspects of the cognitively based approaches to the preparation of administrators was professional reflection. Perhaps the most influential scholar affecting the application of the reflective process to the improvement of administrative practice and the preparation of reflective practitioners was Donald Schön (1983, 1987). Schön explored how professionals think in action, differentiating between reflection-in-action, which occurs during the process of action, and reflection-on-action, which takes place more systematically and after the press to act has passed. Both of these important processes were applied by those seeking more action-oriented preparation programs grounded in an extensive experiential, empirical, and theoretical knowledge base (Hart & Bredeson, 1996). The reflective practitioner became almost a catchphrase of leadership preparation programs in education. It also became a quality that all educational leaders sought.

The research on educational leaders based on a cognitive perspective, as well as some of the redesigned preparation programs relying on this perspective on educational leadership were compiled in a book by Hallinger et al. (1993) under the auspices of the National Center for Educational Leadership. As well as classifying, framing, and defining administrative problems, this effort explored the nature of administrative expertise and presented five approaches applying cognitive perspectives to the preparation of educational administrators. These were: (a) issues surrounding the teaching of problem solving, (b) a cognitive apprenticeship model of problem solving (Prestine, 1993), (c) a design studio for reflective practice (Hart, 1993), (d) teaching problem solving as problem-solving learning (Kelsey, 1993), and (e) problem-based learning in medical and managerial education (Bridges & Hallinger, 1993).

The practical applications described range from apprenticeship problem solving (Prestine, 1993) to lessons imported from medical and managerial education (Bridges & Hallinger, 1993). The authors reported that some of the lessons learned from these collected experiments were that (a) knowledge often remains inert and unapplied; (b) problem solving takes time and requires general problem-solving skills; (c) knowledge, process, and context are interactive; (d) apprenticeship models of cognition require active learners in an authentic context; (e) students often do not know what they do not know and so have difficulty sustaining early engagement in problem-based learning, because although the students know they must look for something, they do not know what that something is; (f) the relationship between formal knowledge and applied or problem-based expertise is complex and difficult to capture in preparation programs; and (g) students who are successful come to view problems in new ways, reformulated while seeking resolutions (Hart, 1993; Kelsey, 1993; Prestine, 1993).

Although the different approaches to cognitively based preparation programs actually were highly varied, those who studied these varied programs offered some guidance about common features. According to scholars reporting research on the outcomes of cognitively based programs in educational leadership, specific conditions to be met in the instructional experience were the following (Leithwood, Hallinger & Murphy, 1993):

1. Provide models of expert problem solving.
2. Provide practice opportunities across a wide variety of problem types.
3. Sequence increasingly complex task demands.
4. Provide performance feedback on individual problem solving.
5. Ensure participation in sophisticated group problem-solving processes.
6. Encourage individual reflection on own and group problem solving.
7. Provide performance feedback on contribution of individual to group problem-solving processes.

Whether the many changes made during the decade actually met these conditions is yet to be demonstrated. One particular approach to cognitively based preparation on which some evaluation data are available, problem-based learning, is also perhaps the most common. This particular approach consequently deserves additional attention.

Problem-Based Learning

When compared with some other professional schools, problem-based learning came late to educational administration preparation programs. Medicine, management, and others applied problem-based learning structures for years before they sparked the interest of educator preparation providers (Barrows, 1988; Bridges & Hallinger, 1993). Even so, many leaders in the field asserted that "a problem-based curriculum seems most appropriate for the preparation of school administrators. [Furthermore], utilizing a problem-based curriculum successfully will require the reorganization of theory, research, clinical history, and best practice around professional problems of practice" (Forsyth, 1992, pp. 23, 24). It also required a tighter integration of formal study, field experiences, and internships and grew naturally out of cognitive science perspectives on administrative practice (Leithwood & Steinbach, 1995a, 1995b).

Among the most well-known of early advocates for problem-based learning in educational leadership programs was Edwin Bridges. Bridges emphasized that two questions commonly surface in relation to problem-based learning (PBL): "How does PBL differ from the case-method and traditional instruction? What happens during a PBL class session?" (Bridges, 1992, p. 1). Bridges answered that problem-based learning fundamentally changes the roles of students and instructors, and that questions about what students learn through this method have been only partially answered.

One way to examine these changes is to compare problem-based learning with two common pedagogies used in educational administration preparation programs—traditional courses and seminars, and the case method. The differences among traditional classroom instruction, the case method, and problem-based learning lie in the nature of the learning materials used, the pedagogical processes dominating the majority of learning activities, and the roles of students and instructors. First, learning materials in traditional settings are familiar to all students—books, journal articles, and other published sources of written discourse on practice, research, and theory; experts in the field and practitioners who present perspectives and information and answer student questions; and other, supplemental resources, such as the Internet and audiovisual materials. Learning materials in the case method consist of a "case," which is a written description of a practice problem/situation that is meant to include sufficient detail to provide stimulus for learning particular administrative or leadership principles. The title of the case often provides a preview of the problem to the students. The case often identifies the problem to be considered by the students. Problem-based learning relies on a project approach (although some also call project stimulus materials "cases"). A PBL project renders a situation of practice through such things as role-playing; written stimulus materials; computer, Internet, or audiovisual stimulus materials; and documents or other archival data meant to simulate the information formats that administrators might encounter. A problem is not identified in the materials provided to students.

Second, pedagogy differs significantly among the three methods. In traditional courses, instructors provide the information and knowledge to the students. Instructors may lead discussions in addition to lecturing; students may present independent projects to their colleagues; and additional learning resources such as guest speakers may be included. The case method relies on the instructor to structure questions about the problem presented in the case and relies on students to provide alternative answers to the problem. Problem-based pedagogy requires that the instructor, the library, expert practitioners, and practice settings provide information about principles of administration and leadership to assist student learners. The instructor provides pertinent readings and, sometimes, guiding questions designed to stimulate discussion and student activity.

Finally, students and instructors play very different roles in these three pedagogies. Traditional methods rely on a view of instructor as knowledge giver and teacher. Case methods rely on a view of instructor as problem-poser and questioner. In problem-based instruction, the instructor functions as an observer and a resource to the team of student learners. Using the materials provided to them and many different problem-finding and problem-solving approaches, students go to multiple authoritative sources of information from practice, research, theory (and the instructor) to identify and seek action alternatives to a practice-based situation. Bridges (1992, pp. 5-6) distinguishes problem-based learning with five characteristics. First, the starting point for learning is a "stimulus for which an individual lacks a ready response." Second, the stimulus represents a situation that "students are apt to face as future professionals." Third, knowledge to be mastered by the student is organized around situations of practice rather than academic disciplines. Fourth, a major responsibility for learning and for activities that stimulate learning are the responsibility of the students. Finally, students' learning groups rather than instructor presentations dominate the learning process. Bridges further differentiates between problem-stimulated learning and student-centered learning. In the former, the instructor provides materials about an identified administrative problem. In the latter, a variety of learning issues are introduced through stimulus materials. Student-centered learning is very common in medical schools and in some other professional fields (Barrows, 1988; Hart, 1993; Hart & Bredeson, 1996).

Proponents of problem-based instruction argued that in addition to the cognitive material and knowledge base available through traditional instruction, students learn teamwork, administrative and project development skills, and problem solving. Many programs also required that students recommend specific action and justify their recommendations with a rationale based on the knowledge base (Hart, 1993). Additionally, students were said to learn to recognize and begin to overcome problem-solving errors common to human cognition (Hart & Bredeson, 1996):

> (1) inappropriate scanning (seeking data or information that will not be helpful), (2) incorrect synthesis (reaching unwarranted conclusions), (3) inadequate synthesis (failure to come to a conclusion that is warranted from the data), (4) premature closure, and (5) anchoring (failure to attend to new, relevant, but unfamiliar information—being anchored in past decisions or experiences). (pp. 49-50)

Bridges applied these techniques to administrator preparation at Stanford University. Additionally, variations of his approach were used in "design studio" models and, in Canada, in a number of programs studied by Leithwood and his colleagues. For example, Leithwood and Stager (1989) examined the problem-solving processes of principals and the differences between those identified as experts and their more typical colleagues to establish a foundation for expert problem solving. As predicted by other research on experts' ability to deal with complex problems, the differences between expert and typical principals were most evident in responses to messy or poorly defined problems. These processes involved five components: interpretation, goals, principles, constraints, and solution processes.

The challenge to preparation programs to improve the problem-solving expertise of school administrators also was addressed by Leithwood and Steinbach (1995b). To assist those seeking to include these components in administrator preparation programs, they offered a number of important suggestions. First, they suggested that although the debate about the relative efficacy of domain-specific knowledge and general cognitive skills rages on, the question remains one of emphasis because research suggests that both are important.

> In the absence of domain-specific knowledge, one has nothing to think about. In the absence of reasonably well-developed general thinking skills, one's knowledge may not be applied in circumstances where it has potential use. For instructional purposes, it seems reasonable to approach the matter in a conditional way. The probability that a person will successfully solve a problem is a function of both the availability of problem-relevant knowledge and general thinking skills or heuristics. (Leithwood & Steinbach, 1995b, pp. 283-286)

Reporting the results of a program designed to maximize problem-solving skills among students, they noted efforts to enhance the initial acquisition of useful, strategic knowledge and efforts to foster the transfer of knowledge from formal instructional settings to the administrative setting.

Second, Leithwood and Steinbach's research led them to conclude that the general approach to teaching problem solving, which closely resembles what is usually meant by problem-based instruction (Bridges, 1992), was promising, and that compared with on-the-job experience, problem-solving instruction was far more effective than "slow and unreliable" processes on the job.

Practice-Based School Leadership Preparation

The case approach to building a knowledge base was closely related to another trend in preparation programs that relied even more directly on knowledge from experience to enhance leadership education. Although some feared that an experience-based approach to preparation might stray seriously close to the normative approach that dominated the field prior to the theory movement, calls for relevance and immediacy were strong, and changes in programs followed.

Among the most visible of these reforms were those sponsored by the Danforth Foundation. For a decade, the Danforth Foundation supported universities interested in reforming their programs to make them more grounded in practice. Eventually, 22 universities participated in the project. Milstein & Associates (1993) described the purpose of the Danforth experiments as trying "to change educational-administration preparation programs in ways that make them more relevant to the roles . . . leaders play" (p. vii). Leithwood and his colleagues (1995a, 1995b), too, found that practice-based programs received considerable praise from practitioners. In a survey of the participants from the first 11 universities participating in the Danforth project, he found that respondents gave their highest ratings for the forms of instruction given in seminars, reflection, and problem-based learning. He believes that effective leadership programs provide authentic experiences, stimulate the development of "situated cognition," and foster real-life problem-solving skills.

Practice-based reforms like those described by Milstein often were closely related to the cognition-based apprenticeships described earlier, although they seldom relied on theoretical arguments based in cognitive psychology. Internships, candidate selectivity, and cooperation with local school districts characterized the programs. Additionally, many universities included school districts in the identification, recruitment, and training of program mentors, and they established university-school partnerships that included steering committees made up of representatives of the school district, the university, state departments of education, community service organizations, business and industry, and school boards (Milstein & Associates, 1993; Milstein, Bobroff, & Restine, 1991). These programs required intense collaboration and the consequent compromises. However, many participants argue that the rewards were great. The authentic measures of competence provided by such evaluation measures as practice-based portfolios and the prevalence of appropriate content in formal study received praise (Barnett, 1995). Barnett (1992b) discussed how alternative assessment can tap into learners' espoused theories of action and ways in which educational platforms and portfolios become strategies for revealing learners' theories. Outcome data, however, are scarce. Entry-level, practice-based programs tended to have a number of characteristics in common.

First, many such programs rely on a cohort structure in which developing administrators move through the program as a group (Jacobson, 1996; Norton, 1995b). These structures were designed to enhance camaraderie and shared learning and to provide a more collegial and supportive, less-fragmented learning experience (Milstein & Krueger, 1993). Many also drew on principles of adult learning and development more deliberately in their structure and pedagogy (Barnett & Muse, 1993). Some also combined preparation programs for teachers and administrators, reasoning that preservice teachers and intern principals working together during field placements enhanced the examination of professionalism, perspectives on schooling, and traditional hierarchical teacher/administrator relationships (Marlow, 1996). In a major survey of participants in cohort preparation programs, Norton (1995b) found that respondents had very idiosyncratic experiences that he characterized as "singular." Although strengths reported were highly varied, Norton felt that major positive outcomes included higher quality of student scholarship in coursework; a greater commitment to the program and program completion; a high level of interaction among students, between students and faculty, and between the students and the institution; higher levels of enthusiasm toward coursework; and generally positive response to the preparation program.

Those experimenting with cohort structures cautioned, however, that they were not without problems (Maniloff & Clark, 1993). They could result in strong cohesiveness that was less than supportive of rigorous work, in which a few members of the cohort were always in the spotlight and leading out in discussions and activities, and in which the variety of ideas and inputs into the overall dialogue could be limited by the limited participants.

Second, practice-based reforms almost always included the active participation of practitioners as clinical or adjunct professors in the program. These expert practitioners might or might not participate in the full spectrum of activities from recruitment and selection through final assessment of students' performance, but they were an integral and important part of the programs. They also might serve as expert mentors and reflective coaches to students during their field experiences (Daresh & Barnett, 1993; Sirotnik & Mueller, 1993).

Third, the programs almost always emphasized the revitalization of the field experience or internship. Accusations against poorly organized field experience ranged from lack of supervision and structured learning opportunities to the assignment of trivial or clerical work by practitioners to fill the requisite internship hours. The new programs sought to provide more meaningful learning experiences through such techniques as shadowing, interviewing administrators, and joint administrator-student projects (Murphy, 1993).

Finally, some of the practice-based programs attempted to ground seminars and coursework in the field, in the schools and districts in which students work. Mims (1993) advocated strongly for preparation programs that include the direct participation of local practitioners. Cambron-McCabe (1993) argued that this process can result in educational work that is more than an academic exercise. Rather, it provides real involvement in school leadership practice as part of the learning experience. More impressively, Pounder (1995) found in her study of one field-based EdD program that from one half to two thirds of student projects resulted in some form of change in educational policy, program, or practice.

Although faculty in educational administration and leadership programs sparked much of this change, state-level policymakers and practitioners also played a role. Bartell (1994) presented the viewpoint of California state governing boards, beginning with the assumption that programs to prepare administrators for their roles are inadequate and are not designed with coming changes in education in mind. She argued that states must take responsibility, translating the knowledge base that administrators really need into an administrator preparation program. Bartell surveyed 2,500 people on the content and structure of administrator preparation programs, professional development experiences, and other credentialing policies. Her respondents identified seven major concerns—management, leadership, academic preparation, community responsiveness, social issues, and civic and political leaderships. Concerns regarding administrator preparation included recruitment, academics, broad skills, early clinical experiences and mentoring, broad preparation and development, and ongoing education. She asserted further that practice-oriented, problem-based approaches to administrator preparation hold the greatest promise for the future.

Describing another reform, Schmuck (1993) reported outcomes of a 2-year experimental administrator preparation program implemented in Oregon in 1988. The program involved seven weekend institutes that included formal study in administration skills and contemporary concepts of instructional leadership. Following the summers, participants completed four school management courses and the NASSP Assessment Center, a field-based mentoring experience, and five seminars for mentoring pairs. Schmuck asserted that (a) most participants were capable of articulating a coherent leadership philosophy and applied the skills learned during mentorship, (b) participants had more favorable attitudes toward their training and a deeper understanding of leadership than did their traditional program counterparts, (c) participants were more successful in procuring administrative positions than were their traditional counterparts, and (d) participants reported that they negotiated their first year quite successfully. Schmuck consequently recommended reforms in administrator preparation based on cohorts, a balance in the curriculum between instructional leadership and school management, and a more extensive use of professor-administrator teams on faculty in preparation programs.

Inservice assistance for new leaders and practice-based initiatives focused on the education of advanced practitioners were a part of this initiative to enhance field-based preparation programs. For new practitioners, programs included such things as laboratory experiences for school-site leaders. For more advanced practitioners, doctoral study was the primary focus (Bratlien, Genzer, Hoyle, & Oates, 1992).

Other practice-based initiatives focused on the education of more advanced practitioners. Doctoral study was the primary focus of these reforms (Bratlien et al., 1992; Cambron-McCabe, 1993; Maniloff & Clark, 1993; Ogawa & Pounder, 1993). These programs frequently sought to blend theory, research, and clinical experiences; included intensive summer seminars; relied on extended clinical weekend sessions; involved senior local administrators as clinical professors; and included ongoing research projects. They also often concentrated on reconceptualizing the PhD or reenergizing the EdD. A major component of reform in these advanced degree programs was the design of an applied or clinical dissertation (Ogawa & Pounder, 1993; Maniloff & Clark, 1993). The applied dissertation also was referred to as a "clinical research project" analogous to the traditional doctoral dissertation but with greater emphasis on a specific problem of practice. . . . [A] student may choose to evaluate an educational or administrative program that has been implemented in his or her employment setting. The clinical research study would be informed by previous theory and research and have defensible methods, but may have a more normative tone in its recommendations for practice. Further, it is not expected that a clinical research study have the degree of generalizability or the theory-building characteristics typically expected in a traditional doctoral dissertation. (Ogawa & Pounder, 1993, p. 97)

Among the stimuli for change in advanced doctoral study for practitioners were faculty desire for a preeminent graduate program and public pressure from governing boards and educational practitioners. For example, the North Carolina reform sprang from a confluence between the desires of a newly configured faculty and recommendations of a major policy report. The combination of policy pressure and professional desires of faculty have led to advanced doctoral degrees that are "designed to prepare educational leaders to confront changing state and local needs and challenges in education" (Maniloff & Clark, 1993, p. 184). Although it would be unfair to say that the changes were foisted on university faculty by the field, the confluence of faculty and field perceptions that major changes were needed sped the development of programs.

Major program restructuring in universities, often described as practice-based and undertaken over the past decade, may not have been as common as many would wish. These changes have been followed closely by Scott Norton (1989, 1995a), whose surveys of program chairs provided some insight into actual changes. In a study of UCEA institutions, Norton (1989) found that only 25% of "chair" respondents said that field experiences were enhanced as a result of program reorganization. In the same study, 50% of respondents felt that classroom experiences were improved, and 60% felt that research experiences were improved. These results fly in the face of the "front-stage" rhetoric that field experiences were the major focus of program reform in educational administration. In a follow-up study in 1995, Norton (1995b) studied 32 non–UCEA and 36 UCEA institutions. In this research, respondents revealed that by far the most common reorganizations involved departmental structure (mergers of units, etc.) rather than fundamental program content and process. Far less common were changes in the structure of degree programs that might have significant implications for practice-based changes. Perhaps Norton's results demonstrated the perennial problem in discussions of reform—that rhetoric about reform was more prevalent than real, lasting change. On the other hand, national and state organizations appeared to be moving forward in making substantive changes in licensure and certification requirements for school leaders that may force changes in preparation programs.

Educational Leadership Licensure, Certification, and Accreditation

The report of the National Commission on Teaching and America's Future (NCTAF, 1996) refers to licensure, certification, and accreditation as "the three-legged stool of teacher quality" (p. 29). In its discussion of these three elements, the Commission emphasizes the need for licensure, certification, and accreditation standards and assessments that are rationally related to one another and to the performance expectations (knowledge, skills, commitments, etc.) of educators. These three elements are equally important contributors to the quality of school leaders and administrators. However, before beginning a discussion of reform in educational leadership licensure, certification, and accreditation, we need a clarification of these three terms. The term *licensure* has largely come to mean the initial "permit" that is granted to allow educators to enter the education profession, whereas *certification* may represent a second authorization granted to practicing educators who may have achieved high levels of professional competence or achievement. This distinction may also include an assumption about differences in authorizing agencies. For example, the National Association of State Directors of Teacher Education and Certification (NASDTEC, 1996) states,

> In recent years, many educators have attempted to make a distinction between certification and licensure based on the definitions used in other professional fields. They argue that states license (e.g. architects, nurses, etc.) and that specialized boards in the respective fields certify. The National Board for Professional Teaching Standards (NBPTS) has accepted that distinction and is "certifying" experienced teachers who meet high and rigorous standards. (p. ix)

However, these distinctions are not universally recognized, and many states and education professionals use the terms *license* or *certify* interchangeably.

The term *accreditation* refers to the review and approval of an educational unit (e.g., schools, colleges, universities, or departments) with respect to recognized standards of educational quality. The U.S. Department of Education recognizes several regional institutional accreditation agencies, such as Middle States Association of Colleges and Schools; New England Association of Schools and Colleges; North Central Association of Colleges and Schools; Northwest Association of Schools and Colleges; Southern Association of Colleges and Schools; and the Western Association of Schools and Colleges.

In the context of educational leadership preparation (or other educator preparation programs), the accrediting agency that is most universally recognized is the National Council for Accreditation of Teacher Education (NCATE). This agency specifically conducts peer reviews of those educational units that prepare teachers and other professional educators. Accreditation by NCATE is voluntary, but to be eligible to apply for NCATE accreditation, a department, school, or college of education must be affiliated with an institution that has been accredited by an institutional accrediting agency that is recognized by the U.S. Department of Education and by the Commission on Recognition of Postsecondary Accreditation (CORPA).

NCATE's mission statement indicates that it seeks to provide professional judgment about the quality of the education unit and to encourage continuous improvement of the unit. Thus, its mission is both evaluation or accountability and development or improvement. In the past decade or more of education reform, NCATE has proactively sought to work with other agencies to improve educator preparation and to ensure that accreditation, licensure, and advanced certification standards are compatible. For example, NCATE has worked with the National Policy Board for Educational Administration (NPBEA) and has entered into partnership agreements with NASDTEC in 40 states to conduct joint program-approval site visits.

One additional point of clarification is probably helpful. That is, NASDTEC is not an accrediting agency, but it does have a standards committee. The NASDTEC Standards Committee was established approximately 30 years ago and has developed standards for states to use when approving programs in specific content areas. Thus, state licensing agencies (e.g., state departments of education) may conduct periodic reviews of educator preparation programs to verify that they are meeting established state or NASDTEC professional standards for educator preparation. This program approval (not accreditation) is especially important in states where educator licensure or certification is met by completion of a state-approved preparation program.

Unlike many of the educational reform initiatives of the 1980s, educational leadership preparation program reform was not initiated or strongly influenced by state-level regulatory agencies, legislative bodies, or governors.

Instead, educational leadership preparation reform preceded (and may have even influenced) changes in regulatory agency standards, policies, and practices. That is, changes in educational leadership licensure, certification, and accreditation have tended to follow, rather than precede, a significant amount of reform activity in leadership preparation programs. Most of the changes in licensure, certification, and accreditation have come about within the past 5 years and are still actively ongoing. At this point, approximately half of the states report no change in requirements for initial administrator licensure/certification; approximately two thirds report no change in requirements for administrator licensure/certification renewal (NASDTEC, 1996).

Where change in licensure, certification, and accreditation has begun to occur, the most notable trend is the emphasis on authentic standards and assessment. That is, standards for the preparation and development of administrators are closely tied to the nature of administrative work, focusing on the knowledge and skills necessary to perform leadership functions. Similarly, assessment of licensure and certification candidates focuses on performance outcomes that are reflective of administrative work tasks and responsibilities. This trend contrasts with a course-driven, curricular approach to standards and assessment. The following discussion will focus on these and other trends in licensure, certification, and accreditation reform for educational leaders that are and have been occurring during the 1990s.

Outcome-Based Standards

The move to outcome-based standards (versus course-driven or curricular standards) is one of the most prevalent changes in administrator licensure, certification, and accreditation. That is, standards are developed based on the analysis of administrators' work—the skills, knowledge, and dispositions necessary for competent job performance. Several agencies and professional organizations have influenced the reform of educator or administrator licensure, certification, and accreditation standards. The NASDTEC Standards Committee reports focusing its attention on developing performance-based standards for educator licensure, and many of the state licensing agencies report a similar trend in educator licensure requirements (NASDTEC, 1996).

NCATE Standards

With specific regard to administrator standards, NCATE, in partnership with the NPBEA and under the leadership of Scott Thomson, developed and adopted new standards for the accreditation of departments of educational leadership. These standards address "the knowledge, skills, and attributes required to lead and manage an educational enterprise centered on teaching and learning" (NPBEA, 1996, p. 6). These are the following:

1. *Strategic Leadership*—The knowledge, skills, and attributes to identify contexts, develop with others vision and purpose, use information, frame problems, exercise leadership processes to achieve common goals, and act ethically for educational communities.

2. *Instructional Leadership*—The knowledge, skills, and attributes to design with others appropriate curricula and instructional programs, develop learner-centered school cultures, assess outcomes, provide student personnel services, and plan with faculty professional development activities aimed at improving instruction.

3. *Organizational Leadership*—The knowledge, skills, and attributes to understand and improve the organization, implement operational plans, manage financial resources, and apply decentralized management processes and procedures.

4. *Political and Community Leadership*—The knowledge, skills, and attributes to act in accordance with legal provisions and statutory requirements, apply regulatory standards, develop and apply appropriate policies, be conscious of ethical implications of policy initiatives and political actions, relate public policy initiatives to student welfare, understand schools as political systems, involve citizens and service agencies, and develop effective staff communications and public relations programs.

5. *Internship*—The internship is defined as the process and product that result from the application in a workplace environment of the strategic, instructional, organizational, and contextual leadership guidelines. When coupled with integrating experiences through related clinics or cohort seminars, the outcome should be a powerful synthesis of knowledge and skills useful to practicing school leaders.

The internship includes a variety of substantial concurrent or capstone experiences in diverse settings planned and guided cooperatively by university and school district personnel for credit hours and conducted in schools and school districts over an extended period of time. The experiences should reflect increasing complexity and responsibility, and include some work in private, community, or social service organizations. An optimum internship would be a year-long, full time experience. Part-time internships involving a limited period of time are insufficient. (NPBEA, 1996, p. 6)

As suggested by the titles of these standards, the NCATE standards are more nearly course-driven than outcome-driven. This is because the origins of the NCATE standards lie in the NPBEA knowledge base project. Also, NCATE has historically had standards rooted in curriculum areas. However, in spite of the curriculum or course emphasis, these NCATE guidelines emphasize that the 11 specific knowledge and skill domains embedded within the broad areas above are *not* to be viewed as separate courses, but rather "universities are encouraged to design curricula in an integrated or problem-based mode to promote an understanding of the connectedness of the various knowledge and skill areas in educational leadership" (NPBEA, 1996, p. 4). The guidelines further suggest that programs should (a) include beneficial bridging experiences between course content and the workplace (e.g., clinical exercises, field applications, internships); (b) employ appropriate adult learning strategies; and (c) use outcomes criteria for program evaluation.

ISLLC Standards

The Interstate School Leaders Licensure Consortium (ISLLC), cosponsored by the Council of Chief State School Officers and the NPBEA, was formed in the early 1990s to develop model standards and assessments for school leaders. ISLLC's primary constituency is the state education agencies responsible for administrator licensure. With consultation from leading educational administration scholars and practitioners, ISLLC developed standards for initial administrator licensure. This consortium of 24 member states has probably promoted the outcome-based approach (vs. curricular approach) more than any other professional group by developing standards with a strong emphasis on administrative behavior necessary to achieve one specific, yet broad, school outcome—the educational success of all students. The ISLLC Standards for School Leaders (CCSSO, 1996) state,

A school administrator is an educational leader who promotes the success of all students by: (1) facilitating the development, articulation, implementation, and stewardship of a vision of learning that is shared and supported by the school community; (2) advocating, nurturing, and sustaining a school culture and instructional program conducive to student learning and staff professional growth; (3) ensuring management of the organization, operations, and resources for a safe, efficient, and ef-

fective learning environment; (4) collaborating with families and community members, responding to diverse community interests and needs,
and mobilizing community resources; (5) acting with integrity, fairness,
and in an ethical manner; (6) understanding, responding to, and influencing the larger political, social, economic, legal, and cultural context.
(p. 10)

These standards are further delineated with indicators that specify the knowledge, dispositions, and performance critical for effective school leadership.

ISLLC's 24 member states believe that these performance-based standards for administrators may be useful for program development and review,
licensure, and advanced certification. A secondary intention is that the creation of a common set of standards will promote interstate collaboration, such
as reciprocity of licensure and assessment of administrative candidates.

Outcome-based (or performance-based) standards such as those just
described reflect the increasing emphasis on authentic standards and assessment. That is, they establish a close connection between licensure, certification, or accreditation standards and effective administrative leadership for
today's and tomorrow's successful schools. Furthermore, outcome-based standards provide a foundation for the development of revised assessment techniques for administrative candidates. These newer assessment or examination
initiatives are described below.

Performance-Based Assessment or Examination

Accompanying the increased emphasis on authentic or outcome-based
standards for administrators is a corresponding emphasis on authentic assessment techniques for educators. To receive licensure or certification, administrators and teachers will be evaluated increasingly with assessment techniques
much different from previous course content-driven, multiple-choice, paper-
and-pencil tests. Recently developed performance-based assessment techniques are being implemented in several states. These performance-based
exams include not only assessments of candidates' job-related knowledge but
also indicators of their job performance skills. They are not without their critics, however. Reitzug (1991) reported that in 1991, 15 states required administrator competency testing, but that these programs were plagued by
ambiguous objectives, questionable validity, adverse effects on minority group
members, and high costs.

For example, the ISLLC administrator assessment model, developed by the Educational Testing Service (ETS), contains four assessment exercises or simulations in which administrative candidates are presented with vignettes, case studies, or documents from realistic school administrative situations. Candidates are required to address the problems or dilemmas presented in these simulations, demonstrating the knowledge, dispositions, and job performance skills outlined by the standards indicators (e.g., information and problem-solving skills, effective communication, instructional program development, resource allocation, collaboration and community relations, ethical behavior, etc.). Although the assessment is a paper-and-pencil exam, it requires narrative responses rather than multiple-choice responses and is designed to capture the higher-order skills of analysis, synthesis, and evaluation rather than lower-level recognition and recall skills.

A content validity study was conducted to determine the extent to which the 25 ISLLC assessment exercises and scoring rubrics reflected the ISLLC standards. An expert panel of principals and university professors verified that the standards were job-related, a necessity in licensure exams. The panel also confirmed that the assessment exercises and scoring rubrics faithfully reflected the specific indicators for each standard that they were designed to measure.

> Ninety-four percent of the exercise-indicator linkages were confirmed and 90% of the rubric-indicator linkages were confirmed. The panel also verified the relevance and importance of all 25 exercises and the authenticity of 24 exercises. The panel similarly confirmed the appropriateness of the overall assessment. (Tannenbaum, for ETS, 1997, p. 2)

Collectively, these results support the content validity of the ISLLC administrator assessment.

Of the 24 ISLLC states, five states (Kentucky, Mississippi, Missouri, North Carolina, and Texas) agreed to pilot the initial "Principals' Licensure Assessment." The initial pilot test was administered to recent or soon-to-be graduates of principal preparation programs in the five pilot states during 1997. Although analysis of scoring results of the exams has not been released to date, initial survey responses from participants suggest that the assessment technique was well received by administrative candidates (CCSSO-ISLLC, 1997). More than 90% of the pilot test participants indicated that they felt that the assessment measured knowledge and skills important to the job performance of beginning school principals; almost 94% felt that the questions dealt with situations and documents similar to those beginning principals are likely to encounter. Participants also felt favorably about the test format, indicating that it was more realistic, fair, and valid than were many traditional standardized testing formats.

Similarly, the ETS recently developed a 2-hour exam for school administrators as part of the PRAXIS Series®. The PRAXIS Educational Leadership: Administration and Supervision exam consists of 120 questions that cover five content areas: determining educational needs, curriculum design and instructional improvement, staff development and program evaluation, school management, and individual and group leadership skills (ETS, 1997). Although the test uses a traditional multiple-choice format, the test of administrator knowledge and cognition is designed to assess higher-order skills such as application, analysis, synthesis, and evaluation.

Authentic assessment techniques for principals and teachers such as those described above have the advantage of considerably more "face" validity with professional educators, legislators, policymakers, and the public. Although the ISLLC licensure exam makes no claim of predictive validity, it is reasonable to ask whether these new assessment instruments may be better predictors of successful job performance than were previous licensure procedures. Certainly, personnel selection research and literature suggests that the more nearly a "test" resembles the actual job performance requirements, the higher the predictive validity of the instrument (Pounder, 1989; Pounder & Young 1996).

Another factor that may influence the long-term efficacy of authentic assessments is the costliness of administering and/or scoring these exams. Because of their labor-intensive nature, authentic assessments may prove to be too costly to sustain over time. The reader is reminded of the Principal Assessment Center, which was developed by the National Association of Secondary School Principals (NASSP) more than 20 years ago as a selection tool to screen administrative candidates. The NASSP Assessment Center used authentic or performance-based assessment techniques similar to those of the ISLLC administrator assessment. Over time, however, fewer and fewer states have used the NASSP Assessment Center due, at least in part, to its labor-intensive nature. It remains to be seen if the reliability, validity, and utility of these exams is strong enough to justify the additional costs associated with their administration and scoring.

Other Patterns and Trends

There are several other patterns in administrator licensure or certification that warrant discussion. These include requirements related to teaching experience, term of license, licensure/certification renewal, licensure/certification reciprocity, criminal background checks, and interstate cooperation regarding license/certificate revocation. Although there has not been a high degree of change in these areas during the past 5 years, where change has occurred, increased rigor in these requirement areas is the trend.

NASDTEC (1996) reports that 46 states require several years of teaching experience (mode = 3 years, range = 1-7 years) to become eligible for an initial administrator license, including four states that recently have increased the length of their teaching experience requirement. Also, 44 states issue the initial administrator license for a finite period of time—often for a period of 5 years or less. To renew the initial license or secure a certificate, 39 states require additional coursework and/or additional years of experience. Of states that require additional coursework, 19 states specifically require some sort of university coursework, 15 states allow a choice between either university or non-university coursework, and one state requires non-university coursework only. Eight states require no additional coursework for license renewal or certification, although at least two of these require some sort of performance or competency assessment. (Three states had missing data on the license renewal issue.)

NASDTEC (1996) also reports two additional licensure/certification priorities in the past few years. First, by establishing the Interstate Certification Agreement Contract, NASDTEC has been trying to promote better licensure/certification reciprocity agreements among states to help educators who find it necessary to move to another state. Currently, 20 states have entered into contractual agreements to establish administrator licensure/certification reciprocity with selected other states; 34 states have entered into reciprocity agreements regarding teacher licensure/certification.

Second, states have always been concerned about the moral character of educators, especially as it relates to the safety of schoolchildren. However, this concern has manifested itself in more stringent educator background checks to minimize the risk to children as well as to reduce the liability to the licensing state. NASDTEC (1996) reports that as a part of the educator licensure application, 49 states currently require applicants to disclose prior convictions; 48 states require applicants to disclose prior license invalidation; 30 states require applicants to disclose prior arrest records regarding moral turpitude charges; 26 states require applicants to disclose prior dismissal; and 34 states conduct some sort of criminal background check of licensure applicants. Although fingerprinting identification requirements are somewhat less prevalent, the trend is toward increasingly stringent requirements. Currently,

14 states require fingerprinting for licensure/certification, and 16 states require fingerprinting for initial employment.

NASDTEC (1996) has gone a step further by establishing the NASDTEC Educator Identification Clearinghouse. The Clearinghouse is a national database for professional educator disciplinary actions taken by the 50 states, the District of Columbia, U.S. Department of Defense Dependent Schools, and U.S. territories. This database contains information on disciplinary actions regarding license/certificate denial or invalidation (i.e., annulled, revoked, suspended, and/or voluntarily surrendered) and the reason for the denial/invalidation. All NASDTEC member states may avail themselves of this information to help determine the fitness of an applicant to receive a license or certificate. The Clearinghouse has proven to be a valuable tool to prevent perpetrators from moving easily from one jurisdiction to another. From 1987 to 1994, the Clearinghouse recorded more than 6,300 disciplinary actions, including more than 3,000 criminal convictions (i.e., violent felonies, sexual misconduct, substance abuse, other); almost 700 self-surrenders for similar offenses; and more than 2,500 cases of noncriminal professional misconduct or incompetence.

The reform trends in administrator licensure and accreditation center largely around authentic standards and assessment. That is, standards for the preparation and performance of administrator candidates increasingly are being tied closely to the nature of administrative work. Program standards and candidate examinations that mirror actual work requirements of administrators promise to be valued and respected more by educators, policymakers, and the public—plus, they promise to be more valid and useful techniques for ensuring high-quality and effective administrators for successful schools. It is important to note, however, that the educational administration profession has not taken active steps to define professional certification (as opposed to initial state licensure).

Other patterns in administrator licensure and certification that are designed to improve the quality of tomorrow's administrators are increased teaching experience and finite terms for initial licensure, with additional coursework and/or experience requirements for renewal or certification. A trend toward interstate licensure reciprocity promises to reduce the employment eligibility problems associated with interstate mobility of administrators and other educators. Finally, to better ensure the safety of schoolchildren and the fitness of educators to teach, a national clearinghouse of educator disciplinary actions is helping to inhibit the likelihood of unfit teachers to cross licensure jurisdictions.

Summary and Conclusions

In this chapter, we have reviewed some of the patterns emerging in preparation programs for educational leadership and administration. We have identified three major themes characterizing these patterns. There was a renewed effort to strengthen and clarify the knowledge base for educational leadership during the decade. This effort was accompanied by innovations in instructional delivery methods congruent with new knowledge. Practice-based reforms of advanced professional degrees and practical experiences for new leaders became a focus of innovation. Finally, new licensure, certification, and accreditation standards and assessment techniques for school leaders were developed in many states.

The innovations seeking to reinvent administrator preparation through changes in the knowledge base and methods for teaching it varied widely. One major project was designed to examine knowledge essential to a mastery of the professional domain of educational leadership and policy. This project included a broader range of perspectives on knowledge, particularly in areas of sociopolitical analysis and critical theory perspectives, but had little impact on pedagogy. Other innovations related to knowledge and knowledge acquisition focused to some extent on content and process. These included an integration of cognition theory, the development of problem-based learning, renewed and refocused uses of the case studies, and the application of technology to teaching the knowledge base and enhancing its application to practice.

Practice-based school leadership preparation programs also marked the decade. They received high praise from many practicing professionals and were the subject of much discussion about the need for authentic professional experience during preservice preparation. They also led to partnership between universities and schools or school districts and to increased use of practicing, expert practitioners, teachers, and coaches. This expanded use of practitioners took place both in formal courses and seminars and in internships and apprenticeships.

Finally, members of the profession sought to institutionalize innovation and growth through revised licensure, certification, and accreditation requirements that reflected changes in the knowledge base and field of practice. Changes in regulatory standards, policies, and practices followed changes in educational leadership preparation, a pattern not characteristic of many of the educational reform initiatives of the 1980s. Like the search for authentic experiences in preservice preparation, changes in regulatory requirements emphasized authentic standards and assessment. They often used performance--based assessment and were strengthened by partnerships among scholarly and professional organizations.

Changes in regulatory requirements aside, few studies to date affirm a widespread revolution in educational leader preparation programs. Many promising innovations have sought to reinvent preparation programs; the proliferation of these innovations across the 400 to 500 college- and university-based preservice programs is not yet certain.

We have described innovations and promising preliminary outcomes in many preservice programs in university programs designed for the ongoing professional development of practicing school leaders. Although these changes have affected the structure, process, and content of many basic and advanced practitioner preparation programs, general surveys of administration program leaders also suggest that they have not revolutionized the basic assumptions and structure of preparation. Few extensive studies of the impacts of these reforms exist, and those we reviewed for this chapter do not support the claim that changes are as yet widespread. Formal, traditionally delivered courses still are prevalent in preservice education for school leaders. However, a strong shift toward programs that better integrate practice and formal knowledge by embedding the educational experience in thought, action, and problems of practice is evident in the decade's changes in many exemplary programs. The reforms in licensure, certification, and accreditation requirements we described may more strongly affect change over time than have reforms in a few leading institutions, simply by virtue of their power to control program graduates' access to the profession.

References

Barnett, B. G. (1992a). A new slant on leadership preparation. *Educational Leadership, 49*(5), 72-75.

Barnett, B. G. (1992b). Using alternative assessment measures in educational leadership preparation programs: Educational platforms and portfolios. *Journal of Personnel Evaluation in Education, 6*, 141-151.

Barnett, B. G. (1995). Portfolio use in educational leadership preparation programs: From theory to practice. *Innovative Higher Education, 19*, 197-206.

Barnett, B. G., & Muse, I. D. (1993). Cohort groups in educational administration: Promises and challenges. *Journal of School Leadership, 3*, 400-415.

Barrows, H. S. (1988). *The tutorial process.* Springfield: Southern Illinois University School of Medicine.

Bartell, C. A. (1994). *Preparing future administrators: Stakeholder perceptions.* Sacramento: California Commission on Teacher Credentialing.

Bass, B. M. (1985). *Leadership and performance beyond expectations.* New York: Free Press

Bates, R. (1987). Conceptions of school culture: An overview. *Educational Administration Quarterly, 23,* 79-116.

Bratlien, M. J., Genzer, S. M., Hoyle, J. R., & Oates, A. D. (1992). The professional studies doctorate: Leaders for learning. *Journal of School Leadership, 2*(1), 75-89.

Bridges, E. (1992). *Problem-based learning for administrators.* Eugene: University of Oregon Press.

Bridges, E. M., & Hallinger, P. (1993). Problem-based learning in medical and managerial education. In P. Hallinger, K. Leithwood, & J. Murphy (Eds.), *Cognitive perspectives on educational leadership* (pp. 253-267). New York: Teachers College Press.

Cambron-McCabe, N. H. (1993). Leadership for democratic authority. In J. Murphy (Ed.), *Preparing tomorrow's school leaders: Alternative designs* (pp.157-176). University Park, PA: The University Council for Educational Administration.

Clark, D. C., & Clark, S. N. (1996). Better preparation of educational leaders. *Educational Researcher, 25*(9), 18-20.

Council of Chief State School Officers. (1996). *Interstate School Leaders Licensure Consortium: Standards for school leaders.* Washington, DC: Author.

Council of Chief State School Officers–Interstate School Leaders Licensure Consortium. (1997). *Work in Progress.* The newsletter of the Interstate School Leaders Licensure Consortium of the Council of Chief State School Officers (CCSSO). Volume 2, No. 1.

Cuban, L. (1993). Foreword. In P. Hallinger, K. Leithwood, & J. Murphy (Eds.), *Cognitive perspectives on educational leadership* (pp. ix-xi). New York: Teachers College Press.

Daresh, J. C., & Barnett, B. G. (1993). Restructuring leadership development in Colorado. In J. Murphy (Ed.), *Preparing tomorrow's school leaders: Alternative designs* (pp. 129- 156). University Park, PA: University Council for Educational Administration.

Educational Testing Service. (1997). *The PRAXIS Series®: Educational Leadership: Administration and Supervision Exam.* Princeton, NJ: Author.

Forsyth, P. B. (1992). Redesigning the preparation of school administrators: Toward consensus. In S. D. Thomson (Ed.), *School leadership* (pp. 23-33). Newbury Park, CA: Corwin.

Foster, W. (1986). *Paradigms and promises: New approaches to educational administration.* Buffalo, NY: Prometheus.

Foster, W. (1994). School leaders as transformative intellectuals: Towards a critical pragmatism. In N. A. Prestine & P. W. Thurston (Eds.), *New directions in educational administration: Policy, preparation, and practice* (pp. 29-52). Greenwich, CT: JAI.

Hallinger, P., Leithwood, K., & Murphy, J. (Eds.). (1993). *Cognitive perspectives on educational leadership.* New York: Teachers College Press.

Hart, A. W. (1993). A design studio for reflective practice. In P. Hallinger, K. Leithwood, & J. Murphy (Eds.), *Cognitive perspectives on educational leadership* (pp. 213-230). New York: Teachers College Press.

Hart, A. W., & Bredeson, P. V. (1996). *The principalship: A theory of professional learning and practice.* New York: McGraw-Hill.

Immegart, G. L. (1990). What is truly missing in advanced preparation in educational administration? *Journal of Educational Administration, 28*(3), 5-13.

Jacobson, S. L. (1996). School leadership in an age of reform: New directions in principal preparation. *International Journal of Educational Reform, 5,* 271-277.

Kelsey, J. G. T. (1993). Learning from teaching: Problems, problem-formulation, and the enhancement of problem-solving capability. In P. Hallinger, K. Leithwood, & J. Murphy (Eds.), *Cognitive perspectives on educational leadership* (pp. 231-252). New York: Teachers College Press.

Kerchner, C. (1993). The strategy of teaching strategy. In P. Hallinger, K. Leithwood, & J. Murphy (Eds.), *Cognitive perspectives on educational leadership* (pp. 5-20). New York: Teachers College Press.

Kowalski, T. J. (1991). *Case studies on educational administration.* New York: Longman.

Leithwood, K., Jantzi, D., Coffin, G., & Wilson, P. (1996). Preparing school leaders: What works? *School Leadership 6*(3), 316-342.

Leithwood K., & Stager, M. (1989). Expertise in principals' problem solving. *Educational Administration Quarterly, 25*(2), 126-161.

Leithwood, K., & Steinbach, R. (1995a). *Expert problem solving: Evidence from school leaders.* New York: SUNY Press.

Leithwood, K., & Steinbach, R. (1995b). Improving the problem-solving expertise of school administrators. In K. Leithwood & R. Steinbach (Eds.), *Expert problem solving: Evidence from school leaders* (pp. 281-309). New York: SUNY Press.

Maniloff, H., & Clark, D. L. (1993). Preparing effective leaders for schools and school systems: Graduate study at the University of North Carolina—Chapel Hill. In J. Murphy (Ed.), *Preparing tomorrow's school leaders: Alternative designs* (pp. 177-204). University Park, PA: University Council for Educational Administration.

Marlow, S. E. (1996). New relationships, new realities: Bringing preservice teachers and a preservice principal together in a professional preparation program. *Journal of School Leadership, 6,* 155-179.

McCleary, L. E. (1992). The knowledge base for school leaders. In S. D. Thomson (Ed.), *School leadership* (pp. 16-22). Newbury Park, CA: Corwin.

Milstein, M. M., & Associates. (1993). *Changing the way we prepare educational leaders: The Danforth experience.* Newbury Park, CA: Corwin.

Milstein, M. M., Bobroff, B. M., & Restine, L. N. (1991). *Internship programs in educational administration.* New York: Teachers College Press.

Milstein, M. M., & Krueger, J. (1993). Innovative approaches to clinical internships: The University of New Mexico experience. In J. Murphy (Ed.), *Preparing tomorrow's school leaders: Alternative designs* (pp. 19-38). University Park, PA: University Council for Educational Administration.

Mims, N. G. (1993). Leadership preparation: A cooperative effort between a college and school district. *Journal of School Leadership, 3,* 421-426.

Murphy, J. (1992). *The landscape of leadership preparation: Reframing the education of school administrators.* Newbury Park, CA: Corwin.

Murphy, J. (Ed.). (1993). *Preparing tomorrow's school leaders: Alternative designs.* University Park, PA: University Council for Educational Administration.

National Association of State Directors of Teacher Education & Certification. (1996). *Manual of certification and preparation of educational personnel in the U.S. and Canada.* Dubuque, IA: Kendall/Hunt.

National Commission on Teaching & America's Future. (1996). *What matters most: Teaching for America's future.* New York: Author.

National Policy Board for Educational Administration. (1996). *NCATE curriculum guidelines for advanced programs in educational leadership. A publication of the National Policy Board for Educational Administration.* Fairfax, VA: Author.

Norris, C. (1990). Developing visionary leaders for tomorrow's schools. *NASSP Bulletin, 74*(526), 6-10.

Norton, M. S. (1989). *Effects/affects of reorganization on programs of educational administration: A study of UCEA institutions.* Tempe, AZ: UCEA Program Center for Preparation Programs.

Norton, M. S. (1995a, Fall). Department reorganization and faculty status in educational administration. *Journal of Thought*, 87-96.

Norton, M. S. (1995b). *The status of student cohorts in educational administration preparation programs.* Tempe: Arizona State University, Division of Educational Leadership and Policy Studies.

Ogawa, R. T., & Pounder, D. G. (1993). Structured improvisation: The University of Utah's Ed.D. program in educational administration. In J. Murphy (Ed.), *Preparing tomorrow's school leaders: Alternative designs* (pp. 85-108). University Park, PA: The University Council for Educational Administration.

Ohde, K. L., & Murphy, J. (1993). The development of expertise: Implications for school administrators. In P. Hallinger, K. Leithwood, & J. Murphy (Eds.), *Cognitive perspectives on educational leadership* (pp. 75-87). New York: Teachers College Press.

Pounder, D. G. (1989). Improving the predictive validity of teacher selection decisions: Lessons from teacher appraisal. *Journal of Personnel Evaluation, 2*, 123-132.

Pounder, D. G. (1995). Theory to practice in administrator preparation: An evaluation study. *Journal of School Leadership, 5*, 151-162.

Pounder, D. G., & Young, I. P. (1996). Recruitment and selection of educational administrators: Priorities for today's schools. In K. Leithwood (Ed.), A. W. Hart (Section Ed.). *The international handbook for educational leadership and administration.* Netherlands: Kluwer.

Prestine, N. A. (1993). Apprenticeship in problem-solving: Extending the cognitive apprenticeship model. In P. Hallinger, K. Leithwood, & J. Murphy (Eds.), *Cognitive perspectives on educational leadership* (pp. 192-212). New York: Teachers College Press.

Reitzug, U. C. (1991). Administrator competency testing: Issues, considerations, and recommendations for preparation programs and policymakers. *Journal of School Leadership, 1*, 190-210.

Scheurich, J. J., & Laible, J. (1995). The buck stops here—In our preparation programs: Educational leadership for all children (no exceptions allowed). *Educational Administration Quarterly, 31*, 313-322.

Schmuck, R. A. (1993). Beyond academics in the preparation of educational leaders: Four years of action research. *OSSC Report, 33*(2), 1-10.

Schön, D. A. (1983). *The reflective practitioner: How professionals think in action.* San Francisco: Jossey-Bass.

Schön, D.A. (1987). *Educating the reflective practitioner.* San Francisco: Jossey-Bass.

Sirotnik, K. A., & Mueller, K. (1993). Challenging the wisdom of conventional principal preparation programs and getting away with it (so far). In J. Murphy (Ed.), *Preparing tomorrow's school leaders: Alternative designs* (pp. 57-84). University Park, PA: University Council for Educational Administration.

Tannenbaum, R. J. (1997). *Content validation of the Interstate School Leaders Licensure Consortium school leaders licensure assessment.* Princeton, NJ: Educational Testing Service.

University Council for Educational Administration. (1993). UCEA IESLP project takes off. *UCEA Review, 34*(2), 1.

University Council for Educational Administration. (1997). UCEA goal activities: The work continues. *UCEA Review, 37*(2), 12-13.

Wendel, F. C. (Ed.). (1990a). *Enhancing the knowledge base in educational administration.* University Park, PA: The University Council for Educational Administration.

Wendel, F. C. (Ed). (1990b). *Reform in administrator preparation programs: Individual perspectives.* University Park, PA: The University Council for Educational Administration.

6

The Persistent Saga: Changing Instruction and Curriculum to Better Prepare School Leaders

EDDY J. VAN METER

It is sobering to note that at least 30 commission and task force reports relating to the reform of education in the United States have been published during the school reform era of the past 15 years (Bjork, 1996). It is equally disturbing to acknowledge that beginning with *A Nation at Risk* (National Commission on Excellence in Education, 1983), the findings from these reports have, with minor exception, been more negative than positive, and almost all of the reports have concluded with a call to improve the existing circumstance (Ginsberg & Plank, 1995).

In part as a response to these reports, but spurred forward by other forces as well, during the past 15 years there also has been a corresponding preoccupation at all levels—national, state, and local—with initiating policies and implementing programs in the name of educational reform (Bacharach, 1990; Elmore & Associates, 1990; Finn & Rebarber, 1992; Murphy, 1990).

The field of educational administration certainly has not been excluded from this climate of reform exhortation and activity. In *Leaders for America's Schools* (National Commission on Excellence in Educational Administration, 1987), to cite one commission report example, 35 recommendations for improving educational administration as a profession were set forth. Several of these recommendations were directed to universities, and within universities to needed reforms regarding school leadership preparation (Griffiths, Stout, & Forsyth, 1988). Additional calls for the reform of school leadership preparation were also being made during this same general period of time (Murphy, 1992, Murphy & Hallinger, 1987).

The record now shows that many school leadership faculty and programs did, in fact, respond to these calls for reform, and numerous reform efforts have been initiated over the past decade (Leithwood, Jantzi, Coffin, & Wilson, 1996; Milstein & Associates, 1993; Teitel, 1997). Obviously, there is much more that remains to be accomplished (Mulkeen, Cambron-McCabe, & Anderson, 1994), and legitimate concerns continue to be raised about changes that have been and are being made (Cibulka, Mawhinney, & Paquette, 1995), as well as the eventual impact of these changes (Haller, Brent, & McNamara, 1997). However, it is important to continue examining what we know about specific aspects of these recent reform efforts because this can help to clarify features of the initiatives that remain problematic, and it can also help point the way toward more needed refinements and improvements.

What follows, then, is such an examination, with attention focused on instructional and curricular aspects of recent school leadership preparation changes. To accomplish this task, I first provide a brief sketch of several reform initiatives that have been reported in the literature. Next, I discuss a number of issues that generally seem problematic regarding these kinds of initiatives, without attempting to examine the specific details of each case reviewed. I then suggest a few actions that might be taken in the future to move this agenda of program improvement forward. Finally, also in brief fashion, I place this latest period of program reform interest into a historical perspective and, in keeping with a thesis set forth by Achilles (1994), suggest that we are engaged in what is really a persistent and ongoing saga of trying to improve the preparation of school leaders.

Recent Instructional and Curricular Initiatives and Changes in School Leadership Preparation

One rather straightforward way to gain an impression of the kinds of curricular and instructional initiatives that have been introduced into school leadership preparation during the past few years is simply to describe several examples in brief fashion. Accordingly, the following is an arbitrary sample of cases, presented out of context and in no particular order. Taken together, they do, however, provide some "flavor" for how school leadership preparation is actually being organized and delivered in new and different ways.

As a way of presenting this selective overview, let me initially reproduce a summary of reform efforts initiated by five departments of school leadership that participated in the Danforth Principal Preparation Program, as reported by Milstein and Krueger (1997):

1. The University of Alabama faculty focused on survival skills and instructional leadership skills needed by entry-level administrators. Content is packaged in 2-hour modules and is presented during the summer. Faculty members are drawn from across the university and from the field. Integrated seminars are held to help students synthesize the modules.

2. University of Central Florida kept its traditional course blocks but increased its use of simulations, case studies, role-playing, and reflective writing. In addition, dynamics at internship sites are being integrated into classroom discussion and a Renaissance strand, which gets students involved in a variety of artistic, cultural, and civic events, introduces students to alternative ideas and different cultures. Finally, student portfolios are used as part of their evaluations.

3. The University of Connecticut purposefully sequenced learning and engaged leading practitioners to team with professors to promote the blending of theory and experience. Learning modules are being developed and long-term field-based projects are being integrated into the academic program.

4. California State University at Fresno also sequenced academic offerings, which focus on instructional leadership and emphasize hands-on participative learning. Workshops designed and presented by students are offered for academic credit. Finally, an advisory committee, composed of leading administrators from the area, is retained to keep the academic content relevant.

5. The University of Washington instituted curriculum design committees composed of faculty, administrators, students, and alumni to guide program design. Academic content is organized around two major themes, which have replaced traditional courses: the moral dimensions of leadership and inquiry, and organizations and educational change. Topics explored are organized so that they parallel the cycle of activities being focused on in school districts (e.g., budget issues are discussed when school districts are working on annual budget presentations). Finally, academic meeting times are offered

during the day rather than in the evening to increase the likelihood of effective learning. (pp. 104-105)

There are six additional and similar examples, not all of them necessarily linked to sponsored reform initiatives of the Danforth Foundation, that may also help to depict the kind of program changes that have taken place over the past several years. I add them as a way to provide a richer mix of descriptions regarding some of the initiatives that have been implemented in the name of curricular and instructional improvement.

Curriculum coherence: University of Northern Colorado. In this example, a principalship preparation program was redesigned in such a way that the practice of students taking disjointed courses in unorganized sequence was discontinued. The old program was replaced by a more integrated curriculum that was based on an articulated vision of effective school leadership (Daresh & Barnett, 1993). This program change featured the creation of a set of core courses designed intentionally to be different from the traditional, discipline-based courses previously required. A sense of this change, which was intended to result in greater curricular coherence, is suggested by the new course titles:

1. Understanding Self—Developing a Personal Vision for Educational Leadership
2. Using Inquiry—Framing Problems and Making Decisions in Educational Leadership
3. Shaping Organizations—Management and Leadership in Education
4. Understanding People—Professional Development and Educational Leadership
5. Understanding Environments—Social, Political, Economic, and Legal Influences (Daresh & Barnett, 1993, pp. 138-139)

The revised program also incorporated additional learning experiences created to supplement the core curriculum. Included was an internship experience, specialized training in teacher evaluation, and a student portfolio requirement.

Demonstrated performance: North Dakota State University. Faculty at North Dakota State University, in this example, redesigned their educational leadership preparation program in a way that was intended to blend the knowledge base of educational administration with the performance skills needed for effective school leadership practice (Van Berkum, 1994). The performance skills were based on leadership dimensions identified by the NASSP Principal Assessment Center. The curriculum was organized into six rather traditionally named areas (e.g., supervision and staff development, fiscal responsibility), with students being required to demonstrate skills within each area. Thus, embedded within each area (i.e., course) were requirements that display some indication of performance skills (e.g., problem analysis, judgment, sensitivity). In addition, a record-keeping system provided a cumulative record of demonstrated skills and performance across the entire curriculum.

Here, the focus was on integrating skills across content areas (e.g., an activity that taps problem analysis skill relating to some aspect of fiscal responsibility; an assessment of judgment regarding a legal issue). There was also a focus on documenting performance and the enhancement of skills across the curriculum.

Experience-based learning: Michigan State University. In this example, which is more instructionally than curriculum focused, faculty at Michigan State University initiated an activity centered on an application of experiential learning (Benham & Shepard, 1995). Selected school professionals participated in a 5-day leadership retreat, during which they were engaged in both "ropes course" activities conducted outdoors and team-centered, problem-based activities conducted indoors. The general design of the retreat was based on an Outward Bound experiential learning model. Interviews conducted with participants after the retreat revealed that three themes of learning were generated by the experience: Opportunities were created to overcome personal barriers, activities enhanced participant relationships by fostering teamwork and shared power, and activities modeled authentic commitments based on trust and respect. A faculty assessment of the retreat pointed out the limitations of using the approach but also included favorable commentary regarding the potential of such experiential learning applications to enhance the preparation of school leaders.

Database exploration: University of Pittsburgh. This example featured a computer laboratory that houses a statewide school systems information database. This database served as a centerpiece instructional tool for a redesigned school superintendency preparation program at the University of Pittsburgh (Wallace, 1994). The computer laboratory and database provided a "unique opportunity for superintendents in training to acquire an understanding of, and facility with, the use of computers and multiple databases for management and leadership functions" (p. 199). Opportunities were created within the preparation program for students to work with school system data, focusing on such issues as human resources management and financial planning.

The superintendency program itself was organized into four interactive domains of study: (a) vision, (b) data orientation, (c) organizational and professional development, and (d) management. Students had some flexibility in taking coursework within each domain, plus they were also required to engage in field studies, clinical experiences, and explorations of data that integrate the domain emphases.

Problem-based learning: Stanford University. In this example, which sparked a great deal of interest when first announced and since then has been emulated widely, a problem-based learning (PBL) approach to instruction was incorporated into a new principalship preparation program at Stanford University (Bridges & Hallinger, 1992). As described, PBL refers to an instructional strategy that organizes knowledge around administrative problems rather than the traditional discipline areas of school administration (e.g., school law, personnel administration, school finance). Using the PBL approach, which was featured in some 40% of the curriculum, students in the Stanford program worked on realistic school-related problems (e.g., implementing an AIDS curriculum; hiring a teacher), and they did this as members of a project team. The overall curriculum, while retaining a series-of-courses-to-be-taken format, was grounded in an emphasis intended to reflect the real-world circumstances of schooling. Course titles included "The Role of Personality and Emotions in Organizations," "Instruction of Socially Heterogeneous Populations," and "School-Based Decision Making" (pp. 119-120).

Clearly, the use of PBL as an approach to instruction in school leadership preparation has expanded greatly since the early Stanford University application just described (e.g., see Bridges & Hallinger, 1997). This sketch of the program as depicted in 1992 does, however, provide an introduction to the concept that is adequate for the purpose to be served here.

Multiple perspectives: University of Kentucky. A final example is taken from a redesign of the doctoral program in school leadership at the University of Kentucky. Here, the inclusion of an enhanced "multiple-perspective" orientation to the study of organizational and leadership issues was featured as one emphasis in the new curriculum (Van Meter & Scollay, 1995). Students take a two-course sequence that incorporates a variation of the "frames theory" approach popularized by Bolman and Deal (1984, 1991). The original Bolman and Deal approach provides a way for individuals to understand leadership and organizational behavior by viewing such behavior through contrasting frames of interpretation (i.e., structural, human resource, political, and symbolic frames). In the two-course sequence created at the University of Kentucky, these four frames were used, but four additional frames are also introduced and discussed as alternative "lenses" through which school-related actions can be interpreted. The four additional lenses are systems, critical theory, postmodern, and communitarian frames.

In contrast to one of the previous examples already noted (i.e., the curriculum change at the University of Northern Colorado), this change was not grounded so much in what is needed for effective school leadership as championed in the literature. Rather, the two-course sequence was constructed to provide students with a richer set of conceptual skills that is expected to be applied to all circumstances of leadership or organizational interaction that might be encountered.

The Problematic Nature of
Many Recent Program Reform Efforts

Again, I want to emphasize that the examples just identified are not intended to represent all of the differing kinds of program changes that have taken place during this latest period of reform. However, collectively, they do provide some illustration of changes taking place, and each has received enough thought and attention to be featured in the literature of our field.

What, then, can we say about these as well as other recent efforts to change the way in which instructional practice and curricular content are defined in programs intending to prepare school leaders?

To start, I would make the observation that most program changes are ultimately a product of individual department and program faculties making improvements on the basis of their interpretation of what is needed and feasible within the context of their institution, rather than attempting to adopt an intact reform model, idea, or program design. I am not saying that faculty pay no attention to external platforms, models, or themes of reform, nor am I suggesting that foundations, education agencies, or professional associations typically promote intact approaches. What I do contend is that when faculty engage in back-home program revisions, whatever the reform idea that has provided a stimulus for the change, the end result is almost always a modified version of the idea that meets the unique circumstances existing within that particular department, college, and university. This observation is, in fact, merely one variation of a well-known story within the existing literature on planned change and the diffusion of educational innovations (e.g., see McLaughlin & Elmore, 1982).

There is certainly nothing inherently negative about the situation just described. Such individualism and adaptation, when applied to one person or an entire program faculty, clearly has a potential to stimulate creativity, and it places decisions about program change at the level closest to the point of delivery. When viewed from a vantage point of attempting to implement a reform policy or program that is targeted to a national or even regional audience, however, it also has a tendency to sometimes lead to uneven approaches to program reform and improvement. This, in turn, can be interpreted by some as an impediment to widespread reform implementation.

What seems most striking about all of this, particularly when thought about within the context of the past 15 years, is the paucity of meaningful attempts to define, develop, and implement specific preparation program reforms that have, in fact, been national in scope. Furthermore, those more-limited attempts that were initiated have almost all permitted participants to become involved in what amounts to a voluntary manner, thus requiring only limited commitment to a degree of implementation that would ultimately meet the requirements of external review and approval, if such were actually to be imposed. There has also not been a great deal of financial backing for efforts having such a national orientation. This is not to say that nationally focused projects should have received more attention or financial backing, but only to make the observation that for whatever reasons, our preparation program improvement efforts during this era of reform seem to have been limited in both scope and funding.

Turning to other matters, another kind of issue I would raise concerning recent program reform efforts relates to the extent to which these initiatives seem not to seriously challenge traditional graduate school policies and requirements that have been adopted by most universities. Among other things, these typically include a well-defined credit-hour structure for coursework, and courses usually are expected to be completed within a designated time frame (e.g., a semester, a quarter term).

It is interesting to note that most new reform practices continue to conform to the established patterns of graduate school and university practice just mentioned. Certainly, attempts are sometimes made to insert creative features within the existing structure (e.g., create a course or practicum that spans two semesters, configure several modules of instruction within a given semester but assign grades for each module separately, etc.). However, few attempts seem to break completely from the organizing structure imposed by institutional requirements and tradition.

Obviously, an argument can be made that such conformity to institutional rules is laudable. It does, however, place a limitation on program variations that could prove worthwhile if attempted. As an example, it might be interesting to design a preparation program composed primarily of curricular modules that are completed individually within a time frame that is completely controlled by each student (even though group activities and meetings with faculty and other students might still be scheduled routinely on a weekly, monthly, or similar basis). The logistics of such a program might be daunting, but the freedom to think about such program delivery flexibility is certainly enhanced once it is possible to work outside the traditional framework of institutional restrictions.

In a similar way, almost universal access to the Internet and to other distance learning technology options obviously creates a potential to configure preparation programs in new ways (Hobbs & Christianson, 1997). Faculty are already implementing such options in many colleges and universities that offer a school leadership preparation program, yet university administrators in some instances are only now beginning to grapple with the implications of this new world of the virtual university.

A different issue that is problematic with reference to program reform is the tension that exists between calls for school leadership preparation to be more grounded in the expectations of job performance versus calls for preparation to incorporate the increased number of perspectives now evident within our field (e.g., critical theory, postmodernism, and feminist perspectives). It is not that these emphases are in opposition; critical theory and feminist perspectives can certainly inform expected standards of performance! Rather, it is an issue of trying to remember that the total amount of time available for preparation is limited. In effect, this tension can evolve into the common dilemma of teaching a smaller number of topics in depth versus addressing a larger number of topics with less depth of discussion, understanding, or coverage.

There is also something problematic about a lack of clarity that persists regarding the curriculum that is needed for initial licensure as a school leader versus the curriculum needed for advanced study at the doctoral level. As reflected in the program examples summarized earlier in this chapter, much of the discussion about school leadership preparation during this latest period of reform has focused on issues relating to the preservice preparation of school principals and how they can better meet the on-the-job challenges they will face once they are employed as building administrators. Discussions about curricular changes needed for doctoral study, on the other hand, have tended to focus on issues such as alternative approaches to designing a research sequence (e.g., a focus on quantitative methodology, qualitative methodology, or some combination of both); contrasting approaches to an understanding of the best way to understand the role and purpose of leadership in school settings; and discussions of how best to ground our field intellectually. A question thus arises about whether it is more appropriate to plan and organize the entry-level curriculum for school leadership and the advanced doctoral curriculum in a way that provides students with either a seamless web of study or a somewhat connected and interrelated curriculum, or in a manner that separates the two curriculum experiences in a fundamental way. This issue remains almost completely unaddressed.

There is, perhaps, another issue to consider with regard to the above observation, this having to do with the possibility that during the past 15 years we may have also seen a shift, particularly in some doctoral-granting universities, from a school leadership faculty that is comprised almost exclusively of discipline-oriented scholars (e.g., the school law professor, the school finance professor) to a faculty that now includes many more epistemologically oriented scholars (e.g., the critical theory professor, the postmodernist professor). Obviously, the realities of the professoriate are more complex than these orientations imply, and faculty cannot be defined in such simplistic terms. Nevertheless, it is interesting to speculate about how such a shift in faculty orientation—or perhaps it is really faculty interest—may affect the way in which a department faculty goes about the business of designing or revising school leadership preparation, particularly when such work centers on programs relating to the preparation of school principals.

Finally, it should be mentioned that decisions to adopt a specific instructional strategy—the use of problem-based learning is a good example—sometimes have a tendency to drive the content of the curriculum in certain directions (e.g., adopting PBL means a focus on "problems"). This is an issue that needs to be given more attention when faculty are considering program reforms that start from an instructional vantage point rather than beginning with the curriculum and then defining the kinds of instructional strategies needed. Program reform that involves changes in how instruction is provided clearly can have unforeseen consequences. This is a simple observation—it is something of which almost everyone is aware—but it does need to be remembered.

Additional Steps in the Path
Toward Preparation Program Improvement

It is trite to say that there is no magic bullet leading to instructional and curricular improvement in school leadership preparation. It is also true that our profession continues to go about the business of trying to improve how school leaders are prepared in many different ways. Given this complex process and circumstance, it can be useful at times to simply set forth ideas for discussion and consideration. It is in this spirit that the following suggestions are made. Most of these actions are intentionally specific and small enough to be initiated without a great expenditure of resources. However, I end with a recommended project that is somewhat larger and more complicated in scope.

I would first propose that one of the national organizations having an affiliation with educational administration (e.g., UCEA, AERA, AASA) should, in the near future, sponsor a one-time meeting targeted to a national level of involvement and focused specifically on curricular and instructional improvements that are needed in school leadership preparation. This might be organized as a follow-up to the reform efforts of the 1980s that resulted in the publication of the *Leaders for America's Schools* report, but with a more focused agenda (i.e., examining only the curricular and instructional aspects of school leadership preparation). The question of clarifying curriculum needs about superintendency preparation was mentioned earlier in this chapter and could be one topic to be addressed. Another topic for discussion could focus on curricular and instructional matters regarding some of the forgotten players in most of the current preparation reform dialogue (e.g., school business administrators, district directors of human resources, assistant principals, directors of special education). A meeting or invited forum such as the one being suggested here could serve to concentrate discussion on specific issues of preparation and could do so without being sidetracked by having other topics considered at the same time.

Another manageable initiative of a similar nature would be for the National Council of Professors of Educational Administration (NCPEA) to organize a task force to examine curricular and instructional ideas that have been widely discussed, presented, and published over the past decade, including those ideas that appear in the new *NCPEA Yearbook* series, which has been published annually since 1993 (e.g., see Wildman, 1997). The charge to the task force would be to compile and then examine the many ideas relating to curricular and instructional reform that they are able to identify, synthesize these ideas in some fashion, and identify a series of recommendations for improvement that are based on the best thinking represented in the sources of information reviewed. The task force might also be asked to present a special report of their findings and recommendations to the larger membership. This report could also be published and distributed to school leadership preparation departments throughout the country and to other interested agencies, individuals, and organizations as well. An external funding source might be identified and financial resources obtained to support this entire effort.

I would also recommend that the Council of Chief State School Officers (CCSSO), as the sponsoring organization, should continue to find new ways to build upon the national recognition that has resulted from the work of the Interstate School Leadership Licensure Consortium (ISLLC) in creating Standards for School Leaders that are now being adopted in many states (CCSSO, 1996). One specific way in which CCSSO might do this is to sponsor, fund, and convene a meeting of school leadership program faculty representatives from around the country to participate in a dialogue about how some programs are already engaged in curriculum reform activities centered around the ISLLC standards, how those not yet engaged might learn from the experience of others, and how everyone might use in back-home improvement activities some of the more recently available materials and sources of information that feature and discuss the work of the ISLLC (e.g., see Murphy, 1997; Sharp, Walter, & Sharp, 1998; Van Meter & Murphy, 1997).

Finally, and again turning to a somewhat different kind of issue, I want to suggest one more idea that may have some merit as a way to improve the curricular and instructional aspects of school leadership preparation. This relates to the potential afforded by the technology explosion of the past decade and centers on a contention that it may be time to think seriously about the creation of a virtual university for school leadership preparation, with all college and university preparation programs across the country being connected and contributing members and partners. The idea is not to eliminate existing preparation programs but rather to incorporate the virtual university as one part of each preparation program, with the amount of involvement to be decided by each program faculty and participating institution. Entire courses, faculty lectures, interinstitutional student conversations, and similar instructional and curricular activities could be offered as part of this national—or international—delivery system. In like manner, course syllabi, instructional modules, and other information resources could be retrieved by computer access as needed (i.e., with the availability of such resources, program faculty at any member college or university could then pick and choose materials to be modified and used as needed rather than have individuals at each location spend the amount of time that is required to create such materials independently). Furthermore, a routine part of the preparation experience at a given site might involve a faculty member meeting with students to debrief materials that the students have downloaded and used in some fashion as a learning resource, or perhaps examining materials that the students have developed themselves and will enter as a potential learning resource.

The irony is that these kinds of virtual university and resource-on-the-Web locations are already being developed and are operational. However, at present, the former are typically organized as a single-institution endeavor or as a limited consortium arrangement, and they emphasize several academic disciplines across the entire university curriculum. Resources on the Web, on the other hand, are usually created by individual faculty members or by academic departments and provide general, department-related information or details regarding a specific course. What has not occurred is the creation of this kind of distance-learning capacity in an integrative way and as a collective endeavor that has a specific focus on meeting our school leadership preparation needs through collaborative involvement. The development of this kind of instructional and curricular delivery and resource support system would appear to be a logical next step in our expanding use of technology; thus, a plan to seek funding for the creation of such a system at least needs to be considered.

A Historical Perspective on
Our Current Preparation Reform Efforts

As discussed in this chapter, there is ample evidence to document that educational administration program faculty and departments have been responsive over the past 15 years to calls for reform in school leadership preparation, while acknowledging that much more needs to be done. As also suggested, at least in terms of curricular and instructional changes, much of this reform has been both incremental in nature and designed to meet unique institutional contexts, needs, and circumstances. It is thus important that we continue to examine our existing reform efforts while we also work toward continuing future improvements. In like manner, it can also perhaps be instructive to place our reform and improvement activities into some kind of historical perspective, and it is to this task that I now want to briefly turn my attention.

There are excellent existing commentaries that examine the historical circumstances of educational administration as a profession and field of study (e.g., Campbell, Fleming, Newell, & Bennion, 1987; Culbertson, 1988; Cunningham, Hack, & Nystrand, 1977). However, for the purpose to be served here, I want to draw on the historical overview that Murphy (1992) provides in his more recent book *The Landscape of Leadership Preparation.* In this book, Murphy outlines the history of our field in a way that differs somewhat from the approach often taken (i.e., the notion of a "scientific management" period being followed by a "human relations" period, followed in turn by a "behavioral sciences" period, which then gives way to a current, more "eclectic" period). Acknowledging the work of previous writers, Murphy instead identifies an "Ideological Era" as being the defining theme within educational administration up to the beginning of the 20th century. He contends that this era was followed by a "Prescriptive Era," which proved to be dominant from about 1900 to 1946, and goes on to identify a "Scientific Era" that shaped and influenced our profession during the period from about 1947 to 1985. Finally, beginning in 1986, we entered what Murphy tentatively identifies as a "Dialectic Era" that continues to the present. In this historical outline, Murphy also includes the useful concept of "Eras of Ferment"; such eras refer to short, 10- to 15-year periods that serve to bridge and overlap with the longer periods of emphasis. What distinguishes these shorter periods of ferment is a questioning of ending dominant-era assumptions and practices, as well as dialogue about these same issues as they apply to the emerging dominant era.

In the commentary just mentioned, Murphy goes on to suggest that the past 15-year period of concern about school leadership preparation reform can be explained at least partially by the fact that we are again positioned in a period of ferment, and that we should recognize and understand the implications of this being the case. If we accept Murphy's thesis, and I find it rather compelling, then it can indeed help to explain the current unsettled situation in which we find ourselves.

This is not, of course, a complete explanation of why so much attention has been devoted recently to our program reform efforts. Certainly, the influence of the larger education reform movement accounts for a great deal of our current activities. There also have been important reform initiatives stimulated by the work of UCEA, NPBEA, and other organizations and agencies as well. It may nevertheless expand our understanding to recognize that part of the impetus for this most recent period of reform thinking and action can perhaps be accounted for as being part of the natural flow of history within our field.

In effect, although we may position our concerns about school leadership preparation improvement as being concentrated in the present, or situated within the 15-year period of recent general education reform, a contrasting view is that we are merely taking part in a current phase of what is really an episodic and ongoing renewal of our profession and practice. Given this view, our recent engagements with change and inquiry can be interpreted as being part of an ongoing saga regarding school preparation improvement, one that extends far into the past and will continue well into the future.

The bad news, perhaps, is that going about the task of curricular and instructional reform has been and will always be a difficult and demanding assignment. The good news is that we have a wealth of creative reform ideas and examples now available, a talented group of people involved, and a growing body of program improvement literature on which to base our continuing work.

References

Achilles, C. M. (1994). Searching for the golden fleece: The epic search continues. *Educational Administration Quarterly, 30*(1), 6-26.

Bacharach, S. B. (Ed.). (1990). *Education reform: Making sense of it all.* Boston: Allyn & Bacon.

Benham, M. K. P., & Shepard, E. (1995). Experience-based leadership training: Reflections of African-American school leaders. *Journal of School Leadership, 5*(3) 272-307.

Bjork, L. (1996). The revisionists' critique of the education reform reports. *Journal of School Leadership, 6*(3), 290-315.

Bolman, L. G., & Deal, T. E. (1984). *Modern approaches to understanding and managing organizations.* San Francisco: Jossey-Bass.

Bolman, L. G., & Deal, T. E. (1991). *Reframing organizations: Artistry, choice, and leadership.* San Francisco: Jossey-Bass.

Bridges, E. M., & Hallinger, P. (1992). *Problem-based learning for administrators.* Eugene: University of Oregon, ERIC Clearinghouse on Educational Management.

Bridges, E. M., & Hallinger, P. (1997). Using problem-based learning to prepare educational leaders. *Peabody Journal of Education, 71*(2), 131-146.

Campbell, R. F., Fleming, T., Newell, L. J., & Bennion, J. W. (1987). *A history of thought and practice in educational administration.* New York: Teachers College Press.

Cibulka, J. G., Mawhinney, H. B., & Paquette, J. (1995). Administrative leadership and the crisis in the study of educational administration: Technical rationality and its aftermath. In P. W. Cookson, Jr., & B. Schneider (Eds.), *Transforming schools.* New York: Garland.

Council of Chief State School Officers. (1996). *Interstate school leaders licensure consortium: Standards for school leaders.* Washington, DC: Author.

Culbertson, J. A. (1988). A century's quest for a knowledge base. In N. J. Boyan (Ed.), *Handbook of research on educational administration* (pp. 3-26). New York: Longman.

Cunningham, L. L., Hack, W., G., & Nystrand, R. O. (Eds.). (1977). *Educational administration: The developing decades.* Berkeley, CA: McCutchan.

Daresh, J. C., & Barnett, B. G. (1993). Restructuring leadership development in Colorado. In J. Murphy (Ed.), *Preparing tomorrow's school leaders: Alternative designs* (pp. 129-156). University Park, PA: The University Council for Educational Administration.

Elmore, R. F., & Associates. (1990). *Restructuring schools: The next generation of educational reform.* San Francisco: Jossey-Bass.

Finn, C. E., Jr., & Rebarber, T. (Eds.). (1992). *Education reform in the '90s.* New York: Macmillan.

Ginsberg, R., & Plank, D. N. (Eds.). (1995). *Commissions, reports, reforms, and educational policy.* Westport, CT: Praeger.

Griffiths, D. E., Stout, R. T., & Forsyth, P. B. (Eds.). (1988). *Leaders for America's schools: The report and papers of the National Commission on Excellence in Educational Administration.* Berkeley, CA: McCutchan.

Haller, E. J., Brent, B. O., & McNamara, J. H. (1997). Does graduate training in educational administration improve America's schools? *Phi Delta Kappan, 79*(3), 222-227.

Hobbs, V. M., & Christianson, J. S. (1997). *Virtual classrooms: Educational opportunity through two-way interactive television.* Lancaster, PA: Technomic.

Leithwood, K., Jantzi, D., Coffin, G., & Wilson, P. (1996). Preparing school leaders: What works? *Journal of School Leadership, 6*(3), 316-342.

McLaughlin, M. W., & Elmore, R. F. (1982). Implementation of federal education programs: Implications for future federal policy. *Peabody Journal of Education, 60*, 8-19.

Milstein, M. M., & Associates. (1993). *Changing the way we prepare educational leaders: The Danforth experience.* Newbury Park, CA: Corwin.

Milstein, M. M., & Krueger, J. A. (1997). Improving educational administration preparation programs: What we have learned over the past decade. *Peabody Journal of Education, 72*(2), 100-116.

Mulkeen, T. A., Cambron-McCabe, N. H., & Anderson, B. J. (Eds.). (1994). *Democratic leadership: The changing context of administrative preparation.* Norwood, NJ: Ablex.

Murphy, J. (Ed.). (1990). *The educational reform movement of the 1980s.* Berkeley, CA: McCutchan.

Murphy, J. (1992). *The landscape of leadership preparation: Reframing the education of school administrators.* Newbury Park, CA: Corwin.

Murphy, J. (1997, November 19). Putting new school leaders to the test. *Education Week,* pp. 34, 52.

Murphy, J., & Hallinger, P. (Eds.). (1987). *Approaches to administrative training in education.* Albany: State University of New York Press.

National Commission on Excellence in Education. (1983). *A nation at risk: The imperative for educational reform.* Washington, DC: U.S. Department of Education.

National Commission on Excellence in Educational Administration. (1987). *Leaders for America's schools.* Tempe, AZ: UCEA.

Sharp, W. L., Walter, J. K., & Sharp, H. M. (1998). *Case studies for school leaders: Implementing the ISLLC standards.* Lancaster, PA: Technomic.

Teitel, L. (1997). Understanding and harnessing the power of the cohort model in preparing educational leaders. *Peabody Journal of Education, 72*(2), 66-85.

Van Berkum, D. W. (1994). Performance skill development of the aspiring principal integrated into principal preparation. *Journal of School Leadership, 4*(1), 52-68.

Van Meter, E., & Murphy, J. (1997). *Using ISLLC standards to strengthen preparation programs in school administration,* Washington, DC: Council of Chief State School Officers.

Van Meter, E. J., & Scollay, S. J. (1995). Curriculum revision in educational administration: An institutional case record and retrospective commentary. *Journal of School Leadership, 5*(6), 512-531.

Wallace, R. C., Jr. (1994). Linking practice and the preparation of school administrators. In T. A. Mulkeen, N. H. Cambron-McCabe, & B. J.

Anderson (Eds.), *Democratic leadership: The changing context of administrative preparation* (pp. 189-200). Norwood, NJ: Ablex.

Wildman, L. (Ed.). (1997). *School administration: The new knowledge base.* Lancaster, PA: Technomic.

7

Changes in Preparation Programs: Perceptions of Department Chairs

JOSEPH MURPHY

After being directionless for a decade, the field of educational administration in the mid-1980s undertook some important efforts to improve school leadership and the preparation of school leaders.

MCCARTHY AND KUH (1997, P. 12)

Almost all of our empirical understanding of the reform of the academic arm of educational leadership, especially its preparation programs, derives from one of four sources. Chronicles of reformation in individual programs or groups of departments engaged in related reforms (e.g., those in the Danforth programs) provide the richest repository of knowledge to date.[1] Second, but less prevalent, are analyses of activities on specific pieces of the reform agenda (e.g., cohort programs, problem-based instructional strategies, the use of technology).[2] Treatments of the strategies that important professional bodies have used to reshape the profession furnish a third useful lens for drawing conclusions about changes afoot in departments of educational leadership (e.g., see the Forsyth and Thomson chapters in this volume). Finally, there are a number of macrolevel analyses of the recontoured landscape of the profession. These, in turn, are of two types: synthetic reviews[3] and empirical studies.[4]

The work described in this chapter falls into the fourth category. It extends empirical investigations undertaken in the mid-to-late 1980s. Specifically, based on responses from 44 chairpersons of educational leadership departments in UCEA institutions, we describe the types of revisions that programs have begun to make in response to three related sets of pressures:

170

(a) pressures bearing on school administrators from the larger reform agenda—that is, improving K-12 education across the board; (b) general critiques of and calls for improvement in educational leadership; and (c) specific analyses of and demands for change in administrator preparation programs. In the next section, we discuss the procedures used in the study. We then turn our attention to the findings. Analysis of the data and discussion of the findings are integrated throughout the chapter.

Procedures

An initial formulation of the protocol used in this study was developed in 1988 and used in an exploratory study with department chairs of administrator preparation programs in Illinois (Murphy, 1989, 1990). The objectives of that study were similar to the ones here, but the focus was primarily on changes resulting from the educational reform movement sweeping over the K-12 public education system at that time.

On the basis of that work and of feedback from two experts in educational leadership—one university-based and one field-based—the original questionnaire was revised somewhat. The resulting protocol contained 21 items—16 combination Likert-scale and open-ended format questions, 3 open-ended-only questions, and 2 Likert-scale-only questions. That instrument was then used to anchor a second study of preparation program reform with 74 chairpersons of educational leadership departments throughout the nation (Murphy, 1991). Of these, 29 were from non–UCEA schools, and 45 were from UCEA institutions.

For the current study, the 21-item instrument was revised slightly. Most important, the questions that focused on the educational reform movement of the 1980s were deleted. Of the 17 remaining items, one was a Likert-scale-only question:

The last decade has brought about changes in the way you prepare school administrators in your college/school of education:

1	2	3	4	5
very little		somewhat		a great deal

Directions for the 16 combination Likert-scale and open-ended format questions (Questions 2a-p) were as follows:

How would you characterize the amount of change in the preparation of school administrators at your school/college of education in the following areas?

1	2	3	4	5
very little		somewhat		a great deal

Please describe important changes, if any:

Chairpersons of educational administration departments in the 54 UCEA institutions were the target audience for the study. Forty-four (81.5%) of those unit heads returned completed questionnaires.

All of the questions were analyzed descriptively. *T* tests were used to assess differences between responses from the 1991 study (questionnaires completed in November and December of 1989) and the current study (questionnaires completed in November and December of 1996).

Results and Discussion

Overall Effect

To ascertain the level of reform influence, we led with a general question that required unit heads to assess the cumulative effect of the reform movement on their programs. In general, these educational leaders felt that preparation programs have undergone moderate to strong changes over the past decade (mean = 3.93) (see Item 1, Table 7.1). As seen in Item 1, Table 7.2, department heads reported considerably more change activity in 1996 at the close of the decade of reform (mean = 3.93) than they did in the late 1980s (mean = 3.18). As shown in Items 2a through 2p, Table 7.2, in the earlier study, chairs assigned scores of 3 or higher to only 2 of the 16 topic areas (2d, 2e). In the current study, 10 items (2a, 2b, 2c, 2d, 2e, 2f, 2h, 2i, 2k, 2p) were scored 3 or higher, and another 3 items were marked 2.9 or higher. The modal score for the 16 programmatic sub-areas in Question 2 was only 2.5 in 1988; in 1996, it was 3.3.

Based on these responses, it appears that the pressures for reform are having a noticeable impact on administrator preparation programs. Although it is difficult to locate the influences afoot with certainty, some or all of the forces discussed below may be at work. On one hand, time may be the salient variable. That is, unlike in the earlier study, most of the reform reports in the

TABLE 7.1 Department Chairpersons' Perceptions of Changes in
Preparation Programs in Departments of Educational
Leadership in UCEA Institutions

Area		*n*	*M*
1	Overall effect	44	3.93
2a	Recruitment of students	44	3.69
2b	Selection of students	44	3.93
2c	Monitoring/assessing progress	42	3.23
2d	Clinical experiences	44	3.86
2e	Content of the program	44	3.82
2f	Teaching and learning strategies	43	3.63
2g	Degree structure	43	2.56
2h	Involvement of practitioners in development	44	3.18
2i	Involvement of practitioners in delivery	44	3.34
2j	Involvement of faculty in schools	44	2.93
2k	Type (mix) of students	42	3.43
2l	Services for practicing administrators	43	2.63
2m	Selection of faculty	42	2.90
2n	Departmental staffing	43	2.95
2o	Faculty development opportunities	44	2.55
2p	Departmental mission/agenda	43	3.60

area of leadership have had a chance to spread across the profession. There has also been sufficient time for programs to engage change initiatives and for some of those efforts to take root.

It may also be the case that the buffering these programs have histori-cally enjoyed—buffering employed to fend off external influences—may be thinning considerably. In short, their option to not act may be becoming re-duced. In particular, the resurgence of more vigorous state control over prepa-ration programs may be propelling reform efforts. This has certainly been the case in the states of North Carolina, Ohio, Mississippi, and Kentucky (see Van Meter, Chapter 6 of this volume). Concomitantly, the introduction of mar-ket dynamics into the licensure system may be influencing departments to strengthen their training programs. At least two such forces have surfaced over

TABLE 7.2 Departmental Chairpersons' Perceptions of Changes in
Preparation Programs in Departments of Educational
Leadership in UCEA Institutions: 1989 vs. 1996

	Area	1989			1996			
		n	M	SD	n	M	SD	t Test
1	Overall effect	45	3.18	1.0	44	3.93	1.13	-3.28**
2a	Recruitment of students	45	2.51	1.2	44	3.69	1.94	-3.42***
2b	Selection of students	45	2.62	1.2	44	3.93	2.01	-3.70***
2c	Monitoring/assessing progress	44	2.54	1.0	42	3.23	1.46	-2.57*
2d	Clinical experiences	45	3.00	1.3	44	3.86	1.13	-3.29**
2e	Content of the program	46	3.26	1.2	44	3.82	1.24	-2.15*
2f	Teaching and learning strategies	45	2.51	1.1	43	3.63	1.13	-4.66***
2g	Degree structure	45	2.11	1.4	43	2.56	1.42	-1.48
2h	Involvement of practitioners in development	45	2.96	1.1	44	3.18	1.32	-0.85
2i	Involvement of practitioners in delivery	44	2.46	1.2	44	3.34	1.22	-3.37**
2j	Involvement of faculty in schools	46	2.57	1.1	44	2.93	1.23	-1.45
2k	Type (mix) of students	43	2.16	1.1	42	3.43	1.13	-5.19***
2l	Services for practicing administrators	45	2.44	1.3	43	2.63	1.38	-0.66
2m	Selection of faculty	45	2.76	1.4	42	2.90	1.43	-0.46
2n	Departmental staffing	41	2.12	1.2	43	2.95	1.36	-2.93**
2o	Faculty development opportunities	44	1.96	1.1	44	2.55	1.32	-2.25*
2p	Departmental mission/agenda	45	2.82	1.2	43	3.60	1.28	-2.92**

$*p < .05$; $**p < .01$; $***p < .001$.

the past decade—the creation of alternative avenues for licensure and the
growth of alternative providers of programs leading to licensure, especially
those offered by professional associations and local educational agencies.

Professional forces may also lie behind the reform work noted by these
department heads. The widespread complacency about preparation programs

among professors of educational administration, which has been highlighted by McCarthy, Kuh, Newell, and Iacona (1988) and McCarthy and Kuh (1997), is perhaps being challenged as older members of the professoriate retire and new faculty begin to assume the reins of the profession. If, indeed, we are witnessing a lifting of the veil of complacency, it may be attributable to the influx of more women professors and of more faculty members who are joining the professoriate from practice (see McCarthy, Chapter 8 of this volume). There certainly appears to be more agitation for program improvement today than was the case in the mid-1980s.

The growth of professional groups dedicated to program reform, such as the new AERA special interest groups on problem-based learning and on teaching and learning in educational administration, are noteworthy markers in the professional area—so, too, has been the development of professional networks of reformers, such as those nurtured through the Danforth initiatives of the late 1980s and early 1990s. In short, it may be that the rather inhospitable landscape of the profession is being remolded to be more receptive to the seeds of change. It is worth noting that many more colleagues than was the case 15 years ago have staked at least part of their professional reputations on work related to preparation program development and reform.

Finally, it is possible that shifting norms in universities in general and in colleges of education in particular may be responsible for some of the increased attention to program reform noted by the respondents in this study. Specifically, at least two forces operating in education schools may be directing, or at least facilitating, program improvement. The first is the increased emphasis "on enhancing the quality of instruction [in] most colleges and universities" (McCarthy & Kuh, 1997, p. 245). The second is the demand by many colleges of education that meaningful connections to practice be established and nurtured. Although sometimes offset by other forces (e.g., the press for research respectability), these two dynamics may be helping to energize efforts to strengthen preparation programs in the area of educational leadership.

Student Recruitment, Selection, and Type of Students

> *Ten years ago, we didn't recruit. We do this now.* (Chair)
> *We are fairly selective now, not at all before.* (Chair)

The two reports at the forefront of reform in preparation programs—the National Commission on Excellence in Educational Administration's (NCEEA) *Leaders for America's Schools* (1987) and the National Policy

Board for Educational Administration's (NPBEA) *Improving the Preparation of School Administrators* (1989)—underscored the need to strengthen
the procedures employed to identify and select students into leadership programs. For example, the NPBEA begins its call for reform by recommending
that

> vigorous recruitment strategies be mounted to attract the brightest and
> most capable candidates, of diverse race, ethnicity, and sex [and that]
> entrance standards to administrator preparation programs be dramatically
> raised to ensure that all candidates possess strong analytic ability, high
> administrative potential, and demonstrated success in teaching. (NPBEA,
> 1989, p. 5)

To measure progress in this area, we asked three questions to determine how
the student population has changed over the past decade. Overall, recruitment
and selection have been heavily affected (3.69 and 3.93, respectively; see 2a
and 2b, Table 7.1). Not surprisingly, there also has been some change in the
type, or the mix, of students (3.43) in preparation programs (see 2k, Table
7.1). Particularly salient is the progress reported from 1989 to 1996 (see 2a,
2b, and 2k, Table 7.2). In the earlier investigation, we described only slight
changes in recruitment and selection and suggested that the results indicated
that efforts to increase enrollments of historically underrepresented groups
in educational administration were still in the early stages. Responses provided in this study allow us to construct a much more positive storyline.

Recruitment

Analysis of the open-ended responses to Questions 2a, 2b, and 2k provides a fairly rich description of the types of alterations that these programs
are undertaking in the areas of recruitment and of selection of students. To
begin with, there is evidence of much more active recruitment of students than
has historically been the case in the profession (Griffiths, 1988). In review-
ing the completed questionnaires, one gets a sense that the calls for greater
emphasis on student recruitment that pepper major reform reports are being
heeded.

Some of this enhanced attention can be traced to concerted efforts to
secure more diverse student bodies, especially in terms of racial composition. Indeed, when discussing recruitment, nine chairs commented on initiatives to increase minority enrollments. Some of the change is attributable to
the widespread implementation of cohort programs, a dynamic mentioned
directly by the chairs of 12 departments. According to respondents, the de-

velopment of cohorts has both permitted and encouraged them to be more thoughtful about recruiting students. More vigorous work in the recruitment vineyards can also be linked to the establishment of collaborative arrangements with colleagues in schools and school districts to identify quality candidates. These partnerships are both a motivating force in and an outcome of the quest to strengthen recruitment in educational leadership programs.

Finally, although harder to pin down, part of the new proactive stance in the area of student recruitment results from enhanced clarity about program goals and conceptions of leadership undergirding individual preparation programs. There is a perception among some respondents that their departments are arriving at more coherent and more shared understandings of leadership as well as more robust knowledge about experiences necessary to nurture leadership among students (see 2p, Table 7.1). As they do so, the picture of the type of student who fits that vision becomes much clearer. In turn, some programs are being more aggressive in seeking out these types of students rather than simply waiting for the traditional drop-in trade. It is important to emphasize that these visions of good leadership and portraits of appropriate students vary across the programs. Some seek out students with demonstrated leadership experience in schools, whereas others deliberately cast a wider net, looking for nontraditional, and in some cases maverick, candidates. The key ingredient seems to be the clarity of perspective in the department. It is this dimension of the department that encourages active recruitment.

In closing, it is noteworthy that although still not heavily emphasized, recruitment is being connected to funding issues in ways not on the radar screen in the 1989 data. A number of programs have entered into collaborative arrangements with school districts that help defray the costs of schooling for students. At least four other departments have established scholarships to assist with recruitment.

Selection

In the area of selection, there is evidence of strengthened standards and greater selectivity, claims made directly by about a quarter of the respondents and indirectly by a considerable number of others. Addressing standards, department heads outlined some places where traditional selection measures such as grade point average and Graduate Record Examination scores had been ratcheted up.

More important, chairs spoke quite forcefully about what might best be thought of as a revitalization of existing selection measures and a broadening of the portfolio of selection tools. In this regard, there seemed to be movement on a number of fronts at the same time. In some places, there appeared to be greater coherence about the relevant mix of measures to be employed in the selection process as well as renewed commitment to employ these tools in a thoughtful fashion in the service of collecting and assessing information about candidates. Personal interviews, examples of written work, and documentation of leadership experiences were all privileged in the responses. There is a sense in these responses that chairs saw a shift from the use of screening tools as rituals to fill slots to the use of screening tools as part of more holistic and vibrant systems of measures for securing more able students.

At the same time, the key issue, as with recruitment, seems to be the thoughtful use of a variety of measures deemed appropriate at a given institution rather than the identification of a particular list of indexes. In some cases, assessment center exercises were employed. In other departments, more traditional measures were used. The essential ingredient appears to be commitment by the faculty to a comprehensive set of measures that is consistent with the demands and expectations of their various programs.

Turning to results, there is some evidence that this more proactive attention to selection helped programs attract candidates that the departments believed were better qualified for graduate study than their peers of a decade earlier. There is also evidence that in at least three programs, selectivity in numerical terms had been enhanced. That is, they were consciously admitting fewer students and a smaller percentage of applicants than they had previously.

Type (Mix) of Students

In our earlier study (Murphy, 1991), we asked colleagues about changes in the mix of students in their program, a concept that caused considerable confusion. In this study, we relabeled the item "type of students" and were rewarded with much richer data in return. Although the responses here covered a good deal of ground, three themes stood out. Chairs told us that the composition of their graduate programs was more diverse than it was a decade before. Four respondents spoke of enhanced diversity in general terms, whereas increased enrollments of women and racial minorities were noted by six and eleven respondents, respectively. Chairs also informed us that the profile of the average student had changed somewhat. Five colleagues reported directly that students were stronger academically, whereas others commented on their sense that students appeared to be more critical and more willing to take risks than did students in the mid-1980s. Finally, there is evidence that at least a few of the programs have more nontraditional students—those from a wider range of educational backgrounds and from outside the mainstream—than has been the case in the past.

Course Content and Clinical Experiences

> *Five years ago we totally reworked our doctoral program—from a*
> *shopping-mall to a cohort, structured sequence of courses. For the*
> *past two years we have been overhauling our Masters and*
> *Professional Diploma (entry-level) programs, bringing some*
> *integration of themes as well as more on-site assignments to every*
> *course.* (Chair)

> *We have required more variety in clinical experiences than we did a*
> *decade ago. We monitor the clinical experiences more closely, and*
> *we are more explicit about what we expect students to have experi-*
> *enced. We also include more clinical experiences in our classes as*
> *opposed to just our internships.* (Chair)

Analysts of the condition of the curriculum that defined preparation programs
in the 1970s and 1980s were generally quite critical (see Murphy, 1992, for
a review). Reviewers also did not discern much interest on the part of faculty
to engage in systemic curricular revision (McCarthy et al., 1988). By 1989,
however, department heads told us that some important alterations had taken
place in the curricular and clinical areas in response to reform pressures in
the larger environment. As can be seen in Items 2d and 2e in Table 7.2, of all
the topic areas assessed, heads reported that the largest amount of change had
occurred in the curriculum provided (3.21) and the clinical experiences offered (3.01) in their departments. In the most recent round of data collection
(1996), they claimed that the earlier reform work was continuing, a position
supported by the statistical analysis presented in Table 7.2.

Course Content

In their replies to the open-ended part of the question on course content,
unit heads sketched out revisions on an array of topics, although commonali-
ties are difficult to discern. The one clear theme was program change and
development. In some cases, this was reflected in the revision of courses to
make them more current or to bring them into line with emerging reform
themes. More often, it was seen in more molar changes; that is, more comprehensive overhaul of programs. There was also some suggestion that the
integration of program content and the sequencing of courses were receiving
attention—trends that were already evident in the 1989 responses. Turning
to content areas, five were highlighted as receiving additional emphasis in at
least three programs: policy and politics (5); ethics and values (4); student

learning/student outcomes (3); diversity (3); and research methodology, especially qualitative methods (3).

A number of points merit comment here. First, in the earlier study, none of the five content areas just listed reached even the low threshold level employed here. Second, with two notable exceptions, these findings are in line with the changes chronicled by program heads in the recent McCarthy and Kuh (1997) study. Third, those two exceptions are striking. In the McCarthy and Kuh investigation, in addressing curriculum changes over the past decade, technology and new conceptions of leadership were the content areas most heavily underscored. In this study, there was a resounding silence on the issue of technology as a content area, although, as we describe later, there was a good deal of attention to technology as a delivery method. Program heads also had little to say about leadership. Whereas a strengthening of the leadership component of preparation programs was the strongest content theme in the earlier study, it did not stand out in the 1996 responses. Finally, certain issues, such as critical theory and feminist theory, were rarely referenced.

Clinical Experiences

Program heads also suggested that a considerable amount of change had occurred in the clinical components (3.86) of their departments over the past few years. Two patterns lace the replies to the open-ended question about shifts afoot in this dimension of UCEA–based preparation programs. First, the focus on clinically based experiences in these programs has increased; there has been a significant increase in the role of fieldwork in administrator preparation. This enhancement can best be characterized as the strengthening of the full array of clinical components, from class-based activities to full-blown internships.

To begin with, department chairs argued that their programs are working to integrate clinical experiences into university-based courses in new ways, that "clinical experiences are becoming a regular part of all courses." There are also assertions of greater use of real-world problems in coursework. The firewall between field activities and university coursework is being dismantled in many programs—clinical experiences are being "integrated into the cohort sequence, rather than [existing] in stand-alone fashion." At the same time, it appears that traditional practicum activities are being fortified. More time is being devoted to the practicum, and it is being done in a more thoughtful fashion. Finally, and consistent with recent NCATE guidelines, it is clear that the internship is being lengthened and deepened throughout these UCEA–

based programs. The overall effect is that these programs are taking the clinical dimension of preparation programs more seriously than they did when the theory era of school administration was coming to an end in the early 1980s. Consequently, these clinical components comprise a larger percentage of the program completed by today's students.

The second theme can be characterized as an upgrading of the quality of the expanded clinical component of preparation programs. Across the programs, unit heads outlined a plethora of methods that they and their colleagues are employing to improve field-based experiences, including providing more structure to assignments, especially in terms of expectations about what students need to learn; increasing the amount and the quality of faculty supervision; ensuring greater involvement of site supervisors; integrating field experiences and academic offerings more effectively; developing better forums for students to debrief on clinical experiences and to reflect on their learning; creating better systems of mentor advisors; establishing more diverse field-based learning opportunities; and monitoring clinical experiences more closely.

In general, personal assessments provided by these unit heads suggest that considerable energy is being devoted to revising the learning components of preparation programs, at least at UCEA institutions. There is also evidence that these efforts are leading to significant and important changes. The comprehensive overhauls regularly noted in the responses do begin to address the fundamental question of what knowledge should anchor our programs, at least at the molecular level of the individual department. Although this is likely to prove insufficient, it is a much better state than the one that existed in the mid-1980s when McCarthy and her colleagues (1988) found little evidence of faculty enthusiasm for curricular reform.

At the same time, it seems that programs have begun to seriously address the well-documented weaknesses and nearly intractable problems that have plagued the clinical component of preparation programs for the past 30 years. A much more aggressive integration of field-based activities into traditional university-based classes has been an especially noteworthy achievement in these programs over the past decade. The continuation of the earlier efforts of the late 1980s to extend and deepen clinical work and to upgrade the quality of field-based experiences also deserves to be acknowledged. The one area in which the data fail to provide much information is the nature of the clinical experiences themselves. We need better information at a micro level about the activities in which students in these longer and improved field experiences are actually engaged.

Teaching and Monitoring Student Progress

> *We have developed a much more active learning philosophy in the
> department.* (Chair)

> *Candidates develop portfolios of their work which are reviewed at
> regular intervals by their mentors and other experienced practition-
> ers.* (Chair)

As the 1980s came to a close, analyses of pedagogy in educational administrator preparation programs concluded that there was ample room for improvement. In most departments, instruction was provided in learning formats and
through instructional approaches least conducive to learning (American Association of Colleges for Teacher Education, 1988; Erlandson & Witters-
Churchill, 1988; Nunnery, 1982). Teaching in school administration training
programs suffered from a numbing dullness of boring and routinized delivery practices.

Monitoring of student progress in many preparation programs also left
much to be desired. Assessments of progress at the key junctures of students'
programs were either absent or conducted in a perfunctory fashion. In most
programs, meaningful competency tests on needed skills were conspicuous
by their absence. A standards-free, nonjudgmental attitude pervaded many
departments of school administration. Performance criteria were ill-defined,
and little monitoring occurred.

Against this backdrop, department administrators described a quite dramatic change in the teaching and learning strategies employed in their preparation programs over the past few years, moving from a mean score of 2.51
in 1989 to 3.63 in 1996 (see 2f, Table 7.2). In the area of monitoring/assess-
ing student progress, they reported more moderate but still significant progress,
rising from a mean of 2.54 in 1989 to 3.23 in 1996 (see 2c, Table 7.2).

Teaching

Although not gainsaying the continued prevalence of traditional "talk and
chalk" methods, unit heads suggested that instruction in UCEA–based departments was richer and more multidimensional in 1996 than it was when
the original calls for strengthening preparation programs were released in the
mid-to-late 1980s. Most noteworthy was the claim that departments were in-
fusing more authentic material and more thoughtful and reflective methods
into programs. Undergirding this shift was an enhanced focus on active learning and a renewed interest in the raw material of practice. This trend played

out most prominently in assertions that programs were employing more case-study inquiry (4) and more problem-based learning strategies (8).

Greater emphasis on the use of technology was also spotlighted. Some of it addressed the expanded use of distance learning (5), almost all of which focused on the delivery of off-campus instruction. Much of it, however, was directed to using technology to strengthen instruction inside the classroom (9), including the use of interactive television, the Internet and e-mail, and computer simulations.

Finally, there was a bundle of changes related to the organization and delivery of program content. Chairs maintained that students were engaging in more group work (6) than their peers of earlier generations. Program administrators also related that team teaching was becoming more prevalent (6) and that there was a more deliberate use of practitioners in the instructional process (3). Finally, and somewhat obliquely, respondents noted considerable reliance on the use of off-campus programs.

In closing, it is instructive to compare the situation in 1996 with the 1989 data. In the earlier study (Murphy, 1991), in concluding our analysis of instruction, we stated "that instructional issues continue to lurk in the background, that the critical mass of attention required to galvanize the collective energy of the profession around issues of teaching [had] not yet been reached" (p. 57). This no longer seems to be the case. The findings in the current study support the conclusion of McCarthy and Kuh (1997) that "educational leadership faculty members, particularly at UCEA programs, seem to have a renewed interest in teaching" (p. 245). The one area in our earlier investigation where there was noticeable energy in the area of teaching was in the application of more practice-anchored material—greater reliance on the "stuff" of practice, if you will. That area continued to be highlighted in the current study. Unlike the earlier report, however, in which discussion of technology was quite limited, technology-based instruction shared center stage in the current study.

Monitoring Student Progress

Analysis of the open-ended responses reveals only two themes. First, nine programs had introduced the application of portfolios over the past few years. Whereas most respondents simply noted the addition of portfolios, some were very specific in describing how they were being used. In one case, portfolios provided the culminating assessment at the completion of each thematic unit. At a second university, portfolios replaced the comprehensive examination for the master's degree. At a third institution, the portfolios provided a running record of students' progress—progress that was evaluated annually.

Second, an extra layer of assessment was added in seven programs. This enhanced scrutiny, which was most noticeable at the doctoral level, took a variety of forms. The most common were the use of a regularly scheduled review at an early stage in the academic program to evaluate the progress of students and the addition of a piece of the qualifying examination earlier in the career of students than has been the norm in preparation programs.

As with teaching strategies, it is interesting to examine the differences between responses in 1989 and 1996. In the early data, unit heads reported the largest increase in monitoring connected with the clinical components of programs. This type of monitoring was discussed by only two heads in 1996. In the 1989 data, the link between external forces such as state legislation or the actions of state agencies and enhanced monitoring of students was underscored. That was not the case here. References to portfolios that marked the 1996 replies were largely absent in the 1989 responses.

University-School Relations

We have an advisory board of practitioners. . . . We report to them each year how we have responded to their suggestions. (Chair)

Faculty involvement in schools is . . . individualistic, not programmatic. (Chair)

In his insightful essay on the study of educational administration, Carver (1988) designated "the absence of any meaningful coupling between the training arm and the employment agents [as] the point in the fabric of educational administration where the threads are weakest" (p. 6). To ascertain what preparation programs were doing to address this critical problem, we asked four interrelated questions. Two assessed the role of practitioners in preparation program development and delivery; two others measured faculty involvement with practitioners, working with them in the schools and providing them with professional development services. The questions were designed to overlap and to provide information on these issues from multiple perspectives.

Chairs reported that their departments had undertaken some, but generally not extensive, alterations in each of the two sub-areas—although they were more active in bringing administrators into their fold than they were in entering the world of practice. As noted in Table 7.2, the involvement of practitioners in the development of preparation programs rose from 2.96 in 1989 to 3.18 in 1996 (see Item 2h). On the other hand, involvement of administrators in the delivery of learning experiences saw a quite significant increase, climbing from 2.46 to 3.34 between 1989 and 1996 (see Item 2i). Involvement of university faculty in schools and with services for practicing administrators advanced only slightly, moving from 2.57 to 2.93 and 2.44 to 2.63, respectively (see Items 2j and 2l).

Practitioner Involvement in Preparation Programs

Development. Chairs reported moderate practitioner involvement in the design and development of preparation programs. At the same time, there is considerable inactivity in many departments. Indeed, a good number of program heads had little to say on the issue. A number of others touched not on development but on delivery issues (e.g., principals serving as adjunct professors). Concomitantly, however, analysis reveals that the profession may be poised to create more meaningful opportunities for school administrators to take a central role in helping to design training programs. A handful of chairs highlighted this as a focus area for their departments in the near future.

Where it does occur, practitioner participation in program development takes on a variety of forms. On the weak end of the involvement continuum, some universities "call groups of practitioners together from time to time" to gather feedback about department operations. In the middle of the spectrum, where the bulk of programs are situated, department heads report using more formalized "advisory boards" to "get input about the program." One end of the middle section of the continuum is anchored by institutions with advisory councils that meet once a year. The other end is defined by more formalized policy boards that assemble three or four times each year. The strong end of the continuum is characterized by collaborative partnerships. Although not heavily underscored by respondents, when they do occur, they tend to extend the traditional adviser and reactor roles of principals and superintendents. They allow school administrators to assume more active roles in program development, working collaboratively with university faculty to design and build the infrastructure for preparation programs rather than simply evaluating completed training models.

Delivery. As noted above, UCEA chairs told of a significant increase in the use of practitioners in the instructional realm of preparation programs. More than half of these men and women provided descriptions of how school leaders were engaged in teaching activities. Overwhelmingly, principals and superintendents were engaged as adjunct professors or as part-time instructors to teach specific courses, especially "practice-related courses" such as school facilities and the principalship. Lingering in the background of the responses was a feeling that although much of this instructional activity was in the service of linking the practice and academic domains of the profession, some of it was arising because of limited resources at the university level. Given the short-answer nature of the replies, it was difficult to develop a sense of the integrativeness of this instruction with the teaching activities of the regular faculty.

Two other trends emerged from the narratives. First, chairs indicated that practitioners were being employed in the clinical domains of the educational program, especially as clinical supervisors and mentors. Second, team teaching was highlighted. Unlike in the adjunct instructional model described above, team teaching paired a principal or superintendent and a university professor in the creation and delivery of a specific class.

Faculty Involvement in Schools

Work in schools. As defined in this study, there is a moderate amount of involvement of university professors in the public schools. The increase in participation from 1989 to 1996—a time during which, as detailed above, UCEA institutions saw fairly dramatic changes in the core technology of preparation programs and in the types of students populating these programs—was relatively slight. Although a number of unit heads chronicled faculty connections to public schools, linkages were highly individualistic in nature. Beyond required practicum supervision, most connections were formed on the basis of the interests of particular professors. Stated alternatively, in only a handful of places did faculty involvement appear to be informed by department frameworks or goals or by formalized arrangements between a department and one or more schools or districts. Neither were there any references to efforts "to exchange professional and [school] administrative assignments" (NPBEA, 1989, p. 22), as suggested in the NCEEA and NPBEA reports. In UCEA programs of school leadership, there does not appear to be an analog for the types of linkages between teacher educators and practicing teachers fostered by professional development schools. Nor is it clear that other arrangements that produce more planful and concentrated involvement of faculty in public schools are emerging.

Services to school administrators. With a couple of noteworthy exceptions, services provided by universities for practicing school administrators looked fairly traditional. In particular, the offering of professional development workshops, institutes, seminars, and conferences was emphasized. As was the case for faculty involvement in schools, much of this activity seemed to be based on the initiative of selected faculty members rather than in response to a departmental plan. However, chairs did provide some clues about the power of services provided to practitioners within partnerships with schools, districts, and state agencies and in the context of established forums, centers, and academies. This cluster of partnerships and centers appears to offer the possibility of more sustained, mutual engagement on problems of practice.

Departmental Structure and Operations

We are actively working on a Long-Range Plan, which, unlike previous initiatives of this genre, may actually prove to be a continuing foundation for program development. (Chair)

Our department has lost two tenure lines in the past ten years. We are doing lots more with less. At the present, we are pretty well stretched to the limit. (Chair)

Five questions were designed to assess changes in the structure and operation of UCEA departments since the release of the NCEEA report in 1987. Unit heads reported fairly robust changes in the missions of their departments, from 2.82 in 1989 to 3.60 in 1996 (see 2p, Table 7.2). Statistically significant shifts were also noted in the areas of departmental staffing and faculty development opportunities (see 2n and 2o, respectively, in Table 7.2). More moderate changes were noted in the domains of faculty selection and degree structure (see 2m and 2g, respectively, in Table 7.2).

Department Mission

The major pattern emerging from the replies of the department heads is action. There is a strong sense of change in the missions of these UCEA–based programs. A few chairs described how external forces such as competition from neighboring institutions or mandates from the state influenced revisions of their departmental agendas. Three others explained how having the educational administration program embedded in a larger organizational unit constrained the development of a focused mission in the area of leadership. The only theme in the changes was a new, or in some cases renewed, commitment to the practice dimension of the profession (see also Staffing and Degree Structure below). Although other responses were scattered, they were almost always consistent with the reform vision spotlighted in the NCEEA (1987) and the NPBEA (1989) documents (e.g., a focus on urban education, and greater attention to the intellectual and moral aspects of leadership).

Staffing

For purposes of analysis, we combined the items on selection of faculty (2m) and department staffing (2n). Two powerful themes emerged. First, there was a palpable sense of loss. Thirteen administrators reported reductions in faculty lines that were not offset by new hires. Only two colleagues listed increases in faculty positions. These reports are consistent with the conclusions of McCarthy and Kuh (1997), who found that UCEA institutions had 0.5 fewer faculty members in 1994 than they did in 1986. Second, the value of experience as a practitioner had increased in saliency in the faculty selection algorithm. Whereas three heads described a shift from a field orientation toward a research focus, nine others reported a bias toward faculty with field experience. A third, but much weaker, theme—one noted by only four chairs—was enhanced attention to faculty diversity, what one respondent labeled "greater diversity in race, gender, ethnicity, and thought."

Faculty Development Opportunities

Although there has been a noticeable increase in development opportunities for faculty over the past decade, the professional development cupboard in these programs remains fairly bare. The only specific topic that was mentioned multiple times (6) was professional development in the area of technology. Most of the answers concentrated on the provision of funding for faculty members to attend professional conferences. A couple of chairs noted a constriction in such funding, whereas others described small increases in these professional development resources. Of the cases when dollar figures were provided, none could be considered generous allotments.

What one sees very little of in these comments are the criteria of quality professional development enshrined in the scholarship in this area. With a few distinct exceptions, nearly all of the professional development opportunities outlined were individualistic in nature (e.g., an individual professor attending a conference to deliver a paper or to learn from others presenting their research). Very little of it seemed to be organizationally anchored; instead, it was determined by individual faculty interests rather than department or program goals. Likewise, again with a few clear exceptions, very few of the professional development experiences were linked to the continuous work of building stronger educational administration programs—the type of improvement work that is at the heart of professional development for school-based educators. Finally, there was almost no sense of continuity of experiences. With one or two powerful exceptions (e.g., a series of nine workshops on technology in one program), development activities were almost uniformly ad hoc in nature.

Degree Structure

There was only a moderate change in the degree structures in these UCEA–based educational administration programs. Fewer than half of the participants completed the open-ended part of this question, and many who did respond focused more on program structure (e.g., the use of cohort groups) than on the ways degrees were structured. For the most part, answers were scattered. The only issue that appeared multiple times (5) was one that was evident in the earlier study (Murphy, 1991) as well. It might best be described as a sharpening of the distinctions between the PhD degree for academic careers and the EdD degree for practitioners, with a concomitant rededication of programs toward preparation for practice.

Notes

1. Some of the best of these stories can be found in the now defunct bulletin of the National Policy Board for Educational Administration, *DESIGNS for Leadership*. Approximately 25 issues of *DESIGNS* were printed between 1990 and 1996. Each issue points the reader to one or more programs engaged in program reform. A particularly thoughtful set of chronicles for nine of these programs can be found in *Preparing Tomorrow's School Leaders: Alternative Designs* (Murphy, 1993b). See also Milstein (1993), Muth, Murphy, and Martin (1994), and Van Meter and Scollay (1995). Recent annual meeting programs from AERA, NCPEA, and UCEA provide additional examples of the individual programs that have overhauled their preparation programs.

2. See, for example, Barnett and Muse (1993) and Basom, Yerkes, Norris, and Barnett (1996).

3. See, in particular, McCarthy (in press), Murphy (1993a), Willower (1988), and the Forsyth and Murphy, Hart and Pounder, and Van Meter chapters of this volume.

4. See, for example, Leithwood, Jantzi, Coffin, and Wilson (1996), McCarthy and Kuh (1997), Murphy (1991), and Norton and Levan (1987).

References

American Association of Colleges for Teacher Education. (1988). *School leadership preparation: A preface for action.* Washington, DC: Author.

Barnett, B. G., & Muse, I. D. (1993). Cohort groups in educational administration. *Journal of School Leadership, 3,* 400-415.

Basom, M., Yerkes, D., Norris, C., & Barnett, B. (1996, January). Using cohorts as a means for developing transformational leaders. *Journal of School Leadership, 6,* 99-112.

Carver, F. D. (1988, June). *The evaluation of the study of educational administration.* Paper presented at the Educational Administration Alumni Association Allerton House Conference, University of Illinois at Urbana—Champaign.

Erlandson, D. A., & Witters-Churchill, L. (1988, March). *Design of the Texas NASSP study.* Paper presented at the annual meeting of the National Association of Secondary School Principals.

Griffiths, D. E. (1988). *Educational administration: Reform PDQ or RIP* (Occasional paper, No. 8312). Tempe, AZ: UCEA.

Leithwood, K., Jantzi, D., Coffin, G., & Wilson, P. (1996, May). Preparing school leaders: What works? *Journal of School Leadership, 6,* 316-342.

McCarthy, M. M. (in press). The evolution of educational leadership preparation programs. In J. Murphy & K. S. Louis (Eds.), *Handbook of research on educational administration.* Washington, DC: American Educational Research Association.

McCarthy, M. M., & Kuh, G. D. (1997). *Continuity and change: The educational leadership professoriate.* Columbia, MO: UCEA.

McCarthy, M. M., Kuh, G. D., Newell, L. J., & Iacona, C. M. (1988). *Under scrutiny: The educational administration professoriate.* Tempe, AZ: UCEA.

Milstein, M. M., & Associates. (1993). *Changing the way we prepare educational leaders: The Danforth experience.* Newbury Park, CA: Corwin.

Murphy, J. (1989). Effects of educational reform on programs of school administration in Illinois. *Administrator's Notebook, 33*(3), 1-4.

Murphy, J. (1990). The educational reform movement of the 1980s: A comprehensive analysis. In J. Murphy (Ed.), *The reform of American public education in the 1980s: Perspectives and cases* (pp. 3-55). Berkeley, CA: McCutchan.

Murphy, J. (1991, Spring). The effects of the educational reform movement on departments of educational leadership. *Educational Evaluation and Policy Analysis, 13*(1), 49-65.

Murphy, J. (1992). *The landscape of leadership preparation: Reforming the education of school administrators.* Newbury Park, CA: Corwin.

Murphy, J. (1993a). Alternative designs: New directions. In J. Murphy (Ed.), *Preparing tomorrow's school leaders: Alternative designs* (pp. 225-253). University Park, PA: UCEA.

Murphy, J. (Ed.). (1993b). *Preparing tomorrow's school leaders: Alternative designs.* University Park, PA: UCEA.

Muth, R., Murphy, M. J., & Martin, W. M. (1994). Problem-based learning at the University of Colorado at Denver. *Journal of School Leadership, 4*, 432-450.

National Commission on Excellence in Educational Administration. (1987). *Leaders for America's schools.* Tempe, AZ: UCEA.

National Policy Board for Educational Administration. (1989). *Improving the preparation of school administrators: The reform agenda.* Charlottesville, VA: Author.

Norton, M. S., & Levan, F. D. (1987). Doctoral studies of students in educational administration programs in UCEA member institutions. *Educational Considerations, 14*(1), 21-24.

Nunnery, M. Y. (1982). Reform of K-12 educational administrator preparation: Some basic questions. *Journal of Research and Development in Education, 15*(2), 44-51.

Van Meter, E. J., & Scollay, S. J. (1995, November). Curriculum revision in educational leadership: An institutional case record and retrospective commentary. *Journal of School Leadership, 5*, 512-531.

Willower, D. J. (1988). Synthesis and projection. In N. J. Boyan (Ed.), *Handbook of research on educational administration* (pp. 729-747). New York: Longman.

8

The "Changing" Face of the Educational Leadership Professoriate

MARTHA M. MCCARTHY

Exemplary leaders are needed to bring about fundamental changes in our nation's schools. Because the vast majority of school administrators have advanced degrees in educational leadership, a crucial step in effecting school reform is transforming the preparation of educational leaders. Unfortunately, increasingly strident criticisms have been directed toward the quality of university preparation programs for school leaders and the caliber of faculty staffing these programs (Griffiths, 1988; Heller, Conway, & Jacobson, 1988; Murphy, 1993a). There is considerable sentiment that universities have been part of the problem rather than instigators of reform.

Given that preservice programs leading to licensure for school administrators are likely to remain the domain of universities—at least for the foreseeable future—educational leadership faculty members will continue to play a key role in determining how future school leaders in our nation are prepared to assume their roles. Developments external to universities, such as the adoption of state and national standards and assessment programs for school administrators (see Council of Chief State School Officers, 1996), certainly have the potential to influence the content and structure of preservice programs, but fundamental transformations are unlikely to take place without substantial commitment from rank-and-file faculty members.

AUTHOR'S NOTE: This chapter is based on the Cocking Lecture, which was delivered at the National Council of Professors of Educational Administration Conference in Vail, Colorado, August 13, 1997, and will be published in the 1998 NCPEA yearbook (McCarthy, 1998).

To gauge the capacity and readiness of educational leadership faculty to undertake such a task, we must understand their characteristics, activities, and attitudes.

This chapter summarizes the results of a comprehensive study of the educational leadership professoriate in the United States and Canada conducted in 1994 (McCarthy & Kuh, 1997). The study was designed in part to replicate studies conducted in 1972 (Campbell & Newell, 1973) and 1986 (McCarthy, Kuh, Newell, & Iacona, 1988) so that longitudinal comparisons could be made. The 1994 study was sponsored by the National Council of Professors of Educational Administration (NCPEA) and the University Council for Educational Administration (UCEA) with support from the Danforth Foundation, the American Educational Research Association/National Center for Education Statistics/National Science Foundation Grants Program, and Indiana University.

The study entailed two strands: (a) a survey of program heads regarding educational unit size, structure, and composition;[1] and (b) a survey of individual faculty members to ascertain their characteristics, activities, and attitudes. This chapter focuses primarily on the faculty survey in which a random sample of 940 faculty members from 371 universities was surveyed.[2] The first section of this chapter presents a profile of educational leadership faculty members in 1994 and highlights changes in characteristics, activities, and attitudes over time. The second section addresses several trends and their implications for educational leadership units and for the preparation of school administrators in the United States. The concluding section explores the prognosis for reform of educational leadership preparation programs. Throughout this chapter, the term "educational leadership" is used to refer to "school administration," "school leadership," or "educational administration" faculty members and units.

Profile of Educational Leadership Faculty Members

From the 1970s to the 1990s, the educational leadership professoriate has reflected both stability and change. The typical unit offering graduate degrees in educational leadership in 1994 had 5.6 full-time faculty members, slightly more faculty members than in the mid-1980s ($M = 5.0$; McCarthy et al., 1988) but fewer than in the mid-1970s ($M = 6.5$; Davis, 1978). Although the mean number of faculty members per educational leadership unit has remained fairly constant since 1986, the modal number increased from only two in 1986 to five in 1994. Nevertheless, about two fifths of the educational leadership units in 1994 had fewer than five full-time faculty members, the minimum number considered necessary to adequately staff educational leadership preparation programs (National Commission on Excellence in Educational Administration, 1987; National Policy Board for Educational Administration, 1989).

The increase in the number of faculty between the mid-1980s and mid-1990s was primarily a function of an expansion in faculty positions at comprehensive universities;[3] educational leadership units at research institutions continued to decline slightly in faculty size. In 1994, comprehensive universities, which have limited doctoral offerings, housed more than half of all educational leadership units and more than two fifths of all faculty members and students enrolled in graduate degree programs. When units that offer only administrative certification courses are also considered, the proportion of school leaders prepared by comprehensive universities increases substantially (McCarthy, in press).

About 40% of the 1994 educational leadership faculty respondents said they were hired within the preceding decade, indicating that there has been a substantial influx of new faculty members. More than one fifth (21%) of the 1994 respondents entered the professoriate within the prior 5 years (new faculty), whereas only 14% of the 1986 respondents were new faculty. Given the number of anticipated retirements, continued faculty turnover seems assured into the 21st century. New faculty in 1994 were overrepresented at comprehensive universities and programs not affiliated with the UCEA, consistent with the finding that non–UCEA programs and those at comprehensive universities have increased in size since the mid-1980s. However, even though UCEA programs and those at research universities have downsized slightly, they still have more faculty members than do other units.

Personal and Professional Characteristics

Certain characteristics of educational leadership faculty members have changed markedly since the early 1970s. The most significant change pertains to female representation in the professoriate; the percentage of women faculty increased tenfold between 1972 (2%) and 1994 (20%).[4] Almost two fifths of the faculty hired between 1984 and 1994 were women. This dramatic influx of women into the professoriate seems to be slowing, however, because the number of women hired in the 5-year period prior to 1994 (39%) was only slightly higher than the number appointed 6 to 10 years earlier (37%).

Among new faculty members in 1994, female representation varied significantly by type of institution and UCEA affiliation. More than half of the new educational leadership faculty members at research institutions (53%) and in UCEA programs (60%) in 1994 were women, whereas women comprised only one fourth of the new faculty at comprehensive institutions and one third of the faculty in non–UCEA programs.

Although not as dramatic as the increase in female faculty members, minority representation increased almost fourfold from 1972 (3%) until 1994 (11%). In 1994, minority representation was higher in units at comprehensive universities and those not affiliated with UCEA than in UCEA units and those at research and doctoral universities. The prospects for race equity do not seem as bright as the prospects for gender equity in educational leadership units. It was disappointing that in 1994, minority representation among those hired during the prior 5 years (10%) was smaller than among faculty hired in the preceding 6- to 10-year period (15%). Unlike the findings in 1986, when minority representation was considerably higher among new than among veteran faculty, the intermediate cohort in 1994 (hired between 1984 and 1989) reflected the highest proportion of people of color. This is worrisome because it is difficult to imagine that the educational leadership profession can respond effectively to the changing demographics of American schools and prepare future leaders for those schools without a racially and ethnically diverse professoriate.

As to rank distribution in 1994, the proportions of faculty members at each rank were more similar to data gathered in 1972 than in 1986. The share of faculty at the assistant professor rank declined from 17% in 1972 to 10% in 1986 and then increased to 15% in 1994. Half of the faculty members were professors in 1972 compared to 59% in 1986 and 54% in 1994. Educational leadership units continue to be top-heavy with professors compared with other disciplines; across academe at comprehensive, doctoral, and research universities in 1993, 41% of the faculty members had attained the rank of professor (National Survey of Postsecondary Faculty, 1993). Almost three fourths (74%) of the educational leadership faculty members had attained tenure in 1994, with an average of 14 years since tenure was granted.

The educational professoriate was older in 1994 than in the early 1970s; that is, the typical educational leadership faculty member in 1994 (M age = 54) was 6 years older than his or her counterpart in 1972 (M age = 48). Faculty members hired within the preceding 5 years in 1994 were, on average, 9 years older when they entered the professorship (M age = 45), compared to faculty with more than 10 years of experience in academe, who entered the professoriate at an average age of 34.

One third of the total 1994 respondents had served as school administrators before joining the professoriate. New faculty (45%) were far more likely than senior faculty members (28%) to have administrative experience, which explains in part why new educational leadership faculty members are entering academe at an older age. Faculty who had been school administrators were disproportionately employed at comprehensive universities. Indeed, of the new faculty *with* administrative experience in 1994, 57% were at comprehensive universities, compared to 24% and 19% at doctoral and research universities, respectively. In contrast, almost one half of the new faculty *without* administrative experience (47%) were employed at research institutions, compared to 22% at doctoral and 31% at comprehensive universities. More than one half of the new faculty in non–UCEA programs, compared to one fourth of the new faculty in UCEA programs, had administrative experience. Recently hired male faculty (54%) also were more likely than their female peers (30%) to have been school administrators.

In terms of compensation, educational leadership faculty members as a group appeared to have lost ground during the past decade, compared with faculty in other disciplines. Campbell and Newell (1973) reported that educational leadership faculty members in 1972 were well paid. McCarthy et al. (1988) also reported that salaries in educational leadership units compared favorably with those in other areas in 1986. But the 1993 National Survey of Postsecondary Faculty (NSOPF) indicated that faculty across disciplines made, on average, over $7,000 more than educational leadership faculty members in 1993. Of course, within the educational leadership professoriate, there were significant salary differences by type of institution, with faculty at research universities typically making $8,000 more than faculty at comprehensive universities ($57,000 compared to $49,000).

An unexpected finding in 1994 was that the gender-based salary differences documented in previous studies of educational leadership faculty members had been eliminated when controlling for rank and length of time in academe. This is particularly gratifying, given that faculty salaries across disciplines still reflect a gender discrepancy in compensation (Magner, 1996).

Professional Activities and Preferences

Many responses pertaining to professional activities and preferences remained quite similar across the 1972, 1986, and 1994 cohorts. As in previous studies, the most enjoyable aspect of the professorial role was teaching graduate students, the most preferred periodical was the *Kappan*, and the most important professional organization was the American Educational

Research Association (AERA). Another constant between 1986 and 1994 was the least enjoyable facet of the professorship: faculty governance activities.

Also similar to prior studies, the largest proportion of faculty members' time in 1994 was devoted to teaching and advising graduate students, with two graduate courses per term the typical teaching load. The difference in average teaching loads of faculty members at comprehensive and research universities was reduced from almost two credit hours per term in 1986 to one credit hour in 1994. Overall, the average amount of time that educational leadership faculty devoted to teaching declined between 1986 and 1994, primarily because teaching loads for faculty at comprehensive universities were lower in 1994, and a larger number of faculty did not have teaching assignments because of administrative roles or funded research projects.

Only two of the content areas recommended by the National Policy Board for Educational Administration (NPBEA) for inclusion in leadership preparation programs were among the most frequently reported content specializations of faculty members in 1994: leadership and organizational theory. Leadership was the most frequently mentioned specialization of the 1994 respondents; 16% listed this as their primary focus. The only other topic listed by more than 10% of the 1994 respondents was school law (13%). A small fraction of faculty members specialized in the board-recommended areas of societal and cultural influences on schooling, teaching and learning processes and school improvement, methodologies of organizational studies and policy analysis, policy studies and politics of education, and the moral and ethical dimensions of schooling. Even though few faculty members listed ethics as their area of primary specialization, the 1994 respondents did strongly support giving greater emphasis to ethics in leadership preparation.

Fewer gender-based differences in content specializations were found in 1994 than in 1986. For example, in 1986, female faculty were far more likely than male faculty to specialize in organizational theory (25% compared to 14%) and far less likely to specialize in economics or finance (1% compared to 8%). By 1994, women were somewhat more likely than men to consider economics or finance their primary specialization (10% compared to 7%) and slightly less likely to specialize in organizational theory (8% compared to 9%). The specializations of women moved more in line with those of men between the two studies.

The content specializations of faculty members in 1994 for the most part mirrored traditional course areas included in leadership preparation programs, which is consistent with the findings of prior studies (Norton, 1992; Pohland & Carlson, 1993). In part, this is due to the strong influence that state certification requirements have on the curriculum by requiring coursework in traditional areas (e.g., law, finance, organizational theory, supervision) for individuals to be certified as school administrators.

Scholarly productivity of educational leadership faculty members, reflected by the mean numbers of books, monographs, articles, and chapters produced, has increased steadily since 1965 (Campbell & Newell, 1973; Hills, 1965; McCarthy & Kuh, 1997), even though comparisons with faculty across disciplines remain unfavorable (NSOPF, 1993). The proportion of educational leadership faculty members involved in research increased from 50% in 1965 (Hills, 1965) to 85% in 1994. On average, faculty members in 1994 had written or edited (either alone or with colleagues) 8.6 books or monographs in their careers and had written 12.6 articles or chapters within the preceding 5 years.

Female faculty members as a group in both 1986 and 1994 exhibited more interest in and devoted more time to research than did their male colleagues. Also, women in 1994 were almost twice as likely as men to designate research as their primary strength (25% compared to 13%). But gender differences in numbers of articles and chapters produced within the prior 5 years were not significant, and men produced more than women in terms of books and monographs, controlling for length of time in academe. People of color were somewhat more likely than Caucasians to list research as their primary strength in 1994, whereas the opposite was true in 1986. The proportion of people of color designating research as their primary strength almost doubled between 1986 and 1994 (from 11% to 19%), and there were no significant differences in numbers of publications by race in 1994.

Faculty members affiliated with UCEA programs and research universities continued to publish more than their counterparts did. However, the substantial differences by type of institution and UCEA affiliation in amount of time devoted to research and level of commitment to research narrowed considerably between 1986 and 1994, especially among new faculty members. Strong commitment to and a track record in research appeared to be more important in hiring educational leadership faculty members at UCEA programs and research universities in the 1980s than in the 1990s.

Attitudes Toward the Field and Professoriate

Using the early 1970s as a baseline, faculty demographic characteristics have changed more than faculty job satisfaction and attitudes toward the field and professoriate. In general, educational leadership professors have remained satisfied with their jobs, their students, and their preparation programs. Indeed, faculty members were even more satisfied with various aspects of their work in 1994 than in 1986. More than four fifths of the 1994 respondents were satisfied with their current positions, and most gave high marks to their own preparation program and their students. Also, they identified few topics as rather or very serious problems in the profession.

However, unlike the findings in 1986, at least half of the 1994 faculty cohort felt that the small number of minorities in the profession and the lack of financial support for graduate students were rather or very serious problems. Other concerns that the 1994 respondents voiced pertained primarily to the institutional environment (e.g., lack of university support for their units and for graduate students, insufficient recognition of service activities, politics in academe); external interference in program matters (e.g., increasing state regulation of graduate educational leadership preparation programs); and issues affecting them personally (e.g., heavy teaching, advising, and dissertation loads; low salaries).

A notable development since 1986 has been an increase in the number of faculty interested in strengthening connections with practitioners and emphasizing field-based components in preparation programs. Thus, the NPBEA's (1989) recommendation that relationships with the field should be strengthened apparently is being heeded by educational leadership units. Both program heads and individual faculty members noted that an increase in number and type of connections with the field (e.g., internships, practica, field-based projects) was among the most significant recent developments in their units. Also, the 1994 group ranked "more attention to problems of practice" as the most critical need in the profession, whereas the largest percentage of 1972 respondents ranked "a more extensive knowledge base" first, and the 1986 cohort felt that "curriculum reform" was the most pressing need. Such a shift in preferences among educational leadership faculty members mirrors the efforts in recent years in teacher education programs to tighten the connections between university faculty and schools (Goodlad, 1994; Sizer, 1988).

Another significant finding was that about five sixths of the respondents in 1994 agreed or strongly agreed that ethics should receive more attention in educational leadership preparation programs. In contrast to Farquhar's (1981) findings that little attention was being given to ethical issues in UCEA leadership preparation programs in the late 1970s, by the 1990s, most UCEA programs as well as others were addressing the moral and ethical dimensions of leadership in their preparation programs (Beck & Murphy, 1994; Murphy, 1993a).

The attitudes of educational leadership faculty members in 1994 generally did not differ significantly across subgroups (e.g., by gender, type of institution, race), nor were the differences found in 1986 by gender and UCEA affiliation as pronounced in 1994. Also, the attitudes of newly hired faculty members in 1994 were like those of their experienced colleagues, and many attitudes have remained strikingly similar since the 1970s.

Selected Trends

Despite calls to alter the dominant paradigm in educational leadership preparation programs (Cambron-McCabe & Foster, 1994), such programs were characterized in the early 1990s as having made only gradual, incremental changes at best (Murphy, 1991; Pohland & Carlson, 1993). Findings from the 1994 study indicate that many features of the professoriate (e.g., faculty attitudes, rank distribution) have endured. At the same time, other results of the 1994 study suggest that the professoriate and university preparation programs may be poised on the brink of a significant transition. Implications of several trends that may determine whether there will be a fundamental realignment of educational leadership faculty members and programs are discussed below: (a) the dramatic increase in the number of female faculty members since 1980, (b) the influx of newly hired faculty members who have served as school administrators, (c) tighter coupling between preparation programs and practitioners/schools, and (d) the escalating homogeneity across units.

The Changing Gender Composition

The impact of the increase in female faculty members on educational leadership preparation programs and knowledge production is difficult to interpret. Although more time must pass to understand the long-range implications of this phenomenon, some things are evident now. Until the mid-1980s, educational leadership units appeared to be inhospitable environments for women. Compared with their male counterparts, for example, female faculty were underpaid and less satisfied with their jobs and their preparation programs (McCarthy et al., 1988). This is no longer the case. Women have become more satisfied, perhaps because they have more female colleagues, and many women have assumed leadership roles in their institutions, which puts them in positions to influence faculty hires, components of the curriculum, teaching loads, program reform, student recruitment, and so forth. Women are also exerting leadership at the national level. Since the late 1980s, women have been well represented among the leaders of UCEA, NCPEA, Division A of the AERA, and specialized organizations that focus on law, finance, and politics of education.

The 1994 data contained some surprises, though. Given the gender-based attitude differences found in 1986, it was expected that the presence of more female faculty members would alter the attitudes and nature of activities that had dominated the educational leadership professoriate (McCarthy et al., 1988). In short, the influx of women was expected to change the professional culture in significant ways. However, this prediction did not materialize. Between 1986 and 1994, the attitudes of women and men toward the field and problems in the profession converged, with women's attitudes becoming more closely aligned with those of men. Thus, instead of women altering the overall culture, it appears that they have adopted the dominant values and beliefs. In addition, gender-based attitude differences were less pronounced among recently hired faculty in 1994 than they were among new faculty in 1986.

According to Shakeshaft (1987), in the mid-1980s, female educational leadership faculty members tended to focus more on instructional issues than did male faculty members. But women faculty members were less likely to list teaching as their primary strength in 1994 (60%) than they were in 1986 (71%). They also were far less likely than their male colleagues (73%) in 1994 to view teaching as their primary strength or to have been attracted to academe by an interest in teaching (27% of males; 16% of females). However, women voiced as much interest as men in preparation program development and reform, leaving some ambiguity as to the impact that the shift in gender composition will have on the instructional program.

As noted previously, more than half of the new hires in 1994 at research universities and UCEA programs were women, and female faculty members exhibited a greater affinity for inquiry and devoted more time to research than did their male colleagues. It is possible that female professors at these institutions will become the primary knowledge producers and set the inquiry agenda for the educational leadership profession as males did in earlier decades. However, it is somewhat puzzling that in both 1986 and 1994, men produced more books and monographs than did women, and women published only slightly more articles than did their male colleagues. Perhaps, because women as a group have been educational leadership faculty members a far shorter time than have men, females have not yet hit their

stride in terms of producing books and monographs and have concentrated
on refereed articles that receive greater weight in tenure and promotion
decisions. Or possibly, men have published more articles that would be classified as service pieces rather than research. The impact of women scholars
on the educational leadership literature warrants study. It would be instructive to examine whether there are gender differences in the research topics
addressed, methodologies used, and publication outlets, as has been discovered in other fields (see Bean & Kuh, 1988).

Increase in Practice-Oriented Faculty Members

In the mid-1960s, 90% of educational administration faculty members
were drawn from the ranks of practitioners; those practice-oriented instructors relied on anecdote and experience in lecturing and conducting class
discussions (Hills, 1965). In the next two decades, fewer practitioners and
generalists were hired, and more scholars with academic specializations in
such areas as law, economics, and political science were appointed. The social
sciences were featured in preparation programs throughout the 1970s, and
during this time, there was a steady increase in the proportion of educational
leadership faculty who thought that the literature in the field should be more
theory based (Campbell & Newell, 1973; Newell & Morgan, 1980). In fact,
"theory" was the topic most frequently emphasized in educational administration coursework (Nagle & Nagle, 1978).

By the mid-1980s, however, serious concerns were being raised about
the relevance of educational leadership preparation to the real world of
schools, the dominant role of the social sciences in the curriculum, and the
large number of faculty without experience as school administrators (Foster, 1988; Greenfield, 1988). In the 1990s, units have been hiring more individuals with administrative experience, reflecting a change in views toward
the value of such experience. The appointment of former practitioners has,
in turn, contributed to the increased interest within the professoriate in field-
based activities and concerns. Also, a substantial proportion of the 1994
respondents indicated that field-based activities warranted greater recognition in university reward systems.

No one argues for a return to the practices of the 1950s, when former
practitioners delivered most of the educational leadership courses, which
lacked firm grounding in theory and research. Yet this renewed interest in
hiring practice-oriented faculty has implications for knowledge production
in our field. In 1994, the large group of newly hired faculty members who
had served as school administrators was older than the new cohort without

such experience and had, on average, worked about 20 years as precollegiate educators and administrators before joining the professoriate. Also, as a group, newly hired faculty members with administrative experience were less likely to designate research as their primary strength, and they indicated greater interest in problems of practice than did their veteran colleagues or their new peers without such experience. Also, they devoted substantially less time to research than did new faculty members without administrative experience.

Respondents in 1994 were far less likely than their counterparts in the 1970s to think that more of the educational leadership literature should be theory based. Educational leadership faculty members' ambivalence about the merits of theory in guiding practice can be healthy if it represents the realization that theory and research are not the only sources of knowledge and understanding (Murphy, 1992; Sergiovanni, 1991). But this ambivalence will be counterproductive to improving the preparation of educational leaders if it means that inquiry in the field is no longer considered important. The 1994 UCEA cohort (especially new faculty members) was less likely than the 1986 UCEA group to mention "more emphasis on research" and "greater support for research activities" as the most critical needs facing the profession. Indeed, only 2% of *all* new faculty members in 1994 indicated that "more emphasis on research" was the most critical need. Also, the gap doubled from 1986 to 1994 between educational leadership faculty members and those in other disciplines as to the mean amount of their time devoted to research (12% compared to 18% across disciplines in 1986; 14% compared to 26% across disciplines in 1994).

Many of the recently hired faculty members have come to academe from school districts, which have norms and expectations that differ markedly from those of the academy. Although program reform and connections with the field are important to the future of the profession, newly hired faculty must be made cognizant of the university's and the profession's expectations for their professorial performance. An appropriate balance needs to be struck within educational leadership programs, one where relevant university resources and inquiry-oriented approaches are used in seeking solutions to problems in the field and in preparing school leaders.

Studies are needed to track the research productivity of practice-oriented faculty and to examine the types of projects being attempted and their influence on preparation programs, leadership practices, and the improvement of learning in our schools. In addition, promotion and tenure patterns of new hires in the educational leadership professoriate should be monitored. How will the new group of faculty with practitioner backgrounds affect the nature and quality of research conducted in the field and the structure and content of preparation programs? Are these faculty members likely to embrace service activities and eschew research? Or will they bring pragmatic inquiry approaches to bear on new and persistent field-based problems?

Strengthening Field Connections

Similar to other applied areas, connections with the field of professional practice are generally considered to be essential, both for preparing educational leaders and for effective performance of these leaders in the field. Contemporary schools need reflective practitioners who understand and approach complex problems with vision, creativity, and resolve (Mulkeen & Cambron-McCabe, 1994; Schön, 1987). At professional meetings, increasing attention is being given to the moral dimensions of leadership and craft knowledge—the combination of skills, attitudes, and knowledge needed to address current challenges facing schools and educational leaders. This has nurtured efforts to connect schools with preparation program faculty and students, elevate the status of field service in educational leadership units, and, as discussed above, underscore the value of preparation program faculty who have practical experience as school leaders.

Some university leaders seem receptive to developing new types of partnerships between the academy and external stakeholders in business, industry, and the local community. National networks linking schools and colleges of education with public schools are also receiving considerable attention (see Goodlad, 1994; Sizer, 1988, 1991). In an ideal world, educational leadership units would model how universities can successfully collaborate with these groups and other agencies in mutually beneficial alliances that harness academic resources to improve the quality of life. Equally important, academe would invest in and reward people who are involved in such university/community/school partnerships. But this ideal is far from being achieved.

Although there is much to applaud in more tightly connecting the professoriate with the field and focusing the preparation program curriculum and faculty research on practical school problems, these shifts can also create tension for some faculty members. Faculty respondents in 1994 pointed to such tensions by indicating that service to school districts and state professional associations is not sufficiently appreciated in university reward systems. Despite efforts to reconceptualize scholarship so that dissemination of innovative instructional approaches and noteworthy observations of practice are valued in addition to traditional forms of inquiry (Boyer, 1990), there is little evidence that institutions of higher education are embracing an expanded definition of research. University cultures are not fickle; they change slowly, usually reluctantly. Academe has always valued discovery more than the application of knowledge. Universities, especially research universities, traditionally have not given high status to applied research and have relegated field-based and other outreach activities to a distant third tier in the reward system.

It is too soon to know if attempts to change these norms have any chance of succeeding. Such changes are unlikely without additional leverage from outside the field as well as support from national groups, such as the NPBEA and professional associations. Unless institutional norms and policies change, educational leadership faculty members who are engaged in field-based activities may find themselves disadvantaged in promotion, tenure, and annual reviews compared with their colleagues in other academic areas (Andrews, 1994). Indeed, if faculty *do* focus on activities that run counter to institutional norms, they simply will not survive in academe. If this happens, the pendulum might then swing back, with the emphasis on field connections diminishing and units seeking scholars with strong research records in traditionally valued areas.

Milstein et al. (1993) suggested that perhaps some faculty appointments should be reserved for clinical professors or other non-tenure-track professional staff who would provide leadership for innovative graduate programs and coordinate field activities. This might ameliorate much of the negative tension that faculty members experience because of the clash between institutional expectations for research and their involvement with field service and program reform. But it raises other questions regarding the composition of the educational leadership professoriate and the value of these activities. Should innovation in graduate programs and connections with the field become the responsibility of nontenurable, clinical instructors? And if so, what are the long-term implications for the status of field-based initiatives in academe and the perceived quality of educational leadership programs?

Other issues pertaining to the renewed interest in field connections warrant attention. For example, it is essential to assess whether the nature of current engagement in the field is different from and qualitatively better than school linkages in the past. Also, data are needed to ascertain whether field-based preparation programs produce more effective school leaders.

Homogeneity Across Programs

There seems to be a creeping homogeneity within the educational leadership professoriate. The substantial spread in faculty size among educational leadership units at different types of universities noted in 1986 had been reduced appreciably by 1994. Many other distinctions by type of institution and UCEA affiliation found in 1986 in resources committed to educational leadership programs (e.g., staff support, funds for professional development) had also diminished by 1994. Similarly, the differences noted in 1986 by type of institution, UCEA affiliation, and gender in faculty members' activities and attitudes toward various problems and issues facing the field were not as pronounced in 1994.

Also, differences were not statistically significant by type of institution and UCEA affiliation as to the proportions of faculty members who designated teaching as their primary strength in 1994. Whereas in 1986, the UCEA faculty cohort was far less likely than the non–UCEA group to make this designation, a larger proportion of UCEA faculty members considered teaching to be their primary strength in 1994. Indeed, UCEA faculty members exhibited a dramatic increase in their interest in and commitment to teaching between 1986 and 1994.

Faculty involvement in research also has become more similar across types of institutions and UCEA affiliation. This can be attributed primarily to faculty members at comprehensive universities and non–UCEA programs increasing their involvement in scholarly activities since 1986. The leveling of scholarly productivity is partly a function of the fact that the majority of educational leadership faculty members are no longer receiving their doctorates from a handful of elite institutions, as was true in the 1960s and early 1970s (Campbell & Newell, 1973). No single institution produced even 4% of the faculty members in 1986 or 1994, and the top 10 producers combined prepared less than one third of all faculty in both studies.

In 1986, respondents from UCEA programs and research universities were much less likely than their peers elsewhere to view their current programs as focusing primarily on the preparation of practitioners, but by 1994, differences were no longer significant in respondents' perceptions of their program orientation by UCEA affiliation and type of institution. More than four fifths of all 1994 respondents indicated that their programs were oriented more toward preparing practitioners than toward preparing researchers and scholars or a balance between the two.

The 1994 respondents listed a much larger number of universities than did the 1986 cohort when asked to rank the five best educational leadership programs nationally (although the top-ranked programs remained quite similar in both studies).[5] Indeed, almost half of all educational leadership units offering degree programs were mentioned at least once across the 1994 respondents' top five choices. Optimistically, this might suggest that more diverse criteria are being applied in judging program quality. Whereas traditionally, a unit was judged based on the research publications of its faculty members, perhaps involvement in preparation program initiatives and other activities is now being considered. An alternative explanation, however, is that there is less distinctiveness because of creeping mediocrity across units.

The factors contributing to the increasing homogeneity in faculty activities and beliefs and unit structure and orientation are not known. Possibly, faculty whose attitudes and values do not conform to prevailing views are winnowed from candidate pools during the screening process. Or perhaps they feel unwelcome and undervalued once hired and thus leave academe after a short time. This lack of diversity is troubling if it means that creative thinkers are being excluded from the educational leadership professoriate, as might be suggested by the similarity in attitudes between new and veteran faculty. However, a more positive spin on the movement toward uniformity is that there has been a leveling up among educational leadership programs in that faculty across more units are involved in program reform and knowledge production than was true in the past. Supporting this premise, recent reform initiatives sponsored by the Danforth Foundation have involved faculty from a range of institutions. The roots of the homogeneity probably spring from multiple sources, and whatever the origin, implications of this leveling across educational leadership units warrants additional attention.

Prognosis for Educational Leadership Program Reform

Signals are somewhat mixed regarding whether conditions are favorable for reform in educational leadership units. The slight increase in educational leadership faculty numbers between 1986 and 1994 may facilitate program reform, and a consensus exists among all of the major groups interested in school leadership that preparation program reform is needed. Since 1987, UCEA conventions have focused attention on the improvement of teaching and preparation program reform, and the NPBEA has sponsored workshops and seminars in this regard. Also, program reform has received attention at NCPEA conventions, and an AERA special interest group was established in 1993 to address teaching in educational administration and to provide a forum for faculty members to discuss innovations in preparation programs. In addition, professional publications increasingly have addressed preparation program reform (e.g., Milstein et al., 1993; Mulkeen, Cambron-McCabe, & Anderson, 1994; Murphy, 1993b), so faculty members engaged in such activities have more outlets for manuscripts that address pedagogical and curricular innovations. These activities have given program reform national attention, credibility, and status.

Also, education has become prominent on political agendas ("Education Ranks," 1996), and state legislatures have been increasingly active in the education policy arena. State mandates focusing on changes in school governance, interagency relationships, student performance standards, school choice, technology, and a host of other topics have affected how and where policy decisions are made, the role of school leaders, and even concepts of what education is and where it takes place. Certain state policies have specifically targeted school administrators and leadership preparation. For example, some states have undertaken extensive assessments of educational leadership programs, resulting in the elimination of some programs. Other states are considering alternatives to traditional certification for school administrators, and a few, such as North Carolina, are making significant fiscal investments in improving the preparation of school leaders (Clark, 1997). Moreover, about half of the states are involved in a consortium to create interstate licensure standards for administrators, which have significant implications for preparation programs (Council of Chief State School Officers, 1996).

The Danforth Foundation has supported two recent initiatives that have encouraged preparation program reform, especially in the participating educational leadership units. One initiative focusing on the improvement of principalship preparation involved 22 universities selected in five cycles from 1987 until 1991. Most of the participating units emphasized clinical experiences and field mentors and collaborated extensively with school districts in offering the principal preparation program. The other project, designed to revitalize educational leadership units, involved 21 institutions from 1987 until 1993. This program created opportunities for faculty members to interact with colleagues from other universities and to engage in comprehensive program development with the assistance of outside consultants. Both of these Danforth initiatives have nurtured a professional culture encouraging "reconstruction rather than simply reshaping existing programs" (Cambron-McCabe, 1993, p. 170).

It is not yet possible, however, to determine how widespread the impact of these initiatives has been and whether leadership preparation has actually improved and become more responsive to the needs of the field as a result of these programs. The effects of recently introduced pedagogical approaches (e.g., use of cohort groups) and curricular innovations (e.g., problem-centered learning) must be rigorously evaluated to determine whether these components of preparation programs are relevant to what school administrators do on the job and if they produce more effective school leaders (see Leithwood, Jantzi, Coffin, & Wilson, 1996).

Despite the promising signs mentioned above, some 1994 findings, in combination with data from other studies, suggest that it is premature to declare that the majority of educational leadership programs are in the midst of something akin to a transformation. For example, most faculty members in 1994 were very satisfied with the quality of their programs and students. One explanation for why faculty are satisfied could be that they have worked hard in the recent past to change their programs and are reveling in their successes. Unfortunately, studies and commentators have not documented such widespread program restructuring (Duke, 1992; Hackmann & Price, 1995; Murphy, 1991; Norton, 1992; Pohland & Carlson, 1993). Also, an adequate supply of new faculty members to replenish professorial ranks, much less assume the leadership in program reform, is not assured. Since the 1970s, there has been a steady decline in the number of educational leadership units that place an emphasis on preparing individuals for the professorship. And those individuals who are entering the professoriate are similar to their veteran colleagues in attitudes and activities.

Cambron-McCabe (1993) observed that the educational leadership professoriate is characterized by a culture of congeniality rather than a culture of collegiality; the latter, she argued, is more conducive to reform efforts. The 1994 results suggest that complacency also is woven into the educational leadership program tapestry. Congeniality and complacency are antithetical to the psychology of successful reform movements. Usually, some combination of external challenges and dissatisfaction with the status quo fosters ferment in the field, resulting in change. Because the majority of faculty do not perceive a need for the radical changes that would bring about a transformation in leadership preparation, it remains to be seen if there is a critical mass of reformers to sustain the momentum and energize what appears to be a relatively complacent educational leadership professoriate. In short, whether faculty members will invest the amount of time required to transform educational leadership preparation programs and whether universities will reward such efforts are open questions.

Notes

1. Questionnaires were sent to program heads of the 371 educational leadership units identified, and this survey yielded a response rate of 68%.

2. A 55% response rate was achieved in this survey. See McCarthy and Kuh (1997) for a detailed discussion of the procedures and data analysis and for a comprehensive treatment of findings. This chapter draws heavily on Chapter 7 of that book.

3. Based on the Carnegie Foundation's (1994) classification of institutions of higher education, 27% of the institutions that offer educational leadership graduate degrees are classified as research institutions (awarding 50 or more doctoral degrees each year and receiving annually at least $15.5 million in federal support), 19% are doctoral institutions (awarding at least 10 doctoral degrees in three or more disciplines or 20 doctoral degrees in one or more disciplines), and 55% are comprehensive institutions (awarding at least 20 master's degrees annually in one or more disciplines).

4. These data are based on the responses from individual faculty members in 1994. Data provided by 254 educational leadership program heads in 1994 suggested even higher female (29%) and minority (13%) representation than reported by faculty. For a discussion of possible explanations for this discrepancy, see McCarthy and Kuh (1997).

5. The educational leadership programs ranked highest in 1994 were the University of Wisconsin—Madison (1); Stanford University (2); Indiana University (3); Peabody College, Vanderbilt University (4); Harvard University (5); University of Texas—Austin (6); The Ohio State University (7); University of Utah (8); Texas A&M University (9); and The Pennsylvania State University (10). In 1986, the highest-ranked programs were Stanford University (1); The Ohio State University (2); University of Wisconsin—Madison (3); University of Texas—Austin (4); Harvard University (5); Indiana University (6); University of Oregon (7); University of Chicago (8); Teachers College, Columbia University (9); and Michigan State University (10) (McCarthy & Kuh, 1997, Table 5-23).

References

Andrews, R. (1994). New directions for preparing school leaders. In T. Mulkeen, N. Cambron-McCabe, & B. Anderson (Eds.), *Democratic leadership: The changing context of administrative preparation* (pp. 49-60). Norwood, NJ: Ablex.

Bean, J., & Kuh, G. (1988). The relationship between author gender and the methods and topics used in the study of college students. *Research in Higher Education, 28,* 130-144.

Beck, L., & Murphy, J. (1994). *Ethics in educational leadership programs: An expanding role.* Thousand Oaks, CA: Corwin.

Boyer, E. L. (1990). *Scholarship reconsidered: Priorities of the professoriate.* Princeton, NJ: Princeton University Press.

Cambron-McCabe, N. (1993). Leadership for democratic authority. In J. Murphy (Ed.), *Preparing tomorrow's school leaders: Alternative designs* (pp. 157-176). University Park, PA: The University Council for Educational Administration.

Cambron-McCabe, N., & Foster, W. (1994). A paradigm shift: Implications for the preparation of school leaders. In T. Mulkeen, N. Cambron-McCabe, & B. Anderson (Eds.), *Democratic leadership: The changing context of administrative preparation* (pp. 49-60). Norwood, NJ: Ablex.

Campbell, R. F., & Newell, L. J. (1973). *A study of professors of educational administration.* Columbus, OH: The University Council for Educational Administration.

Carnegie Foundation for the Advancement of Teaching. (1994). *A classification of institutions of higher education.* Princeton, NJ: Author.

Clark, D. (1997, March). *The search for authentic educational leadership: In the universities and in the schools.* Division A invited address presented at the annual meeting of the American Educational Research Association, Chicago.

Council of Chief State School Officers (CCSSO). (1996). *Interstate School Leaders Licensure Consortium: Standards for school leaders.* Washington, DC: Author.

Davis, W. J. (1978). Departments of educational administration. In P. Silver & D. Spuck (Eds.), *Preparatory programs for educational administrators in the United States* (pp. 23-51). Columbus, OH: The University Council for Educational Administration.

Duke, D. L. (1992). The rhetoric and the reality of reform in educational administration. *Phi Delta Kappan, 73,* 764-770.

Education ranks as major issue in elections. (1996). *College Board News, 25*(1), 2.

Farquhar, R. (1981). Preparing educational administrators for ethical practice. *Alberta Journal of Educational Research, 27,* 192-204.

Foster, W. (1988). Educational administration: A critical appraisal. In D. Griffiths, R. Stout, & P. Forsyth (Eds.), *Leaders for America's schools* (pp. 68-81). Berkeley, CA: McCutchan.

Goodlad, J. (1994). *Educational renewal: Better teachers, better schools.* San Francisco: Jossey-Bass.

Greenfield, T. (1988). The decline and fall of the science in educational administration. In D. Griffiths, R. Stout, & P. Forsyth (Eds.), *Leaders for America's schools* (pp. 131-159). Berkeley, CA: McCutchan.

Griffiths, D. E. (1988). *Educational administration: Reform PDQ or RIP* (UCEA Occasional Paper No. 8312). Tempe, AZ: The University Council for Educational Administration.

Hackmann, D., & Price, W. (1995, February). *Preparing school leaders for the 21st century: Results of a national survey of educational leadership doctoral programs.* Paper presented at the National Council of Professors of Educational Administration conference-within-a-conference at the American Association of School Administrators annual convention, San Francisco.

Heller, R., Conway, J., & Jacobson, S. (1988). Here's your blunt critique of administrator preparation. *The Executive Educator, 10*(9), 18-22.

Hills, J. (1965). Educational administration: A field in transition. *Educational Administration Quarterly, 1,* 58-66.

Leithwood, K., Jantzi, D., Coffin, G., & Wilson, P. (1996). Preparing school leaders: What works? *Journal of School Leadership, 6,* 316-342.

Magner, D. (1996, September 13). The faculty. *Chronicle of Higher Education,* A-12-13.

McCarthy, M. (1998). The "new" educational leadership professor. In R. Muth & M. Martin (Eds.), *Toward the year 2000: Leadership for quality schools.* Lancaster, PA: Technomic.

McCarthy, M. (in press). The evolution of educational leadership preparation programs. In J. Murphy & K. Seashore Louis (Eds.), *Handbook on research in educational administration* (2nd ed.). San Francisco: Jossey-Bass.

McCarthy, M., & Kuh, G. (1997). *Continuity and change: The educational leadership professoriate.* Columbia, MO: The University Council for Educational Administration.

McCarthy, M., Kuh, G., Newell, L. J., & Iacona, C. (1988). *Under scrutiny: The educational administration professoriate.* Tempe, AZ: The University Council for Educational Administration.

Milstein, M., & Associates. (1993). *Changing the way we prepare educational leaders: The Danforth experience.* Newbury Park, CA: Corwin.

Mulkeen, T., & Cambron-McCabe, N. (1994). Educating leaders to invent "tomorrow's" schools. In T. Mulkeen, N. Cambron-McCabe, & B. Anderson (Eds.), *Democratic leadership: The changing context of administrative preparation* (pp. 15-28). Norwood, NJ: Ablex.

Mulkeen, T., Cambron-McCabe, N., & Anderson, B. (Eds.). (1994). *Democratic leadership: The changing context of administrative preparation.* Norwood, NJ: Ablex.

Murphy, J. (1991). The effects of the educational reform movement on departments of educational leadership. *Educational Evaluation and Policy Analysis, 13*, 49-65.

Murphy, J. (1992). *The landscape of leadership preparation: Reframing the education of school administrators.* Newbury Park, CA: Corwin.

Murphy, J. (1993a). Ferment in school administration: Rounds 1-3. In J. Murphy (Ed.), *Preparing tomorrow's school leaders: Alternative designs* (pp. 1-38). University Park, PA: The University Council for Educational Administration.

Murphy, J. (Ed.) (1993b). *Preparing tomorrow's school leaders: Alternative designs.* University Park, PA: The University Council for Educational Administration.

Nagle, J., & Nagle, E. (1978). Doctoral programs in educational administration. In P. Silver & D. Spuck (Eds.), *Preparatory programs for educational administrators in the United States* (pp. 114-149). Columbus, OH: The University Council for Educational Administration.

National Commission on Excellence in Educational Administration. (1987). *Leaders for America's schools: The report of the National Commission on Excellence in Educational Administration.* Tempe, AZ: The University Council for Educational Administration.

National Policy Board for Educational Administration (NPBEA). (1989). *Improving the preparation of school administrators: An agenda for reform.* Charlottesville, VA: Author.

National survey of postsecondary faculty. (1993). [CD-ROM of restricted data]. Washington, DC: U.S. Department of Education, National Center for Education Statistics.

Newell, L. J., & Morgan, D. A. (1980). [Study of professors of higher education and educational administration]. Unpublished data.

Norton, M. S. (1992). Doctoral studies of students in educational administration programs in non-member UCEA institutions. *Educational Considerations, 20*, 37-41.

Pohland, P., & Carlson, L. (1993, Fall). Program reform in educational administration. *UCEA Review,* pp. 4-9.

Schön, D. (1987). *Educating the reflective practitioner*. San Francisco: Jossey-Bass.

Sergiovanni, T. (1991). Constructing and changing theories of practice: The key to preparing school administrators. *Urban Review, 23*, 39-49.

Shakeshaft, C. (1987). *Women in educational administration*. Newbury Park, CA: Sage.

Sizer, T. R. (1988). A visit to an essential school. *School Administrator, 45*(10), 18-19.

Sizer, T. R. (1991). No pain, no gain. *Educational Leadership, 48*(8), 32-34.

PART III

Progress to Date

9

Confronting Fundamental Transformation of Leadership Preparation

Nelda H. Cambron-McCabe

To understand my reflections on recent educational administration reform it is important to know the context that has influenced me. Over the past decade, I have been involved in the ongoing reconstruction of leadership education with 17 colleagues in my own department at Miami University. From 1988 through 1993, I participated with 16 other universities as they struggled with program transformation in a process supported by the Danforth Foundation's Program for Professors of School Administration. For the past 5 years, I have worked closely with the Danforth Foundation's Forum for the American School Superintendent.[1] The Forum provides a looking glass in which I continuously reexamine my assumptions about leadership and the practices of our field. From this work specifically, I am left with substantial concerns about the lack of connection between the nature of educational administration preparation programs and the crisis conditions facing many school administrators in our nation.

Another experience that has shaped how I think about the education of school leaders is Miami University's participation as a pilot site in John Goodlad's National Network for Educational Renewal (NNER). This effort targets three related reform agendas: the performance of the overall school system, the performance of individual schools, and the education of teachers. Goodlad (1994) asserts that renewal must be built into all three parts simultaneously or "the whole will inevitably malfunction" (p. 2). The NNER effort has mobilized significant resources and energy toward reconceptualizing the preparation of teachers as a collaborative enterprise between schools and universities. As my institution struggles in this project with transforming the education of teachers, I am attempting to understand its implications for school leadership.

Few would argue that our field has undergone the radical, comprehensive changes that have been demanded of it. They simply have not occurred. Program focus and structures remain substantially unchallenged. Changes can be described as modest at best and as nonexistent at worst. McCarthy and Kuh (1997) conclude from their study, as well as from data from other recent studies, that it is "premature to declare that the majority of educational leadership programs are in the midst of something akin to a transformation" (p. 251). In fact, most faculty in this study indicated that they are satisfied with their programs. Of 220 program heads responding to the question of what constituted the most significant changes in their units during the previous 10 years, only 36 indicated revisions in leadership preparation programs. This period captures the height of our reform-minded efforts in educational administration, and only 16% of the respondents identified important changes in preparation. McCarthy and Kuh also reported that few reforms recommended by the National Policy Board for Educational Administration in 1989 have been implemented, with the exception of increased emphasis on field-based activities. In their concluding analysis, McCarthy and Kuh ask what it will take to bring about a radical change within the context of a "relatively complacent" educational leadership professoriate.

Although educational leadership programs remain essentially unchanged, the past decade has been a time of ferment and spirited conversation. Through our professional meetings and journals, we have kept this reform effort alive longer than many anticipated. Meanwhile, the nation's attention on the conditions of schooling has remained fixed and trenchant. But arguably, the opportunity for reform is narrowing. If we have not instituted significant reforms (i.e., reforms that make a real difference in children's lives) over a decade, how can we expect substantive changes in the near future? In this chapter, I highlight two areas we have not seriously engaged and that could represent significant leverage points. The first is formulating a vision of schooling and determining what that means for educating school leaders. The second area is examining critically how linkages with schools can be integral to our transformation.

Purpose of Leadership Preparation

More unsettling than the documented lack of urgency to reform our field is the failure to construct a vision of schooling and to determine what that vision means for school leadership. To prepare leaders for school transformation, we must have a clear conception of the purposes of schooling (no inference here of a singular or one-dimensional purpose). Today's children face a tremendous social upheaval that demands a fundamentally different approach to schooling to ensure their preparation for full democratic participation. Schörr (1988) poignantly captures today's risks that affect the lives of children: poverty, premature birth, poor health care, inadequate nutrition, abuse, teenage pregnancy, substance abuse, and marginal housing. She argues that these conditions require a reconsideration of present structures that educate and support children. But we must be clear about our expectations.

Transformation of schools is not simply doing better what has always been done. Goodlad (1990) argues that "educators must rethink what education is, what schools are for; and they must examine and rework the structures and practices that have always been out of sync for some students and are now revealed to be inappropriate for many" (p. 2). Without a recognition that our schools do not educate well, we cannot achieve the radical transformation required to educate all children. Goodlad asserts that this transformation of schools "means much more than tinkering around the edges of what we now have. It means changing our schools in profound ways; the schools of tomorrow must be highly deviant from the schools of today" (p. 27). He goes on to state that the change will not occur if we continue to prepare for the prevailing school circumstances. But have we really confronted what education should be and what it will take to prepare leaders to challenge and change existing practices? I think not.

As a field, we have not established working assumptions (or guiding ideas, according to Senge, Ross, Smith, Roberts, & Kleiner, 1994) to inform our work. Identifying our core educational purposes is central to transforming what we do. In my department's reform work, our first priority in reconstructing the leadership program was to struggle with core purpose. Democratic authority emerged as the guiding idea, which led to our conceptualizing leadership as an intellectual, moral, and craft practice (Quantz, Dantley, & Cambron-McCabe, 1991). This brought us to the question of "Democratic leadership for what?" Our answer was, to promote more democratic constructions of teaching and learning to improve the schooling conditions for all children. These assumptions did not dictate program content but established the framework for creating it. Other institutions might take the same assumptions and construct a different set of experiences to achieve a similar vision. Ultimately, a sense of mission must undergird educational leadership programs if our graduates are to be purposefully engaged in the school reform process.

Coming to terms with purpose or assumptions is not about agreeing to a knowledge base for the field. The knowledge base is a contested arena (see Donmoyer, Imber, & Scheurich, 1995) and will remain so while positivist positions are privileged. My perspective relates to determining what guiding ideas might inform leadership education, ideas that allow for multiple interpretations and multiple voices. For example, the moral dimensions of schooling, which are receiving increased emphasis in programs, represent such an idea. They, however, are more than courses to be taught. Rather, they constitute a foundational perspective to be infused or pulled through all aspects of the educational experience. Depending on our construction of purpose, other areas that might receive attention include the cultural context of education, educative learning communities for all members of the school, and constructions of power and schooling. These abstractions form the context for critical reflection—how to think about the process of schooling; how to think about what we have taken for granted. Bateson's (1994) concept of spiral learning captures my sense of the infusion of guiding ideas. She states that "spiral learning moves through complexity with partial understanding, allowing for later returns. . . . What was once barely intelligible may be deeply meaningful a second time. And a third" (p. 31). Which guiding ideas, perspectives, or images will shape our framework for students' learning?

I find the work of the Forum for the American School Superintendent to be informative in struggling with the question of purpose. The Forum is unequivocal in its leadership purpose, grounding leadership in a vision of effective education for all children. Its participants believe that "without such a vision and the values embedded in it, there is little hope for organizational change" (Danforth Foundation, 1995, p. 1). Consequently, professional development experiences for the Forum superintendents revolve around acquiring new knowledge, understandings, and skills that will support them as they attempt to create conditions that enable all children to learn. For example, one of the special 5-year initiatives launched by the Forum in 1994, Success for All Children, was designed to assist Forum superintendents in developing their capacity to serve as advocates for children from birth to age 9 and in addressing communitywide changes needed to ensure these children's success. Each of the seven superintendents responsible for leading this effort has convened a community-based team and developed a plan to implement early childhood programs and modify district policies, school curricula, and teaching practices to ensure the achievement of desired outcomes for all children.

Activities focus on transitions from home to school, family participation, early childhood care, health needs, and developmentally appropriate education. Technical expertise used in these communities crosses multiple boundaries. Having observed these Success for All Children teams at work, I found the various activities, regardless of their specific content, grounded solidly in the interests and well-being of children (Cambron-McCabe & Harvey, 1997). Such an emphasis is equally present in the other three Forum initiatives (leadership, public engagement, principalship); all are informed by the core purpose or guiding idea of the Forum—enabling all children to experience school success. This powerful purpose organizes the superintendents' learning and work. The Forum's effort is not about mastering a discipline called educational administration; it is about learning across boundaries to acquire the knowledge needed to promote the success of all children.

Sarason (1993) articulates a similar focus on children and learning as he addresses school reform. He forcefully argues that if schools are to change, *"the nature of life in the classroom must change"* (p. 102; emphasis in original). He advocates creating fundamentally new learning environments where the work of both teachers and students radically departs from today's classrooms. Sarason admonishes that altering curricula, performance standards, power relationships, and the like will be self-defeating in reforming schools unless our conceptions of children's learning change. Taking seriously this premise, which Sarason calls the "big idea," means substantially altered roles for students, teachers, and administrators.

If we accept that one of the key purposes of educational leadership is to ensure that all children learn, the skills that administrators need to redesign schools require program content and understandings vastly different from most of today's educational administration programs. Much of this new focus relates to knowledge about curricular and instructional matters. That is, skills are needed for direct involvement in the learning side of the schooling enterprise. In the Forum's Success for All Children initiative noted above, the superintendents identified principals' knowledge of early childhood education practices as the most important factor related to successful implementation of reforms at the school building level (Cambron-McCabe & Harvey, 1997). This finding, at the completion of the second year of the initiative, led to the design of a 2-year professional development academy to provide the principals in the seven school districts with in-depth preparation in areas such as developmentally appropriate instructional practices and child development. Similarly, Boone and Kahle (1997) found in a study of Ohio's Systemic Science Initiative (implementation of the National Science Education Standards) that for effective implementation of the standards, both teachers *and* principals need assistance in understanding the nature of science, the processes of inquiry, and how children learn to think. Kahle (personal communication, August 1, 1997) concluded from her extensive work in this initiative for the past 4 years in Ohio schools that principals must possess basic knowledge of the inquiry process and authentic assessment not only to support adequately teachers who are implementing the standards but also to facilitate widespread implementation in their schools.

Focusing on the success of all students could provide a powerful focus for leadership preparation programs. This concept appears as a pivotal notion in the recent work of the Interstate School Leaders Licensure Consortium's (1996) Standards for School Leaders. Each of the six standards begins with the statement "A school administrator is an educational leader who promotes the success of all students by . . ." Miami University's principalship program, implemented in 1992, was created from nine working assumptions. The first statement is "Student academic success is the responsibility of educational leaders." This is followed by a statement also proclaiming that teacher success is the principal's responsibility. These assumptions form the foundation for a program characterized by substantial attention to teaching, learning, and community building.

Relationship of Preparation Programs to Practice

The relevance of educational leadership preparation to the world of schools continues to be challenged (see Clark, 1997; Greenfield, 1988). Throughout the McCarthy and Kuh (1997) study, faculty identified "involvement in problems of school practice" as one of the most pressing needs in the field along with "strengthening connections with practitioners." The National Commission on Excellence in Educational Administration (1987) iterated this stance in its earlier report, specifically recommending increased clinical experiences, involvement of outstanding practitioners, and adoption of a professional development school model. A growing number of preparation programs have begun to emphasize practice (or craft) dimensions (see McCarthy & Kuh, 1997; Murphy, 1993). This is reflected generally as increased credit-hour requirements for internships, practica, and field-based projects.

Although there is agreement (for the most part) regarding the importance of connecting preparation programs to practice, we have not sufficiently examined how these linkages promote better leadership or school transformation rather than simply maintaining the status quo. Goodlad (1990), in tackling this dilemma in teacher education, raised an important question that we also must confront: "Given the intense national concern over the quality of our present schools, why would we want to risk perpetuating their practices by socializing prospective teachers into them" (p. 226)? He argues that we will need to proceed with simultaneous renewal of both schools and preservice education if we are to have good schools and good teachers. Goodlad (1990; 1994) and his associates, through the NNER, have identified 19 interconnected postulates that address the conditions that must exist for such simultaneous reform to occur. Although the NNER is directed at preparing strong teachers for schools, Goodlad (1990) recognizes that the principles advanced are equally applicable to school administrators.

Many of the postulates guiding the NNER agenda have implications for framing how educational administration programs might structure relationships with schools, ranging from identifying a wide array of quality settings to establishing true collegial relationships between school leaders in these sites and university faculty to permit joint planning and conducting of leadership programs. A central aspect of this renewal agenda is the establishment of centers of pedagogy where a university and its various partners come together for the preparation of educators and for engagement in inquiry. Collaborative inquiry occurs in the centers around the context of teaching (the schools), preparation (what educators need to know), and effectiveness of a setting's own programs. Such partnerships (or professional development schools) permit interrogation of the gap between existing conditions and more desirable futures.

In this partnership context, fieldwork becomes more than an uncritical connection to replicate existing practices. It encourages the building of educative communities where elementary and secondary educators, graduate students, and university faculty can fundamentally reconsider student learning, school structures, and authority relationships. It provides a way to rethink the nature of our inquiry. Our dominant research approaches have been denounced for failure to inform the work of schools (Clark, 1997; Starratt & Foster, 1994). Starratt and Foster assert that for our research to be successful, two considerations are paramount: meaningfulness ("In what ways can research into administrative behavior be meaningful to administrators themselves?") and relevance ("How does our research inform and even change the way we educate children?") (p. 151). Partnerships designed as centers of pedagogy provide a new arena to participate in inquiry that matters, with multiple opportunities for a range of research approaches (e.g., locally based action research, case studies, problem-posing research, problem-solving research, and critical ethnographies).

Formal partnerships provide opportunities not only for critical inquiry but for the development of case studies and problem-based learning (PBL) experiences for instruction. McCarthy and Kuh (1997) found increased use of problem-related instructional strategies within the professoriate. Involvement in partner schools provides a rich context for problem finding and creation of these materials. In Miami University's educational leadership department, a group of doctoral students participating in a partnership curriculum reform effort designed a PBL activity that is now used in an advanced graduate seminar (Badiali, 1995). The students who developed the PBL activity evaluated it as one of the most realistic and beneficial learning experiences they had ever had. In subsequent use of the PBL experience, we found that the student learning and performance related to decision making, group dynamics, and curriculum integration far surpassed traditional seminars. Working with partnership schools also has facilitated access to and involvement of teachers and administrators in our PBL instructional activities.

Additionally, connecting with practice through partnerships provides an opportunity to establish a new relationship between the preparation of teachers and administrators. As power relationships are altered and administrators' and teachers' roles are blurred, leadership can no longer be considered the sole province of administrators. If we are preparing all educators for new schools, dialogue about the nature of those schools and the roles within them must occur among school-based educators and university faculty preparing both teachers and administrators. Through Miami University's NNER curriculum redesign work, the school leadership faculty is creating an undergraduate course on teacher leadership with the teacher education faculty. Central to the design of this course, which will be taught primarily in the Department of Educational Leadership, is the development of a shared conception about what is desired in reconstructing school structures and relationships. Undoubtedly, the outcome of these conversations will affect both departments' thinking about other aspects of our programs.

When we advocate forming partnerships with the field and involvement in problems of practice, we generally think of elementary and secondary schools. Many school leaders, however, are building partnerships or collaboratives with multiple groups, including child care, social, health, and community agencies, as it grows more evident that schools alone cannot address the societal changes affecting children (see Cibulka & Kritek, 1996). As in the Danforth Foundation's Forum for school superintendents discussed above, linking schools and other agencies is becoming a prominent strategy for mobilizing communities to support children and their families. Among the collaboration partnerships formed by the Danforth superintendents, university involvement is negligible. With the coordination of children's services being a major policy issue at every level of government and now affecting most schools, educational administration departments have the opportunity to reconstruct what constitutes practice for our field and what kind of leadership will be needed to invent new arrangements for collaboration.

Although significant rhetoric exists regarding the efficacy of partner or professional development schools, the number of long-term collaborative partnership arrangements is small. Few universities have managed more than several pilot sites on a sustained basis. Miami University has 13 partner schools, but, the partner schools can work with only a small percentage of our students. Developing and maintaining additional sites requires tremendous faculty resources and raises contentious reward questions when faculty investment in building partnerships is not valued by a university. Consequently, field site work still occurs most often through individual faculty relationships in selected schools. The question confronting us is, How do we design our work to make partnerships integral rather than an add-on? The field connection is essential for not only what our students and faculty learn in this context but also how we evolve as a profession.

Concluding Thoughts

Our conversations about reforming leadership preparation may focus too frequently on identifying the right structure/content/approach for preparing leaders when we need to make a commitment as a field to an ongoing evolutionary process (or to a continuing struggle) within a larger partnership with practice. The complacency that McCarthy and Kuh (1997) identified could be the result of a product orientation. We have all experienced revision processes to meet new state standards. The familiar pattern is that departments make the required adjustments and check off each mandate. At the end of the process, a new program is adopted, and faculty move on to other priorities. Over the past decade, we have made some program changes, presumably fixing the problems identified by our critics. More, however, is being demanded of us in this restructuring wave; no check-off list exists. We are being asked to reconceptualize school leadership fundamentally and radically. This brings us back to grappling with the purpose of education and schools.

Note

1. The 60 superintendents constituting the Forum for the American School Superintendent, a 10-year effort, come from urban, suburban, and rural school districts in which at least 50% of the students are at risk of school failure. The Forum superintendents meet together twice a year in 4-day retreats devoted to a single topic identified by the membership. Small groups of 7 to 10 superintendents participate in special initiatives on critical issues (early childhood, leadership, public engagement, principalship) and receive small grants to support the initiative work in their districts.

References

Badiali, B. (1995). School-university partnerships: Restructuring opportunities for leadership. *Ohio ASCD, 2*(2), 33-38.

Bateson, M. C. (1994). *Peripheral visions: Learning along the way.* New York: HarperCollins.

Boone, W. J., & Kahle, J. B. (1997). Implementations of the standards: Lessons from a systemic initiative. *School Science and Mathematics, 97,* 292-298.

Cambron-McCabe, N., & Harvey, J. (1997). *Supporting learning for all children: A report on the Success for All Children initiative.* St. Louis, MO: Danforth Foundation.

Cibulka, J. G., & Kritek, W. J. (Eds.). (1996). *Coordination among schools, families, and communities: Prospects for educational reform.* Albany: SUNY Press.

Clark, D. (1997, March). *The search for authentic educational leadership: In the universities and in the schools.* Division A invited address presented at the annual meeting of the American Education Research Association, Chicago.

Danforth Foundation. (1995). *Danforth Program for School Superintendents: Directory.* St. Louis, MO: Author.

Donmoyer, R., Imber, M., & Scheurich, J. J. (1995). *The knowledge base in educational administration: Multiple perspectives.* Albany: SUNY Press.

Goodlad, J. I. (1990). *Teachers for our nation's schools.* San Francisco: Jossey-Bass.

Goodlad, J. I. (1994). *Educational renewal: Better teachers, better schools.* San Francisco: Jossey-Bass.

Greenfield, T. (1988). The decline and fall of the science in educational administration. In D. Griffiths, R. Stout, & P. Forsyth (Eds.), *Leaders for America's schools* (pp. 131-159). Berkeley, CA: McCutchan.

Interstate School Leaders Licensure Consortium. (1996). *Standards for school leaders*. Washington, DC: Council of Chief State School Officers.

McCarthy, M. M., & Kuh, G. D. (1997). *Continuity and change: The educational leadership professoriate*. Columbia, MO: The University Council for Educational Administration.

Murphy, J. (1993). *Preparing tomorrow's school leaders: Alternative designs.* University Park, PA: The University Council for Educational Administration.

National Commission on Excellence in Educational Administration. (1987). *Leaders for America's schools: The report of the National Commission on Excellence in Educational Administration*. Tempe, AZ: The University Council for Educational Administration.

Quantz, R., Dantley, M., & Cambron-McCabe, N. (1991). Preparing school administrators for democratic authority: A critical approach to graduate education. *Urban Review, 23*(3), 3-19.

Sarason, S. (1993). *Letters to a serious education president.* Newbury Park, CA: Corwin.

Schörr, L. (1988). *Within our reach: Breaking the cycle of disadvantage and despair*. New York: Doubleday.

Senge, P., Ross, R., Smith, B., Roberts, C., & Kleiner, A. (1994). *The fifth discipline fieldbook*. New York: Doubleday.

Starratt, R. J., & Foster, W. (1994). Educational administrators as leaders: Research implications. In T. A. Mulkeen, N. H. Cambron-McCabe, & B. J. Anderson (Eds.), *Democratic leadership: The changing context of administrative preparation.* Norwood, NJ: Ablex.

10

Searching for Authentic Educational Leadership in University Graduate Programs and With Public School Colleagues

David L. Clark

A decade ago, I held a will-o-the-wisp view of improving preservice preparation of school leaders by insisting on full-time doctoral study for an elite cohort of students in a much-reduced number of universities. I now advocate a more modest and more achievable set of reforms. This is not to say that I believe we can claim authenticity for our current programs. In general, they are held in low regard by our faculty colleagues at the university and, unfortunately, by many of our former graduate students who are practicing in the field—and deservedly so! But there is a set of practical reforms that some institutions are pursuing already within their current base of resources, and that all of us could pursue if we had the will to do so.

Actually, my overall theme is not profound—it is what most of us advertise to our consumers. The problem is that too few of our programs deliver what we advertise.

Student Recruitment and Selection

Whatever else we claim, we should not claim that we are miracle makers. We do not transmute mediocre teachers into creative, inspiring school

AUTHOR'S NOTE: This chapter was presented initially as an invited address to Division A, American Educational Research Association annual meeting, March 24, 1997.

leaders. We do not turn below-average academic performers into Rhodes scholars. We do not convert graduate students who dislike contact with children and youth into sensitive, caring school leaders who have a sense of the needs of children and youth.

We must change our mind-set from quantity to quality. No aspect of our preparation programs is more damaging than the perception held by our university colleagues, and by many classroom teachers, that we are a haven for mediocre candidates.

Rigorous academic criteria for admission should be viewed as necessary but not nearly sufficient. Every one of our admissions should be reserved for candidates who love to teach and who are committed to nurturing and working with and for children and youth. If they are not interested in supporting the Children's Defense Fund, we shouldn't be interested in them. We do not "owe" anyone the right to be admitted to graduate study in educational leadership. But we do owe the children, youth, teachers, parents, and citizens who support public education an obligation to prepare only the most promising educators to compete for leadership roles in the schools.

I know that some of you are saying, "That may be all right in some institutions, but in my university, we can't afford decreased enrollments or we'll lose faculty and, eventually, our program." I have no sympathy for that position. First, in most cases, it doesn't work out that way. Most universities do respond favorably to qualitative improvement. Second, the damage suffered within programs that accept and graduate below-standard master's and doctoral students in educational administration extends beyond the university into the school systems, which are plagued by these mediocre performers for years.

We ought to define what we can and cannot do within the resource limits provided by our university. We will gain respect by doing so. Isn't it true that we claim substantial expertise in leadership and management? Don't many of us take on consulting assignments in schools and other organizations that are floundering because of inappropriate decision making about resource allocations and use? Let's take some time to insist on good management practices for departments of educational leadership in colleges and universities— and let's stick by our own recommendations.

Immersion Periods of Serious Study

I referred briefly to my relatively recent advocacy of full-time doctoral programs as the basis for the preparation of principals and superintendents. I was wrong. The effort distracted us from pursuing a more feasible practical alternative to a similar end, that is, creating master's-level and doctoral programs that immerse students in intensive study (preferably in cohort arrangements) for a concentrated period of time—generally no more than 2 years.

In a different world, I would still be arguing for full-time study. But it is just not going to happen for most students in our field. However, this should not stop us from designing programs that engage students in ordered, systematic periods of study that focus their minds and talents on mastering course content and understanding the essence of leadership rather than accumulating courses. Many of you are now operating programs that are built on cohort structures featuring ordered sequences of study within a specified time frame for completion. Executive development programs have employed this design successfully for years, and we now have enough sound models of such programs for preservice preparation that there is no excuse to continue part-time study on a catch-as-catch-can basis. We should label inadequate programs just what they are—diploma mills that tarnish our image within the university. And, more importantly, these inadequacies end up certifying candidates whose academic backgrounds are wholly inadequate to the crucial tasks they will confront in public schools.

Instruction

I will focus on process rather than content in discussing our programs of instruction. I am, of course, cognizant of the fact that many of our programs are offered by instructors who have little or no grasp of the knowledge base produced during the neo-orthodox period of the 1950s, 1960s, and 1970s, to say nothing of the more contemporary, nonorthodox emphases of the 1990s. They are still storytellers! They and their students confront the same dilemma that Herbert Simon described colorfully in the mid-1940s: "Most of the propositions that make up the body of administrative theory today share, unfortunately, [the] defect of proverbs. For every principle one can find an equally plausible and acceptable contradictory principle" (Simon, 1946, p. 53). Although Simon's solution—that the choice would be clear when the issue was subjected to scientific inquiry—turned out to be overly simplistic, the theory movement and the empirical studies of the past 50 years have pushed us beyond proverbs and have stimulated richer forms of inquiry (i.e., qualitative research) and more satisfying theoretical frameworks (e.g., critical theory, feminist theory, postmodernist theory).

All of our programs must include the scope and depth of the contemporary knowledge base that supports our core content. However, I want to emphasize a different dimension of our instructional program—our role as teachers, counselors, advisers, and supporters of our students. By the nature of the reward system within our universities, classroom instruction, counseling students, involving them actively in our inquiry, and being available to deal with their personal dilemmas takes a back seat to exactly what we are celebrating here today—our research productivity. Often, the most prolific researchers and authors avoid involvement with students who aspire to a professional assignment in schools rather than a professorship in a college or university or a position in a research or policy organization. I believe that this is shortsighted. With only a few exceptions, graduate programs in educational leadership exist to prepare school administrative personnel. This is our focal mission. To remove from, or lessen the contributions of, the most active scholars in the preparation of practitioners is an unnecessary and unfortunate choice.

I intend to push this argument one step further. The fact is that the total contribution of the members of Division A of AERA to the development of the empirical and theoretical knowledge base in administration and policy development is so minuscule that if all of us had devoted our professional careers to teaching and service, we would hardly have been missed. This is not to argue that we should abandon our research activity, but only to strip away the aura that some of us should not share equally in nurturing and instructing practitioners-in-training. We must demand outstanding classroom instruction and career nurturance from the leading members of our research community if we intend to instruct and inspire our master's and doctoral students in the contemporary knowledge base relevant to our field. Too frequently, they are retreating from this obligation to pursue esoteric scholarly interests that result in a lesser payoff for our profession.

Linkages "In and Off" Campus

No department of educational leadership is prepared to offer an appropriate program of study on its own. Most departments are staffed to offer instruction in organizational theory, policy studies, management, and such specialized technical fields as law and finance. However, outstanding programs in educational leadership are rooted in much more complicated fields of study. No school leader, for example, should lack expertise in curriculum and instruction. Yet only a few universities have attempted to integrate graduate departments of curriculum and instruction and educational leadership, and most place little emphasis on knowledge about teaching and learning. How many programs require coursework in "Social Foundations"? Yet the essence of success in contemporary American schools cries out for leaders who believe that moral and ethical values are the cornerstone of public education in a bifurcated society.

In much of our scholarly work, we decry the gap between educational services and social services. But the overwhelming majority of our students cannot find the time to take a single course in a "School of Social Work." Most of us maintain an early childhood education program of study in our own school or college, but we do not allocate time for our students to take a course in that department or in a university-based program in child development and family studies. More of us at least have a required course in special education, but how many of us expose our students to a minimal understanding of effective approaches to dealing with ESL youngsters, a population that is exploding in scores of states. We cannot do everything in the abbreviated time available to us in graduate preparation programs, but we can do much more than we are doing.

Summary

I have left out topics about which we all worry. How can we arrange intensive, useful internships in the schools? Where will we find time for the critical content areas of our own specialized field of administration and leadership? How should we relate to the new NCATE guidelines that specify required areas of expertise that were designed to reflect the needs emphasized by our professional associations? I talked about the conflict between scholarly research and time spent in teaching and counseling students. But what about the infringement of service demands from schools? Isn't it true that many of our colleagues are absent from both teaching and research because school systems are willing to pay them for consulting and survey activities?

The conflicts that exist within our programs require constant attention and continuing adjustments. My argument today, however, is straightforward. First and foremost, we are responsible for preparing effective school leaders for the 21st century. To steal from Hillary Rodham Clinton (or, more accurately, from an African folk tale), it takes a whole faculty to prepare an effective educational leader. We need to

- Find budding miracle workers in our public schools and convince these teachers to join us in our preparation programs to make schools better
- Provide graduate students with a challenging program of studies

- Devote ourselves to our students and consider ourselves successful when one of our former students demonstrates how to lead a great school

Communicating With Our Students and Our Public School Colleagues

How can we effectively introduce our students and our field-based colleagues to the emerging (and often confusing and inaccessible) knowledge base of educational administration? Contemporary portrayals of the theoretical knowledge base in educational administration de-emphasize functionalism and embrace alternatives that argue that (a) we are active agents in constructing our world; (b) knowledge and power are related inextricably; (c) facts are embedded in and interpreted through social, value-laden processes; and (d) social structures and hierarchies conceal as much as they reveal. The metaperspectives leading the field toward a more comprehensive and complicated knowledge base include critical theory, feminist theory, pragmatism, and postmodernism.

However, in the midst of this exciting and turbulent reconsideration of what is known about organizations, organizational behavior, and organizational practice, there are some powerful counterbalancing forces that suggest that the traditional knowledge base is not only alive and well but is the dominant perspective held in the "real world" of practice. State and national policies and programs of educational reform reflect extremely conservative interpretations of organizational research and theory, such as

1. National goals and standards for education
2. State and national testing programs to measure goal attainment
3. State takeovers of faltering school districts

The press is clearly toward external control mechanisms as the stimulus to drive educational improvement.

Additionally, the graduate programs of study in our own institutions are not typically avant-garde. The majority of our newer textbooks refer to nonorthodox perspectives, but they report almost wholly on orthodox and neo-orthodox research findings. In some of our classrooms, newer theoretical orientations are introduced, but the practical emphasis is still on functionalist/bureaucratic tools, practices, and mind-sets. Regardless of these obstacles, we must accept the challenge of establishing the connection between emerging nonorthodox theories and research findings and effective practice in schools and classrooms.

A number of years ago, Professor Murray Davis published an article titled "That's Interesting" in which he argued that we need a new field, "The Sociology of the Interesting," to supplement the existing field of "The Sociology of Knowledge" (Davis, 1971). The heart of his argument was the proposition that a new theory or research finding is interesting only if it denies an old truth, but that the "truth" is in the mind of the audience, not of the theorist or researcher. He argued that if we hope to create a dialectical examination with clients we need to avoid propositions that are noninteresting:

- What seems to be the case is in fact the case ("That's obvious").
- What is really true has no connection with what you always thought was true ("That's irrelevant").
- Everything you always thought was true is really false ("That is absurd"). (p. 327)

His basic argument was that the "taken-for-granted world" of the audience is as important to the success of achieving a serious dialogue between the audience and the presenter as the proposition offered by the presenter.

We have paid little attention to this advice in educational research circles in general and in organizational theory in particular. My impression is that our most important work in organizational theory is viewed by educational practitioners as noninteresting for the very reasons enumerated by Davis:

- Most of the codified research findings presented in standard textbooks, such as reviews of the research on leadership, are considered obvious and, consequently, boring by practitioners.
- Much of the exhortative material on school renewal and reform, such as explications of alternative programs that are inaccessible to practitioners because of cost or local norms of behavior, is considered irrelevant.
- Many of the theoretical structures that represent the "new wave" of the field are so foreign to the practitioners' experience and so obscure in presentation that the conclusion is "That's absurd."

Most of the codified research findings presented in standard textbooks are boring. We are still treating situational leadership and the concepts of initiating structure and consideration as if the reader should be surprised by such powerful tools for thinking about leaders and leadership. They think what any intelligent observer would say— "That's obvious." In fact, they might also say it's irrelevant, but we ought to reserve that category for research findings on programs of reform that are clearly beyond the existing resources of American public schools. It is true that we know how to produce high student achievement in schools (public and private) that are characterized by privileged family backgrounds, small classes, and teachers who have excellent backgrounds in pedagogy and content fields. But, as conditions of child poverty and limited budgetary allocations proliferate, an increasing number of American public schools do not share such advantageous positions. Finally, we must confront the lack of simple skills in ordinary communication. The form of presentation at "scholarly" meetings and in "scholarly" journals routinely violates the Davis propositions. In fact, many academics and most practitioners are bewildered as they attempt to access the publications of critical theorists, postmodernists, and poststructuralists. Private languages probably deserve the reaction of "That's absurd" from individuals whose daily lives require language clarity for survival.

What would I do to attempt to introduce nonorthodox thought to educational practitioners? First, I would focus on contrasting the disparities between what most practicing administrators "know is true" and findings that challenge that knowledge in very specific ways. I would introduce them to Kathy Ferguson's discussion of the perniciousness of personnel management in public administration before I allowed them to even consider the intensive study of feminist theory (Ferguson, 1984). I would insist that they examine Alvin Gouldner's "The Unemployed Self" before they gave consideration to critical theory (Gouldner, 1989). I would introduce them to Mary Parker Follett's discussion of "The Giving of Orders," in which she surfaces the complexity of "ordering" in human organizations (Follett, 1949).

Is it my belief that contemporary, nonorthodox theory is inherently uninteresting? Of course not. Quite to the contrary, I believe that it is our responsibility to challenge the often uninformed belief systems of practitioners with powerful alternatives to traditional bureaucratic thought. But I think this challenge has to provide the audience with a fair chance to discuss the alternative within the scope of their knowledge base. This suggests several approaches:

- Emphasizing cubits of usable knowledge that may allow school administrators to at least ameliorate the worst consequences of bureaucratic orthodoxy

- Accepting the responsibility for meeting the criteria of practicality, usability, and applicability for nonorthodox findings that will work in school settings
- Settling for individual findings rather than hard-to-access, complicated systems of findings
- Acknowledging our responsibility as interpreters and translators of theoretical propositions and research findings

I believe that we are professors in programs of educational leadership for the primary purpose of preparing outstanding leaders for the country's schools. This requires authenticity in our preservice and inservice programs of study and in our collegial relationships with practicing school leaders. Most of our current programs fall short of these goals. Many fail because they are staffed with professors whose knowledge base does not prepare them to challenge conventional practice. Others fail because professors have chosen to eschew their responsibility to serve their clientele in exchange for the more esoteric life of the scholar-professor. The time has passed when we can afford to tolerate either of these conditions. We are teachers, scholars, colleagues, counselors, and support personnel to school leaders—or we are nothing at all!

References

Davis, M. (1971). That's interesting: Toward a phenomenology of sociology and a sociology of phenomenology. *Philosophy of Social Sciences, 1*, 309-344.

Ferguson, K. (1984). *The feminist case against bureaucracy*. Philadelphia: Temple University Press.

Follett, M. (1949). The giving of orders. In L. Urwick (Ed.), *Freedom and coordination: Lectures in business organization by Mary Parker Follett* (pp. 16-33). London: Management Publications Trust. (Original work published 1933)

Gouldner, A. (1989). The not-enough-world-of work. In G. Morgan (Ed.), *Creative organization theory* (pp. 260-263). Newbury Park, CA: Sage.

Simon, H. (1946). The proverbs of administration. *Public Administration Review, 6*, 53-67.

11

A Decade Half Full
or a Decade Half Empty:
Thoughts From a Tired Reformer

CHAROL SHAKESHAFT

Examining a decade of progress in preparation programs in educational administration should be a piece of cake, especially because my assignment is to reflect upon the changes that I note and from perspectives that I care about. Why, then, has this chapter been so difficult to write? I approach my computer and then quickly find something else to do: check my e-mail, assign classes, write recommendations for students. Even cleaning closets is more inviting than writing this chapter. After a month of avoidance, it occurs to me that my lack of interest in this project—no, that's too mild; what I'm feeling is stronger than distaste—might have something to do with the content of the assignment. The more I reflect upon my emotional response to the theme of this chapter, the more I am sure that my reaction is connected to my own feelings of failed effort and the fear that in a decade packed with meetings, curriculum discussions, shared ideas, strategies, and program tinkering, there has been meager improvement, at best, and a change of labels at worst.

Even as I write that last sentence, I think, Is this really true? Has the field only inched forward? How do I know this? On what evidence am I basing my dismal evaluation? I have little data on other programs (although there are some self-report studies available); no data on behavioral outcomes from school administrators; and certainly no evidence that schooling and achievement, however measured, are related to anything we do in preparation programs in educational administration.

On the other hand, I do have anecdotal and personal data about changes in teaching practices, focus in research methods, and expansion of the populations we study and about whom we teach. Because my mother never said, "If you can't say anything nice, don't say anything at all," I don't have to feel guilty about putting my mixed feelings on paper. Furthermore, my mother taught me early to find my truth and tell it, no matter what the cost. In this case, the cost, it seems, is personal. As I try to connect the effort I have expended on reforming preparation programs in educational administration during the past decade to the results I and others have achieved, I conclude that I should have spent my time on some other endeavor.

In reflecting on the progress made in the past decade in preparation programs for school administrators, I am reporting my own experience during this decade: as the chairperson of a department that has worked aggressively to shift paradigms and practice, as a vice president of Division A, as a program chair for Division A, and as a member of a national work group to create standards for preparation programs. Although certainly not a leader in the reform movement, I have been an active and enthusiastic participant in both a macro and particularly a micro context.

Beginning in fall 1988, the Department of Administration and Policy Studies at Hofstra University began an overhaul of its preparation program for school administrators (which is also the first 30 semester hours of the doctoral program), followed by additional changes to the doctoral program in educational administration. Some early descriptions of our change process were published in *Preparing Tomorrow's School Leaders: Alternative Designs* (Shakeshaft, 1993).

These changes represent a change of mission in our programs. Whereas our previous program focused on developing educational managers and administrators and had a "public servant" orientation, the department now attempts to prepare administrators who will "demonstrate a commitment to the new mission by exhibiting 'moral leadership' . . . and produce educational leaders who may be perceived more as 'activist reformers'" (Browder, 1995, p. 51).

We have been working on the reform of our programs for a decade. Faculty have come and gone, although there has been a core of seven of us that has not changed. Our struggles in some way reflect the larger teaching community in educational administration; thus, a recounting of my experience might be illustrative of the activity, the change, and the frustrations in the past decade.

Process/Program Decisions

We made structural decisions in the programs early on. Because we be-lieve that students learn not only from professors and mentors in the field but from each other, we have built the structure and sequence around a commu-nity of students. These communities of students (known as cohorts at other institutions) move through the program together, taking all of their adminis-trative certification courses together and the first 2 years of the doctoral pro-gram in sequence in a group.

Rather than have courses on the principalship, the superintendency, school law, school finance, and so forth, we focus the five-course certification expe-rience around particular topics, including in each the legal, managerial, eco-nomic, and organizational analyses important to understanding the subject. Additionally, each course includes experiences in reflective practice and ad-dresses equity issues. These are sequential courses; there are no electives.

After the first five courses and a three-semester internship (which results in administrative certification), the doctoral-only sequence begins with a year-long, team-taught course on doctoral work, methods of inquiry, and a general overview of the historical research of the field (Primis). This is followed by a summer course on philosophical thought and conceptual frameworks. The next 2 years are devoted to a four-semester (with projects over January and throughout the summer) research strand that is team taught. As does the cer-tification sequence, the activities in one "course" overlap and connect to the activities in another. During these years, students take electives, define their research problem and purpose or choose a policy issue, and develop and defend a proposal.

Each course experience includes materials that relate to a range of race, class, and gender experiences. Because textbooks, materials, case studies, and learning activities are more likely to focus on the experiences of males than of females, and of white/Caucasian people rather than people of color, we have included appropriate cases and experiences that address the needs of all students, and the lives of women and males of color in particular.

Not unlike most administrator preparation programs, the majority of our students are female. However, unlike most programs, we are attempting to address the needs of our women students. Our women students and students of color receive direct coaching in the program to combat both sexism and racism in interviews and other job-getting activities. Furthermore, we have sponsored a network for women students for the past 13 years aimed at en-suring that the number of women administrators on Long Island increases. Two studies (1992 and 1995) of our graduates indicate that the majority of our women graduates from both our certification and doctoral programs have attained administrative positions.

Our initial structural decisions have served us well, particularly the learning community groups.

Changes Implemented to Meet Goals

The goals for the Hofstra programs were driven by our own commitment to improve the preparation of school administrators, and they were heavily influenced by the national dialogue. Thus, it isn't surprising that many of the issues we have targeted are central to the National Policy Board for Educational Administration, the new NCATE standards for programs in educational administration, and the changed standards for UCEA membership.

Our department discussions and decisions in the past decade have articulated the following program goals:

- Recruit and retain a capable and diverse student body.
- Improve and expand the research of the field, and connect this research to administrative decision making.
- Keep the department and faculty focus on student outcomes, conceptualized from multiple perspectives, and help our students learn to do the same as administrators.
- Develop reflective practice habits in ourselves and our students, keeping our values connected to our actions.
- Improve the effectiveness of our methods of teaching, and increase the relevance of the curriculum to problems of practice.

> *Recruit and retain a more capable and diverse student body.*

Our goal has been to increase the number of students who are of African descent, Asian descent, and/or are Latina/o. In addition, we have tried to attract students who are interested in educational reform and equity issues and who will work to change existing systems. Finally, we have attempted to increase the number of "out of the box" creative students—those who might not normally think to enroll in programs in educational administration. Obviously, these categories are not mutually exclusive.

Demographic data from other departments nationwide indicate the same student body trends that we have experienced during the decade: a dramatic increase in the number of women students so that the majority of students are female, and a slight increase in the number of racially and ethnically underrepresented students. We have made gains in the decade, but we still have a way to go.

Our traditional recruitment and selection processes did little to help us diversify our student body. Typically, we have expected that word-of-mouth discussions of our programs by graduates and current students would bring in additional students. Although this may be true, this method is most likely to reproduce—not expand—the kind of student we already serve. To begin to meet our goal to diversify, we had to change our recruitment methods by identifying additional types of students that we would like to have in our program and go after them. This proved to be more difficult than we thought it would be.

Although we have been able to incorporate a direct mail campaign to particular demographic segments (teachers, minority teachers, etc.), we found it much harder to knowingly target folks who think out of the box. We tried asking for administrative nominations of the most creative and capable teachers in their schools. Earlier in this process, we found that asking administrators for names of students who might be interested in becoming administrators generates a completely different list than does asking administrators who are the most creative and best teachers in the district. No matter which question we ask, most administrators in our geographic area (unless they are Hofstra graduates) are unwilling to nominate or give us names of possible student recruits on the grounds that to do so is unethical and unfair to other administrative certification programs (there are 10 within easy driving distance) and doctoral programs (five are within easy driving distance) in the region.

Even when we were able to contact nominated students, once they applied to our program, we found our selection criteria irrelevant for screening on the criteria we wanted our students to possess. Although we say we want folks who think out of the box, we have no mechanism for determining who among our applicants might be such a professional. We have no current assessments for determining which of the students who apply are creative, intelligent, confluent, and out of the box, in addition to having skills and abilities more traditionally associated with effective leadership. That doesn't mean we don't get such students; it only means that we have no direct way to ensure that the students we select come with the profile we say we want. We have made little headway in a decade in having our admission criteria reflect our recruitment goals. Changing the student mix requires changes in both our recruiting and selection policies and practices.

One of the by-products of this reform is a decrease in our enrollment. A combination of recruiting highly capable students and the increased demands of our programs on students partly explains this reduction in numbers. We now no longer let students start the program anytime they want and take courses "willy-nilly." Students can no longer take Tuesday night. The result is that we have more serious students who are willing to inconvenience themselves for the program and for their own doctoral and certification work. It also means that the pool of students interested in our program has decreased. Although the faculty is not unhappy that we have a more serious—if smaller— student body, others within the university are not as enthused as we are with this change. Thus, we have come in for criticism and have lost a tenure-track position from the department. The certification and doctoral programs in educational administration have historically generated a pleasing profit for the university. Increasing standards and improving the program aren't neces- sarily compatible with these high profits. Balancing the market requirements of the university with the educational goals of the faculty is a difficult and potentially dangerous activity.

> *Improve and expand the research*
> *of the field and connect this*
> *research to administrative*
> *decision making.*

Our doctoral program has always had a heavy research component em- bedded in the curriculum; we have now added research and inquiry into the administrative preparation strand. In both programs, we have more closely linked research and/or "evidence" with decision making, working to help stu- dents become conscious of their own decision-making processes and be able to articulate on what basis a decision has been made. Additionally, we have added components to our program that help students identify what evidence they need for decisions, how to access or collect the data necessary, and how to determine the adequacy of the evidence.

Throughout the decade, we have struggled with the appropriateness of a dissertation as the capstone experience in a doctoral program that prepares people for administrative positions. To the traditional definition of a dissertation we have added a policy advocacy and the doctoral policy document (Browder, 1995). The doctoral policy document opens with a vision statement, followed by an analysis of need section, and then the advocated policy statement. The policy argumentation section is next. The student must defend and/or explain the impact of the policy on learning, finances, equity, growth, and development as well as describe the potential for successful implementation, discussing the barriers to implementation, the political and legal issues surrounding the policy, and the plan. In this section, existing research is synthesized, action research undertaken, and some analyses (particularly cost analyses) prepared. "The level of scholarship exhibited here should be substantial and comprehensive enough to offer confidence that the arguments advanced are balanced, considered, and reasonable" (Browder, 1995, p. 59).

To improve our focus on the connection between coursework and practice, we have been reconceptualizing the research sequence for students despite the obstacle of having this sequence in another department. Central to this reconceptualization is the commitment to end the polarization of qualitative versus quantitative or statistics versus narrative. In this process, we are having students spend 2 years learning inquiry around the issue of student achievement from multiple perspectives and using multiple methods. Thus, they spend time analyzing the philosophical roots of the concept, connecting it to particular schools of philosophical thought. They map the historical use of the term and what kinds of research have been undertaken on student achievement. Synthesis and meta-analytic studies help students review the literature on achievement. Students in the research strand learn statistics by analyzing their own school's data sets from the New York State Prep and Regents tests. Students undertake surveys, and interview studies are conducted to explore achievement from a variety of contexts: student, teacher, parent. Observational studies illuminate how these concepts look in the classroom. Cost analysis connects spending to various definitions of achievement.

We believe that this approach is more likely to strengthen the practice of connecting evidence to decisions and place inquiry into the administrative day. Most of our students will never do another formal piece of research after the dissertation; we hope to build in them action research approaches to their daily work and an ability to develop and analyze policy applications.

The topics that our students explore in their capstone experience reflect some of the trends that I have observed in the past decade in the field. I compared the Division A presentations at the American Educational Research Association (AERA) annual conference in 1988 and 1998. The presentations in 1998 include more focus on teaching and learning, more work on how to prepare administrators, and more studies on the impacts of administrative work or policy on student outcomes. In 1988, few studies examined race, class, and gender themes; at the end of the decade, a substantial proportion of the presentations concentrated on these issues. Although it is unclear that there has been a change in the number of empirically based papers in Division A during the decade, the methods in the studies that do present data have shifted from surveys, analyzed statistically, to observations or interview studies, analyzed thematically.

> *Keep the department and faculty focus on student outcomes, conceptualized from multiple perspectives, and help our students learn to do the same as administrators.*

Most schools are designed to serve the needs of those who work in these organizations rather than those who attend them; universities are no different. Much of what we do and how we do it suits us as university workers rather than the students from whom we collect tuition. Because so much of what we do was put in place long before any of the members of our department arrived, one of the first things we have had to do is become conscious of who is served by whatever procedure we are examining. We also have to make it safe to admit that one of the reasons—or perhaps the whole reason—why we preferred a particular practice was because it served our personal needs. We have been mildly successful at identifying who is served and then shifting to serving more of the students' needs. This shift has not been without great costs to individual faculty members, as I indicate in the title of this chapter.

Some of these shifts have been that we schedule classes at times that are more convenient for students than for faculty members—weekends, summer, earlier, later, January. Other accommodations have been that we have increased the amount of time that we spend in classes and in advisement, well beyond the university requirements. We have opened our homes as second offices and take faxes and phone calls from there. Most of us communicate daily by e-mail with our classes and individual doctoral students. We have added January and summer to the required class schedule, although we are not reimbursed by the university. We hold extra class meetings, we set up school-site projects that take considerable planning and implementation time, and we read and respond to work as many times as it takes for the student to get it to a professional level. We visit students in their schools, we try to help them find jobs, and we give them extra internships and experiences to strengthen their capabilities as administrators. We assess their learning styles and then try to build experiences that respond to these styles.

In addition to these individual changes, we adopted a department curriculum for the first five courses of the doctoral program (which also serve as the administrative certification strand), which meant that changes in course content or materials were department, not individual faculty, decisions. We tried to rotate the teaching of these courses so that no professor would "own" a course. This proved difficult. Although we have shared classes or team-taught them, it has taken a lot out of those who have done it, requiring them to learn new areas and develop new activities. As a backup, we meet once a month for 3 hours in a work group to discuss these courses and how to keep the five experiences connected, as though one experience. We have tried to team teach these courses as well as the research strand. Because the university does not support team teaching in calculating faculty load, this change requires a commitment from individual faculty members to teach without credit toward load. Although two of us have done this for the past 2 years, it has been very difficult and is not a commitment that I believe we can sustain much longer.

By admitting students in learning communities and having them move through the program together, and by allowing students to begin the program only in the fall semester, we have been able to almost completely eliminate the use of adjunct faculty in our programs. This is an important step for the program, because we believe that a long-term, integrated commitment to the program, not just the course, is necessary. Those few adjunct faculty who are part of the team must attend monthly meetings on the program and involve themselves in department activities. Because we have built the program to be cumulative, full-time faculty have had to agree to teach in the summer—something that we have never been required to do unless we wanted to. Most of us do not want the additional teaching load; this, then, is a sacrifice/hardship.

All of these contributions to student learning take time that we didn't have to spend before we began our work together, and time that the university neither requires us to spend nor rewards us for. The result is that although those of us who have changed our practice are more satisfied with what we do and believe we are better serving our students, we are also worn out from the work. We are close to pulling back and returning to our old ways, particularly because we have no way to gauge whether or not all of our extra work is worth the effort we expend.

We have not developed measures that will help us understand whether our students are more capable administrators, whether they are better able to make change, or whether the systems in which they work serve students better because of the way the administrators in them were prepared. Partly, it's too soon to tell. But mainly, we have not determined how we would know. We have data from students that indicate they like the program and believe it has changed their lives—but we have always had such data. It is the nature of graduate students in educational administration and the self-report formative and summative evaluation process that such data exist. Until we are able to determine whether or not our efforts have any of the impacts that we hope for them, it is not likely that we will sustain the extra work these reforms require.

> *Develop reflective practice habits*
> *in ourselves and our students,*
> *keeping our values connected*
> *to our actions.*

We have considerable evidence that the students in our restructured programs are more reflective and that they report using this reflection in their administrative work more than do previous students (Kottkamp, n.d.). Fiction, platform statements, weekly e-mail, and short paper submissions have helped students develop their reflective skills and become more analytic in determining whether espoused theories are actually the theories in practice. As a group, in department meetings, we have spent some time comparing what it is we believe we do with what we actually do and trying to reconcile or diminish the differences between the two. Reflective group practice has become part of the way in which we operate, at least at a departmental level.

Nationwide, it is my understanding that many programs have added reflective components. I don't know how those initiatives are working, but as Kottkamp often reminds us, "In order to do this work, we first have to change ourselves." That is a daunting task. I have changed myself, but I'm not sure I like the result, nor am I sure that this new "instructor" is the me I want to be. Change at the level that our department has attempted has required deep shifts in individual practice. These shifts have been hard to do and, in my case, have left me wondering where I went and who this new person is.

> *Improve the effectiveness of our methods of teaching and increase the relevance of the curriculum to problems of practice.*

We have worked to include problems of practice into our program. This has been much harder than we anticipated, although we expected that such a change would require an organizational complexity as well as an attention to detail that would challenge us. In an effort to move the program out of the classroom and emphasize experiential learning, we have linked each new community of students that we admit with a local school district. These districts have been chosen as partners based upon their own willingness to work with us over five semesters to transform administrative preparation into a focused and problem-based experience.

Representatives of the partner district work with the APS faculty as a team throughout the five semesters and provide problem-based experiences and/or practitioner perspective in each of the five courses. The district is used to generating problem-based learning situations, shadowing experiences, and internship opportunities. Much of the coursework, then, unfolds in the district.

Experiential content of the courses changes from semester to semester as the needs of partner districts and the particular problems of practice engaged in by the community and the district emerge.

Within the classrooms, we have tried more constructivist approaches and have had energetic debate with each other about the place for lecture in our teaching. For myself, it's hard to give up what I like doing and take on something I don't like to do. However, because my colleagues have convinced me that different approaches are better for students, I have changed the way I teach. I'm still in the middle of this struggle, not liking the new ways much, feeling that I am cheating the students, and totally uncomfortable with myself as a teacher.

Has Anything Worked?

Has all this effort made a difference for our students and for their students? Are we preparing "humane and social critics" who will transform schools? We don't know. We know that students understand the mission of the program and have incorporated this mission into their own descriptions of what they are expected to do (i.e., "I'm going to make a difference"). Students also have considerable opportunity to reflect on the differences on which they want to focus and to develop plans for doing so. Additionally, the doctoral policy document offers them an opportunity to practice moral or social change leadership.

We do collect data on how students are progressing. For instance, in addition to the usual evaluation procedures for students (course assignments, tests), student progress is monitored using a portfolio approach, sampling student work at several points in the academic journey. Beginning with their first course, students begin to compile a portfolio that includes descriptions of class experiences, assignments, connections with the field, and an expanding reflective platform. Using these portfolios, community advisers review the progress of each member of the community every semester. The department as a whole monitors the work of each student several times during her or his career. As a group, we discuss our experiences of the strengths and weaknesses of the student's performance and give that feedback to the student. In several cases, we have counseled students out of our programs.

It is very important to evaluate each student, each semester, on the set of criteria that guides the program. Every professor writes a narrative assessment on five major skill/development areas for each student after each course. The student receives a copy of the evaluation, and a copy is placed in the portfolio. If students don't make sufficient progress, or if students are not administratively skilled by midprogram, the student is sent a letter by the department suggesting another line of study.

Still, this doesn't tell us how the students are performing in the field once they leave us. Although we have anecdotal data in this area, we have yet to develop a method and a process for determining whether or not the graduates of this program are reformers themselves. This is work that is still left for us to do.

Where am I after a decade? I still believe in the mission we set out for ourselves. I'm proud of that statement and the goals we have set. I believe that the direction in which we are headed is better instructionally, prepares analytic administrators, helps administrators clarify their values and see their futures, and challenges them to develop their thinking and to convince others. So I'm on board in this sense. At the same time, I wonder where I fit in the new program. I don't quite understand what I can bring to the students, if it isn't content, and I struggle to try to enjoy what I now do.

Thus, I believe that what we do is best for the students, but I don't like doing it. It isn't work that gives me day-to-day satisfaction or much sense of efficacy. It takes time from my research, it requires an involvement with students that I don't always want, it keeps me away from my home for many hours more than I would like, and it involves me in long discussions with my colleagues as we wrestle with our ideas. I like closure, I hate meetings, I avoid intimate contact, and I like solitary work. The old program supported such behavior. The new program doesn't. The question for me is, "Can I change myself enough to be successful and of service in the new program?" or "Must I change jobs so that I am doing what I like?"

In other words, I like the outcomes, but doing the work to get the program there is not fun. I think I am not alone in this seeming contradiction. I'd like our program to get to another place, but I would like it to get there without me having to travel the road. A decade of this travel has left me tired, unsure of myself, and wondering if there is anything about me that is worth retaining. The critical stance, the disciplined analysis of espoused versus actual practice, and the wide-ranging change in expectations for professors have been good for the program and, I think, the students. At the same time, I've lost my sense of self, my self-confidence, and my sense of purpose. And I was the one leading this change!

Is the decade half full or half empty? I don't know. I'm not even sure that it's the right question to ask. Change is growth. Growth is painful. Maybe I'm not far enough along to know if the destination is worth the journey. If the journey is the destination, I'm sunk.

References

Browder, L. (1995). An alternative to the doctoral dissertation: The policy advocacy concept and the doctoral policy document. *Journal of School Leadership, 5,* 40-68.

Shakeshaft, C. (1993). Preparing tomorrow's school leaders: The Hofstra experience. In J. Murphy (Ed.), *Preparing tomorrow's school leaders: Alternative designs.* University Park, PA: The University Council for Educational Administration.

PART IV

Concluding Thoughts

12

A Decade of Changes:
Analysis and Comment

PATRICK B. FORSYTH
JOSEPH MURPHY

The reports and perspectives on the decade of educational administration reform depicted in this volume lead us to conclude that although there has been some progress, the profession's efforts to create relevant technical knowledge and provide fledgling administrators with both technical and practice knowledge have fallen short of transforming the profession. States are not convinced of the quality and utility of educational administration preparation programs, as evidenced by the growing number of external reviews and forced reauthorization of administrator preparation programs. The public, generally, is disillusioned with education and school leadership, as evidenced by the multitudinous efforts to find education alternatives for children. Those who enter the field of educational administration remain unwilling to devote adequate time and effort to their preparation, and many do not ultimately become school administrators. History would suggest that the kind of change necessary to vitalize this profession is perhaps radical, not incremental.

To examine the decade without simply restating what each of the previous authors has said, we place the events of the decade against the general historical backdrop of professional knowledge and preparation and follow that with an overview of these same events in the narrower field of educational administration. Then we examine reforms and reform claims from the decade and finally take up the advice of George Casper Homans, the renowned Harvard sociologist, who urged that a "last chapter" should resemble a primitive orgy after harvest:

The work may have come to an end, but the worker cannot let go all at once. He is still full of energy that will fester if it cannot find an outlet. Accordingly he is allowed a time of license, when he may say all sorts of things he would think twice about saying in more sober moments, when he is no longer bound by logic and evidence but free to speculate about what he has done. (Homans, 1974, p. 356)

General History of Professional Knowledge and Preparation

Human endeavor is informed by a mixture of knowledge and skill gained through personal experience, as well as knowledge and skill passed on in some organized or codified way from others (see Harris,1993, pp. 17-33). For every endeavor, the appropriate mixture of knowledge and skill derived from these two sources is different and mutable. Technology, for example, has substantially changed the mixture for some professions because it has made codified knowledge accessible to nonprofessionals. What distinguishes human endeavors that can be called "professions" (and we use this term with great trepidation) is that in addition to using an extensive body of technical and codified knowledge, professionals rely on a nonroutine kind of experiential knowledge to be effective. Professional practice ideally holds out the individual client or patient's well-being as its goal, making use of contextual and other idiosyncratic and experiential observations, as well as codified information, to heal, educate, help, or protect.

The nature of the dialectic between technical knowledge and practice knowledge dominates the history of professional education. There has been a continuous tension between universities and practitioners for control of professional induction. As a rule, when universities control professional preparation, they undervalue the knowledge of artistry and the importance of experience, sometimes to the point of making professional preparation irrelevant. When practitioners control preparation, they undervalue technical knowledge and research. Rather than a search for balance, the history of professional education can be characterized as a tug-of-war between purists from these two knowledge camps.

We should say at the outset precisely what we mean by these two types of knowledge, whose definitions have been adapted from the conceptualization of Oakeshott as basic to all sciences, arts, or all human activities (Oakeshott, 1962, p. 7). By *technical knowledge* we mean an organized system of theoretical explanation and systematic evidence related to a set of phenomena making up the focus of a professional practice, or more simply stated, codified, specialized knowledge. It can be taught and learned in lecture halls, laboratories, and so on. By practice knowledge, we refer to a kind of knowledge that exists only in use. Practice knowledge, "know-how, artistry, insight, judgment, and connoisseurship are expressed only in practice and learned only through experience with practice" (Harris, 1993, p. 22). This kind of knowledge cannot be taught, but it can be learned through the extended observation of expert practitioners.

In medieval Europe, the major professions (theology, law, and medicine) were all learned at the university, transmitted primarily by lecture, with virtually no emphasis on practice. This trend continued through the Renaissance, ultimately reaching an extreme imbalance as demonstrated by the study of law at Oxford and Cambridge, which became exclusively academic (based on Roman jurisprudence). Those who intended to practice in the English courts were forced to study elsewhere to be trained in the common law, disdained by the faculties of the two prestigious universities as local law and unworthy of university study (Brubacher, 1962, pp. 52-53). After an initial period of relying on European-trained professionals, colonial America necessarily favored an apprenticeship approach for training. Early professional proprietary schools evolved from the apprenticeship system, and for a while, the two systems operated simultaneously, with the lower standards common to the apprenticeship system prevailing (Brubacher, 1962, pp. 60-61).

At the turn of the century, there was a limited return to an emphasis on technical knowledge as some university-affiliated professional schools began to draw on the sciences and other university disciplines. Still, even as late as the last decade of the century, Paulsen could claim that there were no professional schools of university rank in this country, save Harvard in law and Johns Hopkins in medicine (Paulsen, 1895). Despite these exceptions, professional education was in such a deplorable state early in the 20th Century that the Carnegie Foundation for the Advancement of Teaching commissioned Abraham Flexner to conduct a study first of medical schools and then of law schools in an effort to inspire reform. The first Flexner Report (1910) was highly critical of medical schools and had revolutionary consequences, including a drastic reduction in their number, the merger of proprietary professional schools with universities, and an increasing separation of learning from practice. After Flexner, medical schools continued to have practice training, but only after extended exposure to basic scientific theory and research. Although not as homogeneous as post-Flexner medicine, when law preparation moved to the American university, training for practice was effectively abolished. Increasingly throughout the 20th century, professional training

,affiliated with universities moved away from practice and became preoccu-
pied with "the development of an abstract and systematic body of theory,
sufficiently complex and esoteric to justify the profession's claim to unique
competence over its chosen sphere of activity" (Thorne, 1973, p. 30).

In the 1970s, there was a shift back toward practice knowledge, marked
by the work of the Carnegie Commission on Higher Education and chaired
by Clark Kerr. In one of the Commission's reports, Schein (1972) summarized criticisms of the profession, specifically noting that

> professional education generally underutilizes the applied behavioral
> sciences, especially in helping professionals to increase their self-insight,
> their ability to diagnose and manage client relationships and complex
> social problems, their ability to sort out the ethical and value issues in-
> herent in their professional role, and their ability to continue to learn
> throughout their career. (p. 60)

It is clear from Schein's critique that 30 years ago, there already was an emerging concern that the balance between technical and practice knowledge was
in need of adjustment. Later in the same report, Schein sketches "the new professional school," a precursor of problem-based learning, that he says "should
start with a learning theory that integrates basic sciences, applied sciences,
and professional skills within single learning modules rather than separating
them into successive 'core courses,' 'applied courses,' and [practica]" (Schein,
1972, p. 129).

Ten years after Schein, Schön moved the critique and argument for reform of professional preparation with even greater incisiveness, first in his
widely cited *The Reflective Practitioner* (1983), and again, 4 years later, with
the publication of *Educating the Reflective Practitioner* (1987). Schön argues that professional education has relied on a technical rationalist epistemology that views professional competence as the application of techniques
and theories derived from systematic (scientific) research to instrumental
problems of practice (Schön, 1987, p. 33). In both routine and unfamiliar
situations, thinking like a professional consists of rule-governed inquiry (p.
34). In this epistemology, artistry has little place, and "there is no way [for
professionals] to talk about their artistry—except, perhaps, to say that they
are following rules that have not yet been made explicit" (p. 35).

Advancing the case for an alternative epistemology of practice, Schön
(1987) points to professional artistry, understood in terms of reflection-in-
action, which is central to an understanding of professional competence
(p. 35). According to Schön, practitioners who use this epistemology fre-

quently experience the unexpected, causing them to go beyond the rules, facts, theories, and operations. They respond by restructuring some "strategies of action, theories of phenomena, or ways of framing the problem," and they invent experiments to test new understandings (p. 35). Most of Schön's book focuses on developing a new kind of professional education that might develop practitioners' reflection-in-action, what has earlier been called "practice knowledge."

The argument for this kind of preparatory experience is supported by research on the formation of expertise in cognitive psychology. Gordon (1992), for example, claims that "although we possess static, verbalizable knowledge, much of our learning and skilled behavior is driven by a dynamic, procedural knowledge that is not verbalizable" (p. 114). Thus, much of what a professional does cannot be taught as codified technical knowledge. Indeed, it cannot be articulated at all. Practice knowledge must be learned through experience, the kind of experience that is not acquired in lecture halls, libraries, or even laboratories.

Schön (1987) has raised an important challenge that goes to the heart of the issue: "Can the prevailing concepts of professional education ever yield a curriculum adequate to the complex, unstable, uncertain, and conflictual worlds of practice?" (p. 12). The question is even more threatening for the "minor professions," where there may be no agreement on the question of the very existence of a credible, useful body of technical knowledge and, hence, no persuasive argument for housing professional preparation in the university.

In sum, the general history of professional preparation can be described as the product of legitimate interest and emphasis on two kinds of knowledge: technical and practice. Extreme imbalance has tended to provoke correction. In the United States, control of preparation by practitioners through apprenticeship and proprietary professional schools secured an emphasis on practice knowledge right up until the beginning of the 20th century. In the first decade of the century, the inadequacies of this approach were exposed, and professional preparation was absorbed by universities. Predictably, the universities emphasized technical knowledge and scientific research, often creating extraordinary theoretical advances, but in some cases neglecting practice knowledge to the extreme. Around the middle of the century, there began to be heard among the major professions some grumbling about addressing practice knowledge again. The work of Donald Schön has had a significant role in helping professions understand this problem and in motivating professional curriculum revision and experiments in instructional delivery, such as problem-based learning. We now turn to educational administration, using the historical tension between technical and practice knowledge to frame our discussion.

Educational Administration:
History of Knowledge and Preparation

The human endeavor under discussion here is the organization, maintenance, and improvement of educational enterprises—the profession of school administration. Typical of what Glaser (1964) calls the minor professions, the appropriate preparatory mixture of technical and practice knowledge for this field is somewhat volatile, and it is made more so by the fact that educational administration is eclectic and diffuse. Pedagogy, child psychology, law, finance, organizational analysis, human relations, and perhaps a myriad of other specialties are integrally part of the applied specialty of educational administration. This characteristic of diffuseness sets educational administration apart from focused professions such as medicine and law, complicating the issue of balance.

Historically, the formal training and preparation of school administrators in the United States has essentially been carried out in the university. Control of school administrator preparation during the first half of the century primarily was in the hands of former school administrators who moved to the university and conducted programs and classes. Many of these individuals were intellectual giants, but administrator induction consisted of aspirants hearing lectures relating the experiences of these former administrators. The curriculum effectively conveyed neither technical nor practice knowledge about school administration—merely secondhand experiences as filtered through the recollections of retired school leaders, albeit in many cases, distinguished ones.

Practice Knowledge: Broad Strokes

It was not until nearly midcentury that universities began to foster practice knowledge in educational administration preparation. At a 1947 meeting of the National Conference for Professors of Educational Administration (NCPEA), interest in "internship" for school administrators was stimulated, at a time when only two universities had internship requirements (Milstein, Bobroff, & Restine, 1991, p. 4). In the years following that meeting, programs incorporated clinical experiences (internships), and they did so at an impressive rate. Whereas the internship was virtually unheard of in 1947, by 1987, more than 80% of educational administration programs surveyed indicated that they required the internship (Skalski et al., 1987).

Despite the nearly universal embrace of internship as a way to provide practice knowledge, predictably, universities did not manage and nurture this preparatory exercise adequately. Milstein (1990) chronicles the failure thus:

> Too often field sites are chosen haphazardly and/or are not closely monitored. The potential for interns being constrained to passive observation, being placed in roles which do not fit closely with their career goals, or being used as "go-fers," is great when clear and agreed-upon expectations are not developed. Likewise, campus-based practicums and seminars on a regular basis are rarely available or required and clinical experiences are often isolated from the rest of a student's program flow. Finally, the connecting linkages between on-campus experiences and field-based experiences are rarely adequately developed. (p. 121)

Forsyth (1992) is equally pessimistic, claiming that "administrator preparation either abandons a key element of professional preparation, internship, or it approaches this element with neither enthusiasm nor resources" (p. 324).

In addition to internship, educational administration has experimented with "bringing the reality of administration into the classroom through such media as written cases, simulated situations" (Culbertson, 1962, p. 166). Other professions have also experimented with the fostering of practice knowledge in the classroom. Of particular interest is the use of the simulated patient in medicine (actors trained to mimic the symptoms and complaints of a specific pathological condition). UCEA, among others, has been active in promoting and publishing cases and simulations since the 1950s. Although these materials have been used by some to introduce administration students to practice knowledge, their use has not been widespread.

Technical Knowledge: Broad Strokes

Events around the middle of the century also changed the nature of administrator preparation by promoting the development of technical knowledge. In 1947, Walter D. Cocking gathered a group of professors and academics "to take a measure of the field by considering the changing nature of administrative practice, the growing need for theory and research, and emerging demands on graduate programs" (Campbell, Fleming, Newell, & Bennion, 1987, pp. 13-14). This group evolved into the NCPEA. Its formation was followed by the Kellogg Foundation's funding of the Cooperative

Program in Educational Administration (CPEA), and 10 years later, by the founding of the University Council for Educational Administration (UCEA). These events conspired significantly to change educational administrator preparation.

The field of educational administration is a relatively new one, especially when we think of a field as having claim to a specialized body of knowledge. Prior to the middle of the 20th century, no authoritative claims of this kind were made. It is true that earlier in the century, there were flirtations with scientific management, human relations, and other intellectual "movements," but professors of educational administration were still essentially practitioners who pragmatically embraced popular ideas of the day in their curricula. By midcentury, however, within the university, the press was on for educational administration to have a body of technical knowledge that was "scientific." Thus was born what has been called the theory movement in educational administration, a period whose illusions lasted about 10 years.

Although some of the earliest (1950s) advocates of a scientific approach to building knowledge in educational administration were naively taken with logical positivism, it is not clear that positivism in its essential form was ever embraced by researchers in this field. The movement did raise unrealistic hopes for a coherent grand theory of administration and a science-like corpus of general knowledge that might serve as a platform for practice, but it soon settled for much less. Additionally, the theory movement did raise the bar as far as expectations for defensible systematic inquiry are concerned, for example, introducing notions such as validity and bias. But aside from Getzels and Guba's (1957) initial demonstration theory, there are few examples in the half-century since of theory construction or the nearly mathematical deduction of propositions and claims of objectivity advanced by card-carrying logical positivists. There have been examples of theory development of limited scope and efforts to develop causal models of limited phenomena. This is not, however, the stuff of which logical positivism is made.

The belief in and hope for a scientific theory of administration did create in some an intellectual arrogance that was, to say the least, off-putting and hardly justified. Guba (1975) parodied that attitude at its height:

"Well," we would say, "practice is hardly our concern. We don't know what the practical problems are. It's up to you administrators who have to deal with these problems every day to make the application. And as for not understanding our language, well, you can hardly fault us for that. If we are in the ivory tower, then you are surely in the basement. If we should descend so as to speak your language, why don't you ascend and meet us at least halfway up?" (p. 372)

Momentum for a theory movement in educational administration can be traced to the early 1950s with the presentation of the Getzels-Guba model. But already by 1967, Halpin had declared the movement dead (Monahan, 1975, p. 4). It is somewhat mysterious, then, that Greenfield's notorious critique of the theory movement almost 7 years later (1974) could cause such a stir. Greenfield himself was surprised by the hostile reaction to his attack on social science and the separation of fact from value (Greenfield & Ribbins, 1993, p. 243). His critique would have been more comprehensible if, at the time of its delivery, there was a great cohort of productive positivist researchers turning out sheaves of theoretical explanation about schools and children, socializing fledgling school administrators to manipulate these findings and theories without contextual consciousness, or even a bow to community values and the commonweal. But there was not. During the height of what some think of as educational administration's infatuation with pseudopositivism, there were not enough manuscripts produced that were consistent with that paradigm, even interpreting its features somewhat loosely, to fill four issues of *Educational Administration Quarterly*, making it the only quarterly published thrice yearly.

It did not take the extremes of a flirtation with logical positivism for educational administration as a profession to be wary of placing exclusive trust in technical knowledge. Its history is replete with these messages of caution. None other than John Dewey (1929) warned that "the final reality of educational science is not found in books, nor in experimental laboratories, nor in the class-rooms where it is taught but in the minds of those engaged in directing educational activities" (p. 32). Fewer than 10 years into the theory movement, Culbertson (1962) provides caution against an unwarranted reliance on science:

> Knowledge about the social sciences cannot provide complete guides for dealing with administrative processes. Moral issues face school leaders as they engage in these processes, and such issues transcend scientific theories. Thus, science can provide pertinent understandings through such concepts as "community power structure." However, it cannot give a complete answer to administrators about the manner or the extent to which they should manipulate the "power structure." (p. 161)

Just 2 years later, Willower (1964) makes a similar point:

Commitment to reflective methods is itself a value, and it is an essential one if aims are to be achieved effectively; however, broad educational ideals which reflect sensitivity to human dignity and potentials must guide action as well. Science after all, should be man's servant, not his master. (pp. 94-95)

Most recently, Wiggins (1992) has made the indictment absolutely clear: "The promise of a science of administration has never been fulfilled, and research in the field has made little contribution to the practice of administration" (p. 5). There remain many debatable questions about the theory movement in educational administration and its contributions/effects, and they will not be settled here.

The real questions for us are the following: What were future practitioners of educational administration learning? and What technical knowledge were they being exposed to during the theory movement and in the period after that until the decade under scrutiny in this volume? It may be that the effects of the theory movement have been vastly exaggerated. For example, Hills (1965), writing in the first issue of *EAQ* about those effects, assures us that "there seem to be relatively few concrete indications of any sweeping changes in the field" (p. 58). In that same issue, Andrew Halpin (1965), in characteristic directness, announced that he "started out with high hope. But now as I look at the field ten years later, I find myself dismayed by the trivial progress that we have achieved" (p. 53).

At least two points can be made. First, there was a gradual inclusion of social science content in educational administration curricula after the mid-1950s. Increasingly, professors with interests in sociology, economics, and psychological backgrounds replaced the traditional retired practitioners as program faculty. A little later, law was added as a specialty. But few of these professors were trained social scientists or lawyers; most were graduates of educational administration programs who had emphasized research during their own doctoral training and had been influenced by a like mentor-scholar. General courses in school administration gave way to courses in the specialties, and faculty were expected to teach and do research in their specialties. The courses lacked integration with each other and did not generally constitute a cohesive professional preparation program.

Second, it can be demonstrated that the list of specialties and courses offered in educational administration programs stabilized relatively quickly. By the 1960s, courses in organizational theory, school finance, school business administration, personnel, instructional supervision, facilities planning, and role courses (superintendent and principal) were standard fare. This list is not significantly different from the list of the 1970s (McNally & Dean, 1963, pp. 113-114) or, indeed, the list found by Silver and Spuck in 1978 (Silver & Spuck, 1978).

In sum, early in the 33-year period that covers the theory movement until the NCEEA report (1954-1987), technical knowledge in educational administration programs became specialized. Some of the specialties (law, finance, organizational theory) appeared to gain a place in the curriculum because there was existing or emerging technical knowledge and esoteric content in these specialties that could be borrowed and/or adapted, giving substance and credibility to these specialists and courses. Other curriculum elements remained closer to practice, and the content of these areas of study remained soft. A great part of the enduring corpus of technical knowledge making up the educational administration syllabus was, and continued to be, borrowed from theorists and researchers outside of this field. Self-criticisms by academics in the years leading up to the NCEEA called the technical knowledge of the field marginally relevant, immature, and unrelated to successful practice (see Murphy, 1992, pp. 84-87).

Practice knowledge for preparing school administrators also was severely criticized at the end of this period. Some efforts at establishing internship and the use of cases, simulations, and other practice-oriented learning had all but disappeared from the university. Getting a degree and license in school administration was akin to "getting your ticket punched." No one thought it had much to do with the professional and successful practice of school leadership.

What Has Happened During
the Past Decade in Educational Administration?

In the arena of reform, rhetoric often outstrips reality. The desire to improve this profession is widespread, and we want so much to believe that we are efficacious that it is easy to convince ourselves and others that we have made more progress than the facts might support. A great deal of effort has been devoted to reform and improvement of educational leader preparation during the decade since the NCEEA report. Associations have devoted their energies and funds; state governments, national consortia, foundations, study panels, and countless groups of professional school faculty and practitioners have thought about the leverage points that might be used to stimulate improvement in preparation; and all of these have mounted reform initiatives. The temptation to overestimate our success is nearly irresistible.

There are several stock-taking markers in the decade under consideration. We focus on two: 1992 and 1997, the latter date consisting of data collected for the current volume. In 1992, Murphy's *Landscape of Leadership Preparation* was published, and it provided a comprehensive review and synthesis of research and commentary on professional preparation for this field. In reference to practice knowledge and preparation, Murphy concluded that

> the field-based component continues to be infected with weaknesses that have been revisited on a regular basis since the first decade of the behavioral science revolution in administrative preparation: (a) "unclear or even conflicting objectives" (Cronin & Horoschak, 1973, p. 16); (b) inadequate number of clinical experiences; (c) activities arranged on the basis of convenience; (d) overemphasis on role-centered as opposed to problem-centered experiences; (e) "lack of individualization in 'molding' field experiences to students' individual needs and goals" (Culbertson & Farquhar, 1971, p. 12); (f) poor planning, supervision, and follow-up; (g) absence of "connecting linkages between on-campus experiences and field-based experiences" (Milstein, 1990, p. 121); and (h) overemphasis on low-level (orientation and passive observation type) activities (Clark, 1988; Daresh, 1987; Milstein, 1990). (Murphy, 1992, p. 92)

At the midpoint of the decade, Murphy was equally critical of progress in the development and delivery of technical knowledge:

> The indiscriminate adoption of practices untested (Culbertson, 1988) and uninformed by educational values and purposes (Bates, 1984); serious fragmentation (Erickson, 1979; Willower, 1988); the separation of the practice and academic arms of the profession (Carver, 1988; Farquhar, 1968; Goldhammer, 1983); relatively nonrobust strategies for generating new knowledge (Achilles, 1990; Immegart, 1977), the neglect of ethics (Farquhar, 1968); an infatuation with the study of administration for its own sake (Evans, 1991), and the concomitant failure to address outcomes (Boyd & Crowson, 1981; Erickson, 1977, 1979). . . . In short, preparation programs as a group are not only failing to address the right things, they are also doing a fairly poor job of accomplishing the things on which they have chosen to work. (Murphy, 1992, pp. 85-86)

It is important to note that these evaluations of technical and practice knowledge in professional preparation are based on writings that mostly predate the decade under study here. Murphy's critique of 1992 may not have applied to actual mid-decade conditions. However, McCarthy and Kuh (1997) support this mid-decade view, indicating that "the content specializations of faculty members in 1994 for the most part mirrored traditional course areas included in leadership preparation programs" (p. 247).

The most recent stocktaking we can examine is based on data collected by Murphy from educational leadership department chairs at the end of 1996 (see Chapter 7). Despite the reports contained in this volume by keen observers and participants in all sorts of reform activity (governmental, licensure, knowledge production, program structure, instructional materials development, etc.), perhaps the best indications of just how far the reform has taken us can be had by careful attention to what department chairs say they have changed—hence, the importance of this survey, which compares the department chairs' views of reform for 1989 with those from 1996. In 1989, only one specified area (clinical experiences) was designated by chairs as having been changed "somewhat." In 1996, 10 of the 16 specified areas (recruitment of students, selection of students, monitoring/assessing progress, clinical experiences, program content, teaching and learning strategies, practitioner involvement in development, practitioner involvement in delivery, mix of students, and departmental mission/agenda) had been changed more than "somewhat," according to the department chairs.

Although there is no cause for uninhibited rejoicing, the reports of the department chairs provide hope that, a decade after strident calls for reform, rigorous and relevant scholarship, concern for practice, and closer ties between the academy and practice, there indeed seems to be some movement. The data have their limitations, and the change reported is very moderate, but they may foretell the downfall of complacency that has characterized the educational administration faculty since Campbell and Newell studied them in 1972 and as reaffirmed by McCarthy and Kuh (1997) and McCarthy, Kuh, Newell, and Iacona (1988).

The Future: Some Possibilities

Our last observations are laced with optimism that gradual and incremental reform can work. In the end, it may be the only successful kind of change we can hope for. But there are two questions we are anxious to pose before we give up our careers as fast-change advocates. The first is, Why has our technical knowledge tended to be irrelevant and unrelated to practice when many clearly wanted it to be both relevant and rigorous? Readers should speculate with us, but a number of factors can be considered. Our technical knowledge came after our preparation programs existed, and university conditions required that it come into being in a few short years. Consequently, much of it was borrowed from technical knowledge already existing within university specialties rather than growing out of the tasks of the profession. Often, the fit was far from perfect, and it could even be argued that the wrong specialties emerged because of this rapid retrofit of social science and school administration.

Also, the specialties evolved a system of knowledge organization that linked educational administration specialists with other, noneducation university specialists instead of creating conceptual framework and language linkages with school practitioners. Early research in this field often focused on administrative behavior rather than on the professional tasks of administration and their relationship to school success. That seems parallel to studying how doctors behave rather than how diagnostic tools and intervention strategies maintain or restore the health of patients.

Instead of developing a specialty in school law or organizational theory, it might, for example, have made more sense to create a specialty around building and maintaining positive affective environments in schools. Such a specialty would, of course, have legal, organizational, psychological, and sociological aspects to it. But the technical knowledge that would evolve from the establishment of such a specialty would be directly related to a critical work task of school leaders. Its utility would be evident.

On another level, our technical knowledge is not irrelevant. The *Handbook of Research on Educational Administration* (Boyan, 1988), *Educational Administration: The UCEA Document Base* (Hoy, Astuto, & Forsyth, 1996), and the new *AERA Handbook* about to be published provide a compelling record of 50 years of original scholarship and active borrowing. Practicing administrators, cognitive dissonance aside, often regale academics with claims of the utility for theoretical frameworks. When making a case for change, principals and superintendents will pull together a persuasive array of research findings that support their position. But it does seem to us that this kind of utility is different from the utility that medical education (the acquisition of technical and practice knowledge) has for medical practitioners.

This brings us back to the question of the organization of knowledge and professional preparation. In Chapter 3, an alternative approach to organizing professional knowledge is described that is inductive, that is, arising from the work of school administrators. Instead of having preparation and knowledge organized around university-evolved disciplines, the project developed "problems of practice"—focal work tasks of school administration specified at a middle range of abstraction (Forsyth & Tallerico, 1993, p. ix). Advantages to such an organizational approach, it seems to us, include its obvious relevance to practice, the potential for a distinctive technical and practice knowledge base, and the formation of a common and useful language for scholars and practitioners in our field.

Ilene B. Harris, dual professor of medical education at the University of Minnesota Medical School and College of Education, has written a great deal about professional education from her unusual vantage point. At the conclusion of a chapter examining professional competence, she asks,

> How would education for the professions change if these perspectives were taken seriously? If accreditation bodies, licensure boards, professional schools, institutions of practice, educational policy committees, course directors, teachers, students, and consumers—everyone holding a stake in professional education—were to take these recommendations seriously, what would they do differently? (Harris, 1993, p. 51)

Her answer to her rhetorical question is that "with respect to the content and process of professional education, [ ] education for the professions, at every level, should be organized to a greater extent around the problems of practice" (Harris, 1993, p. 51).

The move to a "problems of practice" organization of knowledge, scholarship, and delivery in educational administration would not be easily accomplished. Experimentation with the delivery aspects of this approach have been going on in medical and law schools for some time. Educational administration has also had advocates for problem-based learning (Bridges, 1992). But it seems to us that the organization of technical and practice knowledge for law and medicine has always more closely paralleled their respective problems of practice than has been the case with educational administration. Without a major restructuring of technical knowledge, research agendas, and specialties around a set of problems of practice, adopting a problem-based learning approach could easily trivialize preparation in this field, eliminating both breadth and depth in professional preparation.

A second question is, Why have practice knowledge experiences such as the internship been so unstable, despite nearly universal agreement about their importance to the preparation of practitioners? It could be argued that the professors of educational administration of recent decades don't know much about practice. Consequently, they are not very interested in practice or designing practice learning experiences. Moreover, the modern research university will punish them for this kind of effort because it will destroy their focus on publication.

Take, for example, an educational administration equivalent of grand rounds in medicine. At a weekly gathering of an advanced practicum, an educational administration intern reports on a field case to which she has been assigned, reporting that over a period of 6 months, a large group of middle school parents have become extremely divided over curriculum decisions made by the school the previous year at the urging of a progressive group of history and literature teachers. Some of the upset parents have children who were previously in gifted programs and who, their parents claim, are now bored to tears because they are in classes covering old material. A parent group of similar size is distraught at what they view as the unfair placement of their children in a series of classes that moves too quickly through the curriculum. The children have not learned the foundational material, and they are unprepared to move on.

A professor of educational administration may not be very well equipped to shepherd a sophisticated analysis of the above situation, one that produces understanding and reviews administrative, legal, policy, psychological and sociological theory, and research related to the case under consideration. A professor's instincts may be entirely wrong for a practice environment. The professor may have never practiced school administration or anything except research design. The professor may, in fact, have no practice knowledge. His or her ability to sift through salient context, separate what is unique about this volatile situation from what is pattern, focus on the important features, and generate potential strategies that help children may not be very impressive. This, despite the fact that he or she may be a highly regarded scholar. Having separated the delivery of practice knowledge and technical knowledge for so long, and having effectively removed practice preparation from the university, professors are not well prepared to plan, organize, and provide this critical part of professional preparation.

It is our view that the paradigm wars of the past 25 years have done little to make schools better or more effective places. Moreover, debates about the philosophical underpinnings of acquiring knowledge do little to equip future school leaders for their very important roles. We have discussed our profession from the perspective of technical and practice knowledge, arguing that a balance of these two is needed, and that both knowledge domains need further attention in the field of educational administration. Some directions for future movement have been hinted at—work to be done that builds on a foundation of reform efforts that has already been laid.

References

Achilles, C. M. (1990, February). *Research in educational administration: One position.* Paper prepared for a Danforth Foundation meeting, San Francisco.

Bates, R. J. (1984). Toward a critical practice of educational administration. In T. J. Sergiovanni & J. E. Corbally (Eds.), *Leadership and organizational culture: New perspectives on administrative theory and practice* (pp. 260-274). Urbana: University of Illinois Press.

Boyan, N. J. (Ed.). (1988). *Handbook of research on educational administration.* New York: Longman.

Boyd, W. L., & Crowson, R. L. (1981). The changing conception and practice of public school administration. In D. C. Berliner (Ed.), *Review of research in education* (Vol. 9, pp. 311-373). Washington, DC: American Education Research Association.

Bridges, E. M. (1992). *Problem-based learning for administrators.* Eugene, OR: ERIC.

Brubacher, J. S. (1962). The evolution of professional education. In N. B. Henry (Ed.), *Education for the professions: The sixty-first yearbook of the National Society for the Study of Education* (pp. 47-67). Chicago: National Society for the Study of Education.

Campbell, R. F., Fleming, T., Newell, L. J., & Bennion, J. W. (1987). *A history of thought and practice in educational administration.* New York: Teachers College Press.

Campbell, R. F., & Newell, L. J. (1973). *A study of professors of educational administration.* Columbus, OH: The University Council for Educational Administration.

Carver, F. D. (1988, June). *The evaluation of the study of educational administration.* Paper presented at the EAAA Allerton House Conference, University of Illinois at Urbana–Champaign.

Clark, D. L. (1988, June). *Charge to the study group of the National Policy Board for Educational Administration.* Unpublished manuscript.

Cronin, J., & Horoschak, P. O. (1973). *Innovative strategies in field experiences for preparing educational administrators* (ERIC/CEM State-of-the-Knowledge Series, Number 21; UCEA Monograph Series, Number 8). Danville, IL: Interstate.

Culbertson, J. (1962). New perspectives: Implications for program change. In J. A. Culbertson & S. P. Hencley, *Preparing administrators: New perspectives* (pp. 151-173). Columbus, OH: The University Council for Educational Administration.

Culbertson, J. (1988). A century's quest for a knowledge base. In N. J. Boyan (Ed*.), Handbook of research on educational administration* (pp. 3-26). New York: Longman.

Culbertson, J. A., & Farquhar, R. H. (1971). Preparing educational leaders: Methods employed in administrative preparation. *UCEA Newsletter, 12*(4), 11-14.

Daresh, J. C. (1987, February). *The practicum in preparing educational administrators: A status report.* Paper presented at the Eastern Educational Research Association meeting, Boston.

Dewey, J. (1929). *The sources of a science of education.* New York: Liverright.

Erickson, D. A. (1977). An overdue paradigm shift in educational administration, or how can we get that idiot off the freeway? In L. L. Cunningham, W. G. Hack, & R. O. Nystrand (Eds.), *Educational administration: The developing decades* (pp. 114-143). Berkeley, CA: McCutchan.

Erickson, D. A. (1979). Research on educational administration: The state-of-the-art. *Educational Researcher, 8,* 9-14.

Evans, R. (1991, April). *Ministrative insight: Educational administration as pedagogic practice.* Paper presented at the annual meeting of the American Educational Research Association, Chicago.

Farquhar, R. H. (1968). The humanities and educational administration: Rationales and recommendations. *Journal of Educational Administration, 6*(2), 97-115.

Forsyth, P. B. (1992). Fury, flutter, and promising directions: Notes on the reform of educational administrator preparation. In E. Miklos & E. Ratsoy (Eds.), *Educational leadership: Challenge and change.* Edmonton, Alberta, Canada: Department of Educational Administration.

Forsyth, P. B., & Tallerico, M. (1993). *City schools: Leading the way.* Newbury Park, CA: Corwin.

Getzels, J. W., & Guba, E. G. (1957, Winter). Social behavior and the administrative process. *School Review, 65,* 423-441.

Glaser, B. (1964). *Organizational scientists: Their professional careers.* Indianapolis, IN: Bobbs-Merrill.

Goldhammer, K. (1983). Evolution in the profession. *Educational Administration Quarterly, 19,* 249-272.

Gordon, S. E. (1992). Implications of cognitive theory for knowledge acquisition. In R. R. Hoffman (Ed.), *The psychology of expertise: Cognitive research and empirical AI* (pp. 99-120). New York: Springer-Verlag.

Greenfield, T., & Ribbins, P. (1993). *Greenfield on educational administration: Towards a humane science.* London: Routledge.

Guba, E. G. (1975). Development, diffusion and evaluation. In W. G. Monahan (Ed.), *Theoretical dimensions of educational administration* (pp. 371-396). New York: Macmillan.

Halpin, A. (1965). Essay. *Educational Administration Quarterly, 1*, 49-53.

Harris, I. B. (1993). New expectations for professional competence. In L. Curry & J. F. Wergin (Eds.), *Educating professionals: Responding to new expectations for competence and accountability* (pp. 17-52). San Francisco: Jossey-Bass.

Hills, J. (1965). Educational administration: A field in transition. *Educational Administration Quarterly, 1*, 58-66.

Homans, G. C. (1974). *Social behavior: Its elementary forms.* New York: Harcourt Brace Jovanovich.

Hoy, W. K., Astuto, T. A., & Forsyth, P. B. (Eds.). (1996). *Educational administration: The UCEA document base.* New York: McGraw-Hill.

Immegart, G. L. (1977). The study of educational administration, 1954-1974. In L. L. Cunningham, W. G. Hack, & R. O. Nystrand (Eds.), *Educational administration: The developing decades* (pp. 298-328). Berkeley, CA: McCutchan.

McCarthy, M. M., & Kuh, G. D. (1997). *Continuity and change: The educational leadership professoriate.* Columbia, MO: The University Council for Educational Administration.

McCarthy, M. M., Kuh, G. D., Newell, L. J., & Iacona, C. M. (1988). *Under scrutiny: The educational administration professoriate.* Tempe, AZ: The University Council for Educational Administration.

McNally, H. J., & Dean, S. E. (1963). The elementary school principal. In D. J. Leu & H. C. Rudman (Eds.), *Preparation programs for school administrators: Common and specialized learnings* (pp. 110-122). East Lansing: University of Michigan Press.

Milstein, M. (1990). Rethinking the clinical aspects in administrative preparation: From theory to practice. In S. L. Jacobson & J. Conway (Eds.), *Educational leadership in an age of reform.* New York: Longman.

Milstein, M., Bobroff, B. M., & Restine, L. N. (1991). *Internship programs in educational administration: A guide to preparing educational leaders.* New York: Teachers College Press.

Monahan, W. G. (Ed.). (1975). Overview. In W. G. Monahan, *Theoretical dimensions of educational administration* (pp. 1-10). New York: Macmillan.

Murphy, J. (1992). *The landscape of leadership preparation: Reframing the education of school administrators.* Newbury Park, CA: Corwin.

Murphy, J., & Hallinger, P. (Eds.). (1987). *Approaches to administrative training in education.* Albany: SUNY Press.

Oakeshott, M. (1962). *Rationalism in politics: And other essays.* New York: Basic Books.

Paulsen, F. (1895). *German universities: Their character and development.* New York: Macmillan.

Schein, E. H. (1972). *Professional education: Some new directions.* New York: McGraw-Hill.

Schön, D. A. (1983). *The reflective practitioner.* New York: Basic Books.

Schön, D. A. (1987). *Educating the reflective practitioner.* San Francisco: Jossey-Bass.

Silver, P., & Spuck, D. W. (1978). *Preparatory programs for educational administrators in the United States.* Columbus, OH: The University Council for Educational Administration.

Skalski, J., Lohman, M., Szcepanik, J., Baratta, A., Bacilious, Z., & Schulte, S. (1987). *Administrative internships.* Paper presented at the annual meeting of the American Educational Research Association, Washington, DC.

Thorne, B. (1973). Professional education in medicine. In The Carnegie Commission on Higher Education, *Education for the professions of medicine, law, theology, and social welfare.* New York: McGraw-Hill.

Wiggins, T. (1992). The mythology of reform in educational administrator preparation: Antecedents of paradigms lost. In F. C. Wendel (Ed.), *Reform in administrator preparation: Myths, realities and proposals* (pp. 4-12). Tempe, AZ: The University Council for Educational Administration.

Willower, D. J. (1964). The professorship in educational administration: A rationale. In D. J. Willower & J. A. Culbertson (Eds.), *The professorship in educational administration.* Columbus, OH: The University Council for Educational Administration.

Willower, D. J. (1988). Synthesis and projection. In N. J. Boyan (Ed.), *Handbook of research on educational administration* (pp. 729-745). New York: Longman.

Index

CORWIN
PRESS

The Corwin Press logo — a raven striding across an open book— represents the happy union of courage and learning. We are a professional-level publisher of books and journals for K–12 educators, and we are committed to creating and providing resources that embody these qualities. Corwin's motto is "Success for All Learners."